The Body in Context

Also by Gareth Moore
Believing in God. A Philosophical Essay
(*T. & T. Clark*)

THE BODY
IN CONTEXT

Sex and Catholicism

Gareth Moore OP

CONTINUUM
London and New York

#45488211

Continuum
The Tower Building, 11 York Road, London SE1 7NX
370 Lexington Avenue, New York, NY 10017–6503

Copyright © 19920 Gareth Moore

First published in 1992
by SCM Press Ltd

First published by Continuum 2001

British Library Cataloguing-in-Publication Data
A catalogue record for this book is available from the British Library.

ISBN 0-8264-5356-2

Typeset by Paston PrePress Ltd, Beccles, Suffolk
Printed and bound in Great Britain by Creative Print and Design, Wales.

Contents

Acknowledgments

During the course of writing this book I have been greatly helped by discussions with many friends and colleagues. That these are too numerous to name does not lessen my indebtedness to them.

The following have read part or all of the book at various stages in its formation: Todd Breyfogle, Brian Davies OP, Robert Dodaro OSA, Nicholas Hammond, Fergus Kerr OP, Herbert McCabe OP, Roger Ruston OP, J. O. Urmson and Hugh Walters OP. My thanks are due to all of these for their friendly and helpful criticism. Above all I must thank Simon Tugwell OP for his long and patient assistance, without which this book would be much worse than it is.

Preface

This book is intended principally as a help to the church in its moral thinking about sex. I write from within the Catholic Christian tradition, and many of the things I have to say will perhaps be of interest only to Christians. Such will be my comments on the meaning and use of certain passages of the Bible. But I hope to show, even to those of other faiths or none, that the church has something valuable and important to say in the field of sexual ethics. Hence many of my remarks presuppose no religious faith and may be properly appreciated and criticized by all.

My aim is to examine some of the principal arguments and styles of argument which Christians, among others, have advanced in support of Christian standards in sexual ethics. The church has from the beginning thought it right to speak on sexual matters, and when it speaks it sometimes claims to do so with the authority of Christ himself. But on the whole, the church has not been content simply to rely on the divine authority it claims for itself, to lay down the law or urge people to behave in this way or stop behaving in that way. It has sought to commend its views to Christians and non-Christians alike by the use of various kinds of argument. The aim has been to present Christian sexual standards and values not simply as arbitrary, unknowable except to those to whom they have been revealed by God, but as reasonable, standards which primarily Christians but also others will see to be right if only they trouble to think about these matters properly. This way of presenting its moral teaching has been especially important in the Catholic tradition, which regards reason as one of the greatest natural gifts we have from God. This should not be allowed to obscure the fact that the church professes to proclaim a teaching which, at least in its fundamentals, is revealed by God; it does not teach what it does because it has worked it all out from first principles. Nevertheless, it has been held important that the church's teaching in moral matters be shown to be in accordance with natural reason. Hence the constant attempt by church leaders and theologians to generate arguments in support of what the church says. These arguments have been of two broad types: arguments from scripture and arguments from philosophy and experience. While the former are expected to carry weight only with Christians, the latter, it is hoped, should appeal to all who examine them honestly in the light of natural reason. But appeal to natural reason has not only been made to those outside the church; since there is comparatively little explicit teaching on sexual morality in the Bible, arguments derived from natural reason, without any but the most general scriptural basis, have been prominent.

The use of such arguments is particularly important in the modern period, when so many do not recognize the divine right of the church to speak on such matters. It can no longer lay down the law, and must earn the right to be heard by those who disagree with it. It can only do so if it seeks to persuade and convince of the rightness of its position, if it appeals to reason. Even within the church the use of argument is important, since even those who accept the church's authority must be convinced that the church's teaching is rational if their conscience is to be formed aright. As far as concerns sex, this use of argument is particularly vital nowadays, when many people who in general accept the teaching authority of the church find they cannot do so in the sphere of sexual ethics, where what the church teaches on, say, extra-marital sex or contraception or homosexuality seems to them so plainly wrong. To be so in disagreement with a church of which one wishes to be a loyal member is to be in an awkward, sometimes painful position. Such people are not helped by a simple re-assertion of the church's authority to teach, or by repetition of the disputed teaching. For those in difficulties authority is not enough. They may be clear about *what* is taught, and they know that the teaching body claims authority, but their difficulty expresses itself in the question *why* it is taught. They need to be convinced. They may in the course of time be convinced by their own experience of life, but meanwhile arguments – from scripture, reason and observation – are an essential tool of persuasion.

In so far as the church speaks to the world in general, to those who are not Christians, it may be speaking to those who do not acknowledge that the church has any teaching power at all, and who deny the authority of scripture. Many of these engage quite happily and with a good conscience in all kinds of sexual activity which the church regards as unacceptable. In its engagement with this audience, the church's use of secular rational argument, convincing argument which makes no appeal to revelation, is even more important.

People can be taken in by fallacious arguments, or by arguments which, though sound in themselves, rest on false premises. However, such arguments are of little use to the church; since their rationality is specious they do not show the rational nature of the church's teaching. And while they may convince for a while, some bright person is going to come along one day and detect the fallacy or mistake involved. Also, too often, one gets a sense that arguments are merely *devised*, drummed up, to support a predetermined conclusion. This can be innocuous when it is done to put on a firm theoretical footing something that everybody already knows, but it is not so appropriate or harmless in disputed cases, like the details of sexual morality. Further, the sense of a putative proof's being devised is increased by the sometimes obvious distortion of text and argument that is gone through in order to give the appearance of establishing the point under dispute. As if, since the conclusion must be right, there *must* be support for it, even conclusive support, in scripture and reason. Whatever the actual motives of the author, this procedure appears disingenuous, and one gets the impression of being cheated. The only result in the long run is that the church is discredited in the eyes of thinking people; it may even appear dishonest, seeming to drum up any argument it can, however specious, in support of its position, which then itself appears unreasonable, unjustified and unjustifiable. It may then be harder than ever for many Christians to remain in dialogue with the church in these matters, and its voice will not be heard in the wider world.

This is a prospect which no Christian can view with equanimity. It is therefore vital that, if the church and its theologians use arguments in support of traditional or indeed new teaching, those arguments be sound ones. The reasoning has to be free of fallacies and based on true premises; and if scripture is used it must be interpreted plausibly. One of my aims in this book is to examine a number of arguments to see whether they are in fact sound. I conclude that many are not. In some cases this is not particularly serious, and it may only need minor adjustments to make the argument cogent. In others the difficulty seems to me more substantial and I do not see how the argument can be salvaged. Different types of argument will have to be generated if church teaching is to be shown to be rational.

Thus, much of what I say is critical. But the work of criticism is a necessary one. It is no service to the church's teaching to attempt to support it, both to believers and to non-believers, with bad arguments. One way this book can be seen is as an aid to clarity, and therefore an aid to the better rational support of church doctrine. Where I am critical of theologians and church documents, this should not be taken as a dismissal of the worth of what they say. Even if an argument is fallacious, its author may well be trying to make a very valuable point by means of it; anybody who has engaged in serious thinking knows that it is quite possible to have an important intuition and then find it very difficult to articulate or substantiate it in formal argument. If I take issue with certain arguments, I am also aware that it is much harder to build up arguments than to knock them down. And my purpose in all this is a positive one. It is not to expose the irrationality of the church's teaching, but to stimulate better, clearer and closer thinking. Of course I myself will have made many mistakes, both in the interpretation of what others have said and in my own argumentation. If I have misinterpreted anybody, I apologize. I look forward to having my reasoning corrected so that I myself will be able to think more clearly about these matters.

But my own argumentation is not only critical; my hope is that it is also constructive. If I find some ways of thinking about sex unsatisfactory, it appears incumbent on me at least to adumbrate what it seems to me might be a way forward. Accordingly, in counterpoint with my criticisms of some styles of reasoning, and sometimes arising out of those criticisms, I sketch some positive suggestions of my own which I hope may be helpful. These, while scattered throughout the book, centre around ideas developed in chapter 1 on the primacy of love, in chapter 4 on pleasure, and in chapter 6 on context, gesture and meaning.

My primary concerns are the phenomena of sex in general and how to think clearly about them. To get thus far and to cover so much ground in a reasonably short space I have had to gloss over many complications, as well as taking certain fundamental things for granted. For example, while I argue about sexual activity, I do not raise the question what counts as sexual activity and what does not. There are difficulties in the way of a short answer to this. Plainly it is not just activity that involves use of the genitals that is sexual for us (and when does use of the genitals count as sexual?). Are there any features common to all sexual activities? Or are they connected rather by family resemblances? A kiss is sometimes sexual, sometimes not. What makes the difference? The sexual is no doubt partly socially defined, a matter of what we regard as sexual in our particular culture. Many more things are seen as sexual since Freud than were before. Without tackling the issues involved here, I simply assume that we by and large recognize sexual behaviour when we see it and that we all more or less agree about what kinds of behaviour we classify as sexual, at least in our everyday discourse. I am confident, at any rate, that the activities I allude to will be recognized as sexual. A related omission is that I do not discuss the nature or origin of sexual desire, why it strikes where it does, why it takes the different forms it does, and what one person who is erotically attracted to another seeks in or from that other. I just take it for granted that some people are attracted to others in a way that we see to be sexual, while others are not. I do not believe that such omissions vitiate my discussion.

Thus the scope of this book is very limited. It is principally concerned with method and styles of argument, not with establishing substantive norms of sexual behaviour. My aim is not directly to defend the traditional sexual ethic of the church, still less is it to attack it. Neither is it to go through a catalogue of sexual activities and pronounce on the rights and wrongs of each one. Neither do I attempt to offer any direct pastoral guidance or support to those in doubt or difficulty regarding sexual matters or the church's teaching. Finally, what is presented here is not meant to be a theology of sex. Apart from this book's other restrictions and shortcomings, one thing that would fatally disqualify it from being regarded as a theology of sex is the complete omission of any discussion of the value Christians attach to virginity and celibacy. Also, since I am concerned chiefly with argument, my focus is more on disputed areas of sexual behaviour (from which, therefore, many of my examples are taken), to the comparative neglect of the loving physical communion of husband and wife which is the central case in any Christian theology of sex. The task of doing full theological justice to the church's teaching on sex I leave to wiser heads. My hope can only be that what I have written may be some aid to clarity in the task of generating such a theology.

1

Sex and Ethics

One way to understand the Christian life is as a preparation for the restoration of all things when Christ comes as king. Christians look forward to the coming of the kingdom of God. We hope to be made citizens of that kingdom. That looking forward and that hope are expressed in our living, by grace, in such a way as to be fittable to live in the kingdom. We cannot ourselves bring about the kingdom, or make ourselves fit to live in it: that must come as a gift of God. But we can, by the grace of God, live in such a way that the life of the kingdom is the perfection of our present life rather than its destruction. If we live in contradiction to the life of the kingdom, then the kingdom, when it comes, will mean the destruction of our life; but if we live, as far as we can, in accordance with life in the kingdom, with that life as our end, then we will grow towards it, and its coming will see our perfection and consummation rather than our destruction. So our business is to orientate ourselves towards the kingdom and turn away from all that is incompatible with it.

Life in the kingdom is a social life. It has to be, if it is to be our perfection, since we are social animals. One of the most important aspects of our lives as individuals is how we relate to others – to particular individuals who are close to us, to those we meet in the course of our daily business and to people at large, the network of groupings and institutions that goes to make up 'society'. Genesis 2 says that when God created the first man he saw that it was not good for man to be alone, and so set about making a companion for him (2.18). This is not an insight peculiar to those who believe in God, but an undeniable fact about human beings, given that we are the kind of animal we are. Even if it is good to be alone sometimes, even if we have to learn to be alone more than we would like and some people have to learn to be alone a great deal, still it is not good for us to be alone in the long term; most of us need others if we are to be reasonably happy.

But our being social animals goes deeper than that. We are not essentially pre-existing human atoms who then find that it is a good thing to be with other human atoms. Rather, it belongs to us to be with others. Our being human involves our relating to other people in a special way. Other people characteristically affect us as other, non-human elements of our environment do not. At a basic level we are affected by, for instance, the way somebody else looks at us; depending on circumstances, a look can make us uncomfortable or angry, it can make us giggle, it can make us ecstatic or crush us; or it can make us go outside and weep bitterly.

Depending on circumstances: this simple bodily gesture, like so many others, takes its power and meaning from the context, from what is going on around it. A look can have the ability to do all these things because of all the numerous complex ways in which people can relate to each other, through shared or differing interests or beliefs, common or separate life histories, and so on. A man may be affected by the look in a dog's eyes and he can be affected by the look in a woman's eyes. But a woman's eyes can be more important, because they can express more; and that is because a man can relate to a woman, and the woman to him, in ways more subtle and complex than the ways he can relate to a dog. We may love a particular person or hate him or her, just as we may love cabbage or hate it; but we are in general liable to see our attitude to the person as a more important element in our life than our attitude towards cabbage. People are more important to us than cabbage because we can share or fail to share our life with people as we cannot share it (or fail to share it) with cabbage; there simply are not many possibilities of relationship with a cabbage (and so not many possibilities of failure of relationship). Flies can sometimes be annoying and so can people, but an annoying human being generally annoys in a deeper and more absorbing way than a fly. We may want sometimes to be surrounded by people, and we may sometimes give anything to be able to get away from them for a while, but in one way or another it generally matters to us whether we are with others or not in a way that it does not in general matter to us whether we are with giraffes or worms. In this sense, our life is social, a life that is concerned with people. We live with other people in a way that we do not live with cabbages or flies or giraffes or worms.

And so too life in the kingdom will be life with other people. If the beginning of scripture points up our fundamentally social nature, the end of scripture suggests that our future, what we are moving towards, is also social. The great vision at the end of the Revelation is of the new Jerusalem, the city of God, to which all the nations will come and whose doors will remain ever open:

> And I saw no temple in the city, for its temple is the Lord God the Almighty and the Lamb. And the city has no need of sun or moon to shine upon it, for the glory of God is its light, and its lamp is the Lamb. By its light shall the nations walk; and the kings of the earth shall bring their glory into it, and its gates shall never be shut by day – and there shall be no night there (Rev. 21.22–25).

Our destiny, according to this vision, is not a solitary communion with God, but a life in a city, in society with other people. Here God, far from being the chief or even the only one we shall live with in heaven, is not an individual we shall relate to at all; he is rather the light in which we shall live together, who will illumine all our dealings with each other. To be fit to live in the kingdom is to live with others in a particular way or range of ways. If a Christian ethic may be seen as eschatological, it is also social. It is about learning to be with each other. We are not being prepared for a solitary life with God, but for life in God with others. So if we wish to ask ethical questions about our actions, these must cluster around the central questions: How do these actions touch other people, and how do they affect or reflect our relations with them? Christian ethics is not a concern with self-indulgent self-'perfection'. If it is possible to speak of Christian life as the pursuit of some kind of self-perfection, the moulding of oneself, this can never be understood in an isolationist sense: that in which our perfection lies is in the ability to live with others.

This is hardly a surprising conclusion. If we look at the ethical teaching of Jesus, it is overwhelmingly concerned with the ways people relate to each other. Jesus is not typically concerned with what people do alone and in a way that affects nobody else, nor is he concerned with prescribing practices which have no relevance to social life. (I am not saying that it is impossible to find Jesus teaching such things, only that you have to look very hard to find them, if they are there at all.) Typical are teachings such as:

If anyone strikes you on the right cheek, turn to him the other also (Matt. 5.39).

Judge not, that you be not judged... Why do you see the speck that is in your brother's eye, but do not notice the log that is in your own eye? (Matt. 7.1, 3).

Whoever would be great among you must be your servant, and whoever would be first among you must be slave of all (Mark 10.43f.).

As you wish that men would do to you, do so to them (Luke 6.31).

We are told to develop habits of service, consideration, generosity, justice, and so on: all those things we summarize as Christian love, qualities which shape a particular way of living with each other. Much of what we do may not particularly concern or affect others, but in so far as it does the questions we are to ask about it are: Is what I am doing just rather than unjust? Is it generous rather than mean? Is it an attempt to dominate? And so on. In short: is this a loving action, or a habit of loving action?

Because love is a matter largely of our habits there are questions to be asked, too, about those areas of our behaviour that do not directly affect others, such as many of the things that we do in private, alone and unobserved. There are many such things that we can do neither lovingly nor unlovingly, since they concern nobody else. Such actions may nevertheless affect our capacity or our inclination to act lovingly. If I drink whisky alone and in private, when there is nobody whose needs I have to attend to, my action is neither loving nor unloving, since it has nothing to do with anybody else. However, if I do it too much – if I develop the wrong kind of habit – I may eventually become, because of dependence or physical degeneration or simply the strength of habit, incapable of attending to others when that is required of me; or if I become too engrossed in the pleasure it gives me to drink whisky, if I form a habit of constantly thinking about and looking forward to the next whisky, this may mean that I have become too self-centred and have simply ceased to think naturally about others, unwilling to act generously.

It is important to note that this has nothing to do with any idea that drinking whisky might in itself be a suspect activity. Exactly the same considerations apply to the habit of drinking carrot juice or any other habit, however laudable the activity involved might be in itself. Prayer is normally reckoned by Christians to be a good thing to do, but if I spend so much time in prayer that I do not eat, or if I am so obsessed with praying that I will not be distracted by the needs of others, then my habit of prayer is vicious.

There is a point to be mentioned here that will become important later. If I drink too much (or simply want to), or I pray too much, so that I no longer can or no longer want to act lovingly towards others, we will say that I have become ungenerous and unloving. How we are as people is a matter of our habits of action. In the same way, one who habitually acts generously, justly and so on is a loving person. This means that it is also possible to talk of Christian ethics as being concerned partly with what kind of people we are or are becoming: Christians want to become and be saints. But here lurks the possibility of a misunderstanding. It is possible to think that Christian ethics is to do with what we essentially are, as opposed to what we merely do. This is connected with the idea that what we really are is something 'internal' (in a sense not quite specified), whereas our actions are a matter of mere externals. But this is a false conception. What and how we are, whether we are loving and saintly or mean and evil, is a matter of how we normally, habitually act. To be a particular kind of person is to be one who habitually acts in a particular way or range of ways.[1] So also to be concerned about the kind of person I am or am becoming is to be concerned with what I do. I may say, confronted with a particular example or model of humanity: 'I don't want to become that kind of person,' and that means that I do not want to be the kind of person that does that sort of thing. For Christians, their Christian concern with themselves is that they become loving persons, people fitted to live with others in the kingdom, in the light of God; and that means people who habitually act lovingly.

There is nothing selfish or self-centred about this kind of concern with ourselves, for it is a concern precisely that we be the kind of person who cares about others and is not self-centred. This is a kind of self-regard that we may and indeed should have. It is a proper form of self-love.

Social sexual ethics

What I want to suggest is that these observations I have been making about Christian ethics in general apply also to Christian sexual ethics in particular. Since we now live our lives together and the future we are promised is a future together, and since therefore Christian ethics is fundamentally a social ethic, the same social considerations will apply to our sexual behaviour as to the rest of our behaviour: does it fit us to live in the kingdom? It is an empirical question in what ways our sexual behaviour affects other people. Like some of the rest of our activities, some of our sexual behaviour may not affect others at all. On the other hand, it may turn out that sexual activities which are often defended as harmless or even promoted as healthy in fact harm others either directly or indirectly. That is a question that has to be answered empirically. This is not necessarily a simple matter. Sometimes, indeed, the answer will be obvious to common sense, but sometimes it will have to be arrived at through careful investigation, perhaps over a long period. There is the added complication that to an extent the precise empirical questions that we ask, and where we look and what we see when we look, may depend on what our prior beliefs are. But nevertheless we do have to look and see. In so far as what we do sexually does affect others, the prime questions to be asked about it are: does it manifest the kind of virtue that is to inform our whole lives? Is it just? Is it generous? and so on; in short, is it loving? If it does not affect others, does it nevertheless affect me, by affecting my capacity to love? Does doing this kind of thing tend to make me more generous and sensitive to others, or more self-centred and less capable of love? The virtue traditionally associated with sexual behaviour is chastity. What I am arguing is that chastity is not a virtue independent of the commandment to love our neighbour. Chastity is love as it appears in the realm of sex.

That is to say, there is in an important sense no special Christian sexual ethic: there are not special rules governing our sexual behaviour that do not apply to the rest of our activities. Sex is a very specialized area of human activity, and specific questions and problems have to be faced if we are to come to a proper understanding of it. But sex is not exceptional in that. Banking and finance too are special areas with their own specific problems, but we do not stand in need of a special Christian ethic of banking; what we have to do is to be just, considerate, generous, and so on in that area of our lives. Thinking about banking from a Christian point of view does not mean generating a special set of principles, different from those that apply in the rest of our lives; rather, it means asking how the general principles that we already have are best applied in this part of our lives, or indeed whether our general principles allow banking to be part of our lives at all. In the same way, sex is a special area in which Christian principles will be applied, but it is not an area with its own special principles. If we want to think of Christian ethics as a set of rules, a law, laid down by God for us to follow, a divine law, then there is not one set of rules concerning our relationships in society – that we should be just, respectful, etc. – and another, further set concerning our sexual activity.

Here it is easy to point to well-known and central texts of the New Testament. St Paul writes to the Romans:

> Owe no one anything, except to love one another; for he who loves his neighbour has fulfilled the law. The commandments: 'You shall not commit adultery, You shall not kill, You shall not steal, You shall not covet,' and any other commandment, are summed up in this sentence: 'You shall love your neighbour as yourself.' Love does no wrong to a neighbour; therefore love is the fulfilling of the law.[2]

This is an inescapable saying for Christians. It is inescapable because it is central to the tradition. What love means here has to be spelt out, but it is very important that what is required is precisely love of neighbour. It is, in this sense, a social requirement and nothing else. Nothing else is necessary except to do what expresses and promotes love of neighbour and to remove obstacles to it. There is no virtue or vice but touches on how we relate to our neighbour. Note particularly how the law on adultery is also subsumed under the commandment to love; adultery is forbidden not because of any special sexual law, but because it infringes the law of love. We have here a strong indication that for Paul sexual behaviour in general is, no less than activity in any other area of life, to be judged in terms of love of neighbour. The attempt to impose any other law is an attempt to rob us of the freedom for which Christ has set us free (cf. Gal 5.1).

Jesus himself speaks in a similar vein. In the Sermon on the Mount he says: 'Whatever you wish that men would do to you, do so to them; for this is the law and the prophets' (Matt. 7.12).[3] According to Jesus, there is nothing that God demands of us, either in the law or through his prophets, that is not dependent on the law of love. This saying of his is particularly important in that it does not simply repeat the love commandment; it also interprets it for us. The good things we are to do to one another are ordinary, natural human goods, the kind of thing that reasonably mature people ordinarily want to have done to them. What people want can be a complicated matter; an individual can want something complex, and his or her different wants can be related in complex ways. There are superficial wants and deep wants, whims and needs; what is a superficial want at one time can become a deep one at another, and vice versa. People can be unsure or unaware of what they really want. Unhappily, an individual's wants can conflict with each other, as well as with the wants of others. But still, it is human wants that matter; needs and desires that arise in the course of human life because of the kind of creature we are and because of the circumstances we find ourselves in.

According to the Christian vision, one need that is deep in people, essential to them even if they are sometimes unaware of it, is the need for God; as our life has its beginning in God, so it is fulfilled and perfected and has its end in God. As Augustine says: 'You have made us for yourself, and our heart is restless until it rests in you.'[4] Hence the work of the church in trying to remind people of their need for God and to keep them open to God is itself an act of love, an attempt to minister to their deepest need. If Christians are right, the need for God is not a special, rather rarefied need; it is the most common and ordinary need of human beings. If people need God, and the gifts of God that draw us towards him, this can be talked of as a spiritual need, but God and his gifts are not something that we need if we want to be a special kind of 'spiritual' human being; they are what we need in order to be human at all. There is no question of there being special 'spiritual' goods divorced from the ordinary needs of people, that are to be recommended to or even imposed on people regardless of what they need and desire as human beings. We are not, for instance, to burn people so as to 'save their soul', for people do not ordinarily want or need to be burned. There may be higher goods than ordinary human ones, but if so they build on and perfect those ordinary human goods; they do not contradict them. One reason why we want now to live in the kingdom is because we recognize that living the life of the kingdom will bring us the perfection of all those ordinary human goods, the things that we value now; otherwise there is no reason why the prospect of the coming kingdom should be at all attractive to us.

All you need is love

The fundamental importance of the love commandment for Christian ethics has been recognized consistently in the tradition. It has, though, sometimes been said that to put such an emphasis on love is to distort the New Testament and provides in any case an obviously inadequate basis for regulating our social life. This is perhaps an arguable point, but there is here a possible mistake that has been made more than once, stemming from a mistaken notion of what a motive is. As an example concerned with sexual ethics I will take David Field's booklet *The Homosexual Way – A Christian Option?*[5] In line with Christian thought in scripture and tradition he asserts that 'an interpretation of Christian ethics which stresses love has plenty to commend it'. But then, in reply to the suggestion that a homosexual relationship based on love is therefore acceptable, goes on:

Despite the stress Jesus laid on the necessity of a loving motive, he nowhere taught that a motive of love can justify anything... He was certainly explicit in emphasizing the importance of the inward thoughts and feelings of a man's sex-life, but there is no hint that he meant his condemnations of extra-marital *hetero*sexual intercourse to apply in cases of bad or mixed motives only.[5]

There is something essentially right about what Field says. The main point seems to be that it is what you actually *do* that is important. People often do what is in fact the wrong thing, even though they do it from the best of motives, and doing something from a good motive does not make it right. The agent may sometimes not be culpable for doing the wrong thing if his motive was a good one, but still he has made a mistake and if he later realizes it he will regret what he did as wrong. A novice goldfish owner may, out of generous good will to his new fish, give them a whole tin of food at once. His motive is good, but his action is not, as he will discover. In his action he is well-disposed, but mistaken. A similar distinction is essential in the moral field. To take a sexual example, a woman may enter into a sexual relation-ship with a man married to another woman, and her motives for doing it may be good ones. She may, for example, want to bring love and comfort to a friend whose marriage is in difficulties. But Christ says, and so does the Christian tradition following him, that what she does is actually wrong. Her love impels her to do the loving thing, but she is mistaken about what the loving thing is. If she later comes to regret her action, that amounts to her seeing it as wrong, and she could not properly do that if her good motive made the action right. Similarly, a man may become involved in a homo-sexual relationship through the desire to give of himself to another in love. His motive is certainly praiseworthy, but his action is still, according to the tradition, wrong. Wrong actions do not have to spring from an evil will; they may not be malicious, but simply mistaken. That is why we can regret doing things which we did from good motives.

That is Field's substantive point, and it is plainly right. But in the way he makes his point there are a number of mistakes lurking. They are small, and incidental to what he has to say, but are potentially a source of considerable confusion, and will have to be cleared up if we are to make progress in thinking about sex. First, note how Field apparently equates motive and 'inward thoughts and feelings'; a motive for him seems to be the thoughts and feelings you have while you are doing something, or perhaps just before you do it. But such a picture of motive is false. My motive for playing this chess game is to get the prize for winning, but my thoughts and feelings while playing may have nothing to do with money and, if I am to play well, should not have; my thoughts should be concentrated entirely on how to outwit my opponent, and I should be quite calm, have no feelings at all to speak of. If I have particular motives for what I do I will also be inclined to have certain thoughts on occasion. At some stage or other I will no doubt have said to myself how good it would be to have the prize money, and will have fantasized about how to spend it. But to have the motive is not now to be thinking or recently to have thought those thoughts, or any thoughts like them. For my motive for concentrating exclusively on the chess game is my desire for the prize; and I am indeed concentrating on the game, not on thoughts of how I am going to spend the prize. To ask what my motive is is to ask, among other things, what I would honestly reply if asked why I am doing it, or what I sincerely tell myself when I think about it. It is not to ask what inward thoughts and feelings I am now having.

Secondly, this false picture of motive leads to a wrong picture of the relation between motive and action. It makes it look as if motive and action are in a sense independent of each other, just as you can do one thing and have your thoughts and feelings occupied with something quite different. It is of course right that the thoughts and feelings you are having while you do something, even if they are very, very good thoughts and feelings, do not justify what you are actually doing; they cannot turn a bad act into a good one. So if you think of having a motive as a matter of having thoughts and feelings it is certainly wrong to say it doesn't matter what you do provided you do it from the right motives. But that is *not* what it is to have a motive. For having a motive *is* (one way of) its mattering to you what you do. My desire to win the prize does not make it irrelevant to me whether or how I actually play. It is precisely my desire for the prize that makes it matter to me that I play and that I play well. Similarly, if I love my neighbour, and my actions towards him are therefore motivated by love, that does not make it irrelevant to me what I do to him or with him. On the contrary, it is precisely because I love him that it matters to me what I do. It is my love of neighbour that makes me careful to do the right thing by him. It is love that leads us, according to the Christian vision, to the standards, insights and laws by which we are to guide our actions towards our neighbour. If we love people we may have particular characteristic thoughts and feelings about them; we may, for instance, feel warm and happy when we think of them. But such feelings, though they may be characteristic and pleasurable, are not the stuff of love. What is essential is what we do. (This, remember, is Field's actual, and important, point.) If we love people we will be concerned to find out their likes and dislikes, so as to be sensitive to them. We will be at pains to discover what is good for them, so as to promote it, and what is bad for them, so as to avoid it. And so too it is love that makes us try to regulate society or influence its regulation so that people may in general be treated rightly.

Here Field does seem to be led into a real error, for he speaks of 'replacing all other absolute standards by the single command to love'.[6] He is very much against that idea, apparently because he believes it leaves it open for people to do terrible things to each other while thinking nice 'loving' thoughts. So we need absolute standards, standards independent of what we happen to be thinking at the time. His insistence on independent standards must be right, but there is not in fact the competition between the love command and other standards that he appears to think there is. For love does not compete with other standards; rather, if we are Christians, it is love that gives us our standards and that makes it vitally important to us to live according to proper standards in our relationships with others. Augustine said: 'Love and do what you will.'[7] Whatever he himself may have meant by this, if we are to understand that as a genuinely Christian remark, we cannot take it as meaning: if you have nice-sounding thoughts and warm feelings about people you can actually be as awful to them as you like. We can only understand it as saying: so long as you love people, so long as it matters to you to do the right thing by them, you need not be bothered about any other rules.

Sexual phenomena, then, I wish to suggest, come into ethical consideration for Christians in so far as they are social phenomena, because they come under the scope of the commandment to love our neighbour. This is certainly the preponderant view of both the Old Testament and the New Testament; and it informs a great deal of the Christian tradition of thinking about sex. One example from later tradition will suffice for now. St Thomas Aquinas, discussing the question 'Is every act of lechery a mortal sin?' in his *De Malo*, considers the following objection:

> Every mortal sin is contrary to charity. . . But simple fornication is against neither the love of God, as it is not a sin against God, nor the love of neighbour, because it does no injury to a neighbour.

He replies not by invoking any special law unconnected with love, but as follows:

> All the vices of lechery, which are beyond the legitimate use of marriage, are sins against a neighbour, inasmuch as they are against the good of the offspring to be generated and educated.[8]

Whatever the merits of this particular answer (on which something will be said in chapter 5), Aquinas' determination to account for sexual ethics in terms of love is clear. A similar way of regarding sexual sins is apparent also in his *Summa Contra Gentiles*. Answering the question whether fornication is a sin according to the divine law, he writes:

> It does not seem a sufficient answer to say that it does injury to God. For God is not offended by us except through that by which we act against our good.[9]

In view of scripture and tradition it is fitting, then, that the love commandment be the foundation for our thinking about sex. There may be all sorts of ways that we want to organize our sexual activity, and for all sorts of reasons: aesthetic, ascetic, economic, etc., but unless they are related to considerations of love these reasons are not components of Christian ethical judgment.

This can be given a sense in which it is truism. If we take as our paradigm of sexual activity two people having sexual intercourse, then since this is an activity in which they relate to one another they are also having a social encounter, so it is up to them to be just and considerate to each other, to respect each other, and so on, as in any other encounter. But our considerations have to go beyond that. Jane and Peter having sexual intercourse do not constitute a complete and isolated society. Each of them is related in various ways to other people. For example, Jane is married to Andrew, who is also Peter's best friend. Social relations carry with them certain expectations, rights and obligations. Keeping those obligations and respecting those rights is a large part of what we mean by justice and love. In our society it is normally one of the expectations of marriage that each partner has exclusive sexual rights over the other. It is also normally part of the love due from a best friend that he or she does not have an affair with your wife or husband. The various institutions and customs of any society bind its members together in all sorts of ways, and it is in observing those institutions that justice consists, if they are themselves just institutions; and our standard for that is whether they allow people to relate to each other in a Christian way, a way in which we can live together humanly now and in the coming kingdom. It is in this sense that I mean that sexual relations are social relations, that our sexual relations involve relations not only with our present sexual partners but also with others, and they can be just and loving or unjust and unloving to those others as well as to our partners. And it is whether they are or not that is the proper criterion of whether a particular sexual activity or relation is a good one.

If this in one way sounds very reasonable, it may at first also seem somewhat surprising. Are there not after all in scripture laws and precepts relating specifically to sexual activity? Examples are not difficult to find. In the Old Testament, the book of Leviticus tells us: 'You shall not steal, nor deal falsely, nor lie to one another' (19.11). It is obvious that this kind of activity is unjust; this is a law relating to social justice. But Leviticus also says: 'You shall not lie with a man as with a woman: it is an abomination' (18.22), and activity like that doesn't seem to have wider social implications; it does not, if both partners are willing and they do it in private, appear to infringe anybody's rights or fail to show respect to anybody. It does not seem to be an application of the law of love, but looks like an independent law, one which is irreducibly about sex.

In the New Testament, Jesus tells us to be generous, to give to one who begs from us (Matt. 5.42), and this is obviously about the way we are to live together with others, but he also says: 'You have heard that it was said:

"You shall not commit adultery." But I say to you that every one who looks at a woman lustfully has already committed adultery with her in his heart' (Matt. 5.27f.). Surely that is not about our life in society; it is about what takes place not in the public arena, but in the secret places of the heart. It is not about what we *do* at all, but about our sexual thoughts, what is inside our head. Apparently, the point of it is not that we should as members of society behave according to the standards of Christian love, but that as individuals we should be sexually pure internally.

There do then, at least at first sight, seem to be standards laid down for us in scripture that are nothing in particular to do with our public life, but which quite simply seek to regulate our private sexual activities and our interior life. If this is really so, that is quite a serious matter, for it does compromise the paramount importance given to the love commandment by Jesus and the New Testament writers I have mentioned. It also makes it problematic what the relationship is between the love commandment and these other standards. I believe the idea that there are such independent standards concerning sexual behaviour is mistaken. The impression given by a cursory reading of the passages I have cited and others like them is deceptive. In the following pages I want to take a closer look at these passages and show that, despite appearances to the contrary, social considerations and social relations are indeed the dominant concerns in them.

2

The Lustful Eye

You have heard that it was said: 'You shall not commit adultery.' But I say to you that every one who looks at a woman lustfully has already committed adultery with her in his heart.

I shall start by taking the example from the Sermon on the Mount that I mentioned at the end of the last chapter. I will deal with it in some detail, as it, and the ways it has been commented on, raise a number of points which are important in Christian discussion of human beings and action in general and human sexual behaviour in particular.

To begin with, this passage has sometimes been used to make the point that morality is not just concerned with what we do to each other, and to focus attention more on what we think – on the thoughts, fantasies and images that pass through our heads – than on what we actually do. With many modern Catholics, at least, this has led to an almost obsessive concern with 'impure thoughts', and on a more formal level it has had its influence on some theological thinkers, both Catholic and Protestant. Remember how Field, in the extract I quoted in the last chapter, takes it as certain that Jesus was 'explicit in emphasizing the importance of the inward thoughts and feelings of a man's sex-life',[1] and it seems to be this passage in Matthew that he has in mind. In another recent book, *Catholic Sexual Ethics*, Lawler, Boyle and May write:

> Jesus' condemnation of a man's looking lustfully at a woman indicates that for him sexual morality is not merely a matter of external behaviour but of a person's internal disposition and will as well. This focus on the person's heart is characteristic of Jesus' moral teaching. It is not so much an extension of moral rules to cover wider areas of human life as it is a focusing on the true nature of morality, for morality is not directly concerned with external behaviour and its effect but with the immediate effects one's choices have on one's self – that is, with the kind of person one makes oneself by one's own free choices.[2]

There are a number of points being made here, but the importance of the 'internal' for these writers is clear enough. 'Internal disposition and will' are contrasted with 'mere external behaviour'. But in fact this passage from Matthew means something quite different from what they, Field and others think it means.

First, contrary to what they say, Jesus is indeed talking here about what people do, their 'external behaviour'. He is telling people not to look at others in a particular way. We all know what it is to look at somebody lustfully, and we all know what it looks like. In the appropriate circumstances we can tell that somebody is looking lustfully at somebody else. There might be a protracted gaze, a particular set of the eyelids and maybe of the eyebrows, perhaps a certain play of the lips, an attitude of the head or stance of the body. Or it might be something much more subtle, the merest glance of the eyes; we might only be able to characterize somebody's look as lustful with hindsight, in the light of what they subsequently did. If we ourselves are the lustful looker, even we ourselves may be unaware that our look is lustful, and only realize it in retrospect. Others may be able to tell us that our look is or was lustful. All sorts of behaviour may count as looking at somebody lustfully, many difficult to describe and some hard to recognize. But nevertheless to look at somebody lustfully is a perfectly public and observable piece of behaviour.[3] That is what Jesus is telling people not to do. There is no suggestion here that 'external' behaviour is 'mere'.

Second, the above translation of these verses from Matthew is from the well-known Revised Standard Version. It obscures important features of the original Greek. The phrase 'every man who looks lustfully on a woman' translates the Greek *pas ho blepōn gunaika pros to epithumēsai autēn*. The Greek word *gune* can mean simply an adult woman, but it is also the word for 'wife', and here it almost certainly means a married woman. Even if, as a Greek word, it could mean an unmarried woman, the presupposition in Jewish society, where girls normally married very young (around fourteen or so) would certainly be that any female old enough to be called *gune* would be married. This is in any case just what we should expect, since at this point in the Sermon on the Mount Jesus is commenting on the commandment 'You shall not commit adultery.' At this point he, like the commandment itself, is concerned with the behaviour of men towards married women.

Third, the words of Jesus, as found in the Greek of Matthew's Gospel, are slightly misleadingly translated in the Revised Standard Version. The translation talks about looking at a woman *lustfully*. The Greek is more literally rendered: 'Anyone who looks at a woman *to covet her* ...' Jesus is here probably referring to the ninth (or tenth in some versions) commandment: 'You shall not covet your neighbour's wife', which in the Greek translation most commonly used in the time of Jesus, the Septuagint, is *ouk epithumēseis tēn gunaika tou plēsion sou* (Ex. 20.17; Deut. 5.27). That Jesus is alluding to this is especially probable in the light of the fact, already mentioned, that he is here commenting on the sixth commandment, forbidding adultery. It confirms that it is a married woman that is in question here. But the main point I want to make concerns the verb. The meaning of *epithumeō* has nothing to do with 'internal' thoughts as opposed to 'external' actions. It means seriously wanting something, setting desire on something and acting accordingly, if you can and if you have no stronger reason not to do so.

A particularly apposite example of the use of *epithumeō* comes from the Greek version of I Enoch, an apocryphal work composed in various stages around the beginning of the Christian era. Chapters 6 and 7 are about the period just before the flood. There we find:

> In those days, when the children of man had multiplied, it happened that there were born unto them handsome and beautiful daughters. And the angels, the children of heaven, saw them and desired (root *epithumeō*) them. And they said to one another: 'Come, let us choose wives for ourselves from among the daughters of man and beget us children.'... And they took wives unto themselves, and everyone chose one woman for himself, and they began to go unto them.[4]

The children of heaven do not just have thoughts running through their heads: they desire and are in a position to take, so they do take. Desire is what normally leads to action. And the action is typically, as in this instance, one of taking, assuming possession. The children of heaven do not want to enjoy the women, but to *have* them.

Behind the Greek *epithumeō* in the ten commandments and therefore also in Matthew is the Hebrew verb *ḥmd*, which similarly refers to desire, leading, as desire typically does, to action. For example, in chapter 7 of the book of Joshua, Achan is admitting to a theft: 'When I saw among the spoil a beautiful mantle from Shinar, and two hundred shekels of silver, and a bar of gold weighing fifty shekels, then I coveted (root *ḥmd*) them, and took them.'[5] Achan's desire, his coveting, issues naturally in action. And the action once again is one of taking so as to possess.

I have talked here about Greek and Hebrew verbs, because Hebrew and Greek are our scriptural languages. But the point is not a recondite or scholarly one. It is about the nature of desire, about what it is to desire something, and the point can be made equally well in English. Put simply, desire, if it is at all a serious desire, leads to action, if you are in a position to act and have no countervailing reason not to act. Suppose in April I say I want to take my holiday in Portugal this summer. In October you see me and ask me how my Portuguese holiday went:

> 'I didn't go'.
> 'Did something stop you?'
> 'No.'
> 'Did you change your mind?'
> 'No. I wanted to go, and I was quite able to go and had no reason not to. I just didn't go.'

A reply like that would be bemusing; you would be entitled to suspect either that I was joking or that, if I were speaking seriously, there was something wrong with me or that I did not quite understand how the English vocabulary of desire and wanting actually works. If you seriously want to do something and yet do not do it, that requires an explanation. If you want to do something, and have nothing preventing you from doing it, and see no reason not to do it – in short, if there is nothing that would explain your not doing it – then you do it. If in these circumstances you do not do it, then in fact you do not want to do it. You may say that you want to do something and genuinely believe you want to do it, and perhaps you have all sorts of fantasies running through your head about doing it. But if you find yourself in a position to do it and yet do not do it, and can give no reason for not doing it, then you do not desire or want to do it.

In fact we often find out in just such a way that we do not after all want to do something we thought we wanted to do. Maybe we got the impression we wanted to do it because we fantasized so much about it; whereas we actually want very much not to do it. (It may be that what we really wanted to do was to fantasize about it. Though it is no doubt true that once we have discovered we do not want to do it we will no longer be so inclined to fantasize about it). Peter has constant fantasies about committing adultery with Jane. Jane also spends her waking hours dreaming of sexual bliss with Peter. The chance comes when Andrew is away for the weekend on urgent business. A drink, a dinner, another drink, and they find themselves in the bedroom. Now that it comes to it, Peter is suddenly horrified and rushes from the room in shame and confusion, to the annoyance and frustration of Jane. Jane actually did want to commit adultery; Peter, for all that he thought he did, did not, and had to discover that he did not.

Whatever the complexities of our language of desire, desire always retains some link with action. In this passage of the Sermon on the Mount Jesus is not talking about inner thoughts divorced from action, or about thinking you want somebody when actually you don't, but about really setting desire on somebody and if possible setting about getting them, or at least trying it on a bit; he is talking about *doing*, about looking at somebody and setting your desire upon them, setting about taking or trying to take them.

And it is not primarily sexual desire that Jesus is criticizing as out of place here, but the desire to have, to possess. Since it is a married woman involved, the action means breaking in on a marriage; it belongs to a spectrum of activities which ends in adultery.[6] In the Hebrew marriage tradition that provides the context for this saying of Jesus, the husband has rights over his wife akin to property rights. This is well attested; here a few examples will suffice.[7] First, note that in the very commandment which lies behind Jesus' comments coveting your neighbour's wife is put alongside coveting his house, his manservant, his ox, 'or anything that is your neighbour's' (Ex. 20.17). At the very least this listing strongly suggests that a man's wife is considered roughly as, or as analogous to, his possession.[8] This placing of wife (and indeed children) alongside material goods as one possession among others is not uncommon. Another example is Deut. 28.29–32, which is part of the description of the curses, principally depredation by victorious enemies, which will befall the Israelites (i.e. the Israelite men) if they do not obey God's commandments:

> and you shall grope at noonday, as the blind grope in darkness, and you shall not prosper in your ways; and you shall be only oppressed and robbed continually, and there shall be no one to help you. You shall betroth a wife, and another man shall lie with her; you shall build a house, and you shall not dwell in it; you shall plant a vineyard, and you shall not use the fruit of it. Your ox shall be slain before your eyes, and you shall not eat of it; your ass shall be violently taken away before your face, and shall not be restored to you; your sheep shall be given to your enemies, and there shall be no one to help you. Your sons and your daughters shall be given to another people, while your eyes look on and fail with longing for them all the day; and it shall not be in the power of your hand to prevent it.

More briefly, Jeremiah threatens the wise men of Judah:

> The wise men shall be put to shame, they shall be dismayed and taken; lo, they have rejected the word of the Lord, and what wisdom is in them? Therefore I will give their wives to others and their fields to conquerors (Jer. 8.9f.).

A man did not own his wife precisely as he owned land or cattle; wives were not sold as were cows and slaves, and there is evidence, if it is needed, that personal relationships with wives were valued in a way that relationships with cows and slaves were not.[9] But the analogy is a strong one nevertheless. This idea of wife as property explains why only the husband had the right of divorce (Deut. 24. 1–4); only he could *disown*. The wife, as the one owned, had no freedom to dispose of herself; and she could not rid herself of her husband, since she did not *have* him in the sense in which he had her.

This background is crucial to understanding Jesus' remarks. Setting your heart on another man's wife will no doubt involve or even consist in wanting sexual intercourse with her. This does not, however, mean committing some special type of sexual sin, but preparing to infringe that man's property rights by taking what is his. It is setting in train a course of action that amounts to injustice against him.[10] So Jesus is not talking, either, about 'lust' in isolation but as infringing on an important social relationship, that between man and wife. Jesus is not aiming to promote something that might be called 'inner purity', if by that is meant a putative mental state divorced from any reference to activity. Neither is he merely wanting to stop particular thoughts and fantasies going through people's heads. He wants to stop people being unjust to each other.

There is in fact nothing at all about thoughts in the text of this passage from Matthew. The man who looks at a married woman so as to covet her need have no thoughts passing through his head at all; indeed, the more engrossed he is by the sight of this woman, the more intent he is on looking at her, the less likely he is to have his mind full of thoughts. Jesus is speaking in defence of a particular important social institution, marriage, by discouraging certain kinds of behaviour.

None of this is to say that our fantasies or the thoughts that run through our heads are unimportant, or to suggest that the Catholic tradition is in any way mistaken in the significance it attaches to sin in thought, as well as in word and deed. Thoughts and fantasies can indeed be very important, but their importance does not lie in their being inner rather than outer, mental rather than physical. On the contrary, they can be important precisely because they can influence the way we behave. What we say to ourselves and the fantasies we have and indulge can convince us we want to do particular things, and can actually bring it about that we want them. And then we will *act*, if we have the liberty to and see no compelling reason against it. Thus what goes on in our head may affect the way we live with others and behave towards them. It may make us rob them or tend them, rape them or serve them. The importance of thoughts lies precisely in their intimate relation to what we do, to the external, not in their being divorced from it. So it is indeed important to cultivate certain ways of thinking and resist others. It is important to think justly that we may act justly, to avoid thinking adulterously that we may avoid acting adulterously.

Morality and the heart

Behind much of what authors like Lawler, Boyle and May say there appears to lie a false antithesis between human behaviour and what people are, a wrong way of looking at the distinction between the internal and the external that we sometimes make when we speak about people. Morality, they claim, 'is not directly concerned with external behaviour and its effect but with the immediate effects one's choices have on one's self – that is, with the kind of person one makes oneself by one's own free choices.' As we saw earlier, it is perfectly in order to say that Christian morality is at least partly concerned with the kind of person one is or is becoming, and with the effect of one's actions and habits on oneself.[11] But, as we again saw earlier, the kind of person you are is a matter of the kind of thing you habitually do. If certain kinds of action have an effect on the kind of person you are, that means they have an effect on the kind of actions you will tend perform. If morality is concerned with the kind of person you are, this is *because* of its concern with 'external behaviour', not in opposition to any such concern.

Another symptom of this mistake is the antithesis Lawler, Boyle and May set up between internal disposition and will on the one hand and external behaviour on the other. Just as thought or fantasy can appear more essential to a person, because somehow interior, than 'mere external behaviour', so can the will, a person's disposition. But, just as in the former case, so here too the reference to external action is indispensable to any proper understanding of the will. Disposition is disposition to *act* in a particular way, and the existence of the disposition is shown by the action, in general. If you don't act, you don't have the disposition, unless you stop yourself from acting, or are prevented from acting. The language of 'internal' and 'external', while it may have its uses, is dangerous, since it can give the impression that the internal and the external are two different, almost independent spheres of human life, whereas the two are intimately linked.

This point can be brought out by looking at another passage from the Gospel, one that Lawler, Boyle and May refer to in this context, and in which they pick up the important biblical use of the word 'heart'. They say:

> This focus on the heart, on the person's disposition and will, is also central to the catalogue of vices Jesus presents (Matthew 15.19; Mark 7.21–22). These vices proceed from the human heart and, unlike those things which are taken into the body, defile the human person.[12]

The passage they refer to is the one in which Jesus criticizes the pharisaic concern with ritual cleanliness, including the ritual washing of hands before eating and (perhaps) their care to avoid the foods designated unclean by the law of Moses. But this passage is far from establishing the point Lawler, Boyle and May seem to want to make, the importance of 'the heart', the 'internal', as opposed to 'mere behaviour', the 'external'. The point here is that what Jesus calls 'the heart' is where actions proceed from. A person's heart has such and such in it if that person acts in such and such a way, or wants to. (And our criterion for somebody's wanting to do something is that he does it if he sees no reason why not.) Jesus does not talk about a person's heart separately from what he does. This is clear from the list of vices: they are all certain ways and habits of acting out here in the world, not funny goings-on in some putative internal theatre of the mind. The heart is what behaviour comes from, and that is why it is so important: 'Out of the heart come evil thoughts,[13] murder, adultery, fornication, theft, false witness, slander. These are what defile a man.'[14] The point is that these things come out of the heart; what is in the heart does not just lie there and make no difference to what you do. And what comes out is various kinds of activity, external, in principle observable (though no doubt often secret) behaviour. The heart is precisely the source of action. If it is in your heart to do it, then you do it, unless you are prevented from doing it. Likewise, if you are free to do it and yet do not do it, it is not in your heart to do it.

Morality, then, *is* concerned with 'external' behaviour and its effect, at least the morality that Jesus talks about. And this is only to be expected, if he is concerned with living in the kingdom, living with others. It is your behaviour that affects people; it is in behaving that you live with people. And this is as true of sexual behaviour as of any other behaviour. Jesus' teaching in Matthew 5 is in full conformity with the social thrust of so much of his other teaching. It no doubt raises questions about his view of marriage, and I will have a little to say about that later, in chapter 8. But the point I want to establish for the moment is simply that Jesus is not here propounding some special principles governing private sexual fantasies. He is concerned with justice in relationships, an aspect of that love which he consistently lays down as the basis of our public activity.

Varieties of fantasy

Let me cite some sentences from another modern work which well illustrate the possibilities of confusion in this area. This is from an essay by Grisez, Boyle, Finnis and May entitled 'Every Marital Act Ought To Be Open To New Life': Toward a Clearer Understanding'.[15] The main concern of these authors is with the morality of contraception, but here they plainly have our passage from Matthew in mind:

> Although the goodness of the life that is destroyed provides the reason why deliberate killing is wrong, the moral evil of killing primarily is in the killer's heart.
> The New Testament makes it abundantly clear, against false, legalistic conceptions, that morality is in the heart. A man can commit adultery without ever touching a woman. And he need not wish to commit adultery with some real woman. Perhaps there is no real woman in the world with whom he wishes to commit adultery. But if he imagines an ideal playmate and freely consents to his wish that she were real so that he might commit adultery with her, he commits adultery. Indeed, any sin is in one's heart before it is in one's deed, and one's sinful deed is wrong because of one's evil heart. Therefore, deliberate homicide is immoral primarily because the contralife will that it involves cannot be a loving heart.[16]

A fundamental misconception here is related to one we have already met elsewhere: the idea that having something in your heart is the same as imagining doing it, or at least that if you imagine doing it that means you have it in your heart. But this is not so; we have already seen how to have something in your heart is to set your desire on it, so that you may end up acting on it. This mistake vitiates the entire paragraph I have quoted, but there are other related errors that deserve special attention.

Note first the sheer exaggeration here. A man simply cannot commit adultery without ever touching a woman. Whatever we may think of the moral importance of the imagination, committing adultery in your imagination is not the same as committing adultery. We can be misled by the preposition 'in' into thinking there is some special realm of the imagination, a special intangible place where we act in special ways, apart from the everyday ways we act in our common physical space; so that we may play the piano in the parlour, but also play it in the imagination. But this is not so. To do something in the imagination is simply to imagine doing it; and generally speaking, you imagine doing something when you are *not* doing it. So even if we pass over the erroneous notion that the heart is concerned with the imagination, and specifically that doing something in your heart is the same as imagining doing it, still committing adultery in your heart is not the same as committing adultery, just as robbing a bank in your imagination is not the same as robbing a bank. It is not committing adultery in a special place or in a special way; it is imagining committing adultery, and people in general imagine committing adultery only when they are not in fact committing adultery. It may still be wrong to imagine committing adultery, but the wrongness of such imagining is not the wrongness of committing adultery.

Even if somebody wanted to insist that the heart is connected with the imagination, the point of what Jesus is saying here can be put without making mistakes of this kind and without exaggeration. It is surely right to stress the importance of what goes through your head. Imagination is sometimes not *mere* imagination, since it may lead to action of various kinds. But it is to misunderstand what Jesus is saying to think that there is somehow a kind of inner adultery quite divorced from what people may actually do. To commit adultery in your heart is a serious thing to do (that is the point of describing the desire or fantasy in those terms), but it is not to commit adultery.

So too, if I imagine an ideal playmate and freely consent to my wish that she were real so that I might commit adultery with her, I may be doing something reprehensible, perhaps something so reprehensible that it deserves to be described as adultery of the heart, but I do not commit adultery. Here it is worth mentioning a variant of a point that was raised earlier. If I imagine committing adultery with such an ideal partner, or for that matter with a real one, part of what may be going on is that I imagine I *want* to commit adultery. And I may in fact want to commit adultery; but in fact I may not want to, as I may discover if the ideal partner materializes. This is true of any imagined partner, real or imaginary. But there is a further point concerning the ideal playmate. What I do not and cannot do in the matter of a fantasy partner is actually to set my desire on somebody. I am at most imagining somebody on whom I imagine I set my desire. So this situation is far removed from what Jesus is actually talking about when he speaks of committing adultery in the heart.

A further though less prominent mistake in what these authors say is the over-simple way they talk about imagination. The concept of imagination is in fact far richer and more variegated than the above discussion allows for. What has been said so far more or less equates imagination with fantasy. Such a limitation, if explicit, is not harmful. More important is the variety of ways imagination, so limited, can be linked to desire. Our authors appear to think that imagining doing something involves wanting to do it. But it does not. Here are some of the things we might talk about under the name of imagination or fantasy:

1. Imagining something that you would like to do if you got the chance (and you might well get the chance if you are lucky, or if you work for it). This kind of imagining is something you might do if you have set your desire on somebody, or on doing something. It is not the same as setting your desire on somebody or something, but one of the things you may well do if you have so set your desire. It is a symptom or accompaniment of desire, not the desire itself.

2. Imagining something you would have liked to do if circumstances were/had been different (if she had not been married, if he had not already been committed, if I were not a priest), but would not now do.

3. Imagining what is clearly impossible for you, e.g. what you would do with a million pounds if you had it, when you have no reason to think you will ever have so much money.

4. Imagining yourself doing something you know you would actually not want to do if you got the chance, 'but it's nice to think about it'.

5. Imagining what it would be like to do something you have no particular feelings about (perhaps in order to find out what you feel about it, or generate a feeling about it). This can take the form of an exercise, formal or informal, like role-play.[17]

There are no doubt other forms of imagination. Some of them may be dangerous or liberating. Some of them are also clearly necessary if we are to develop imaginative sympathy with others, or to appreciate the moral dimension of some acts. If I imagine committing adultery with my neighbour's wife, it may be because I want to commit adultery with her – because I am committing adultery in my heart. But no such thing need be in question. It may just be a pleasant way to idle away a few spare moments; in this case it is not a very laudable thing for me to do, and I should probably be discouraged from doing it, but it is not adultery of the heart. Or I may be confused about whether I want to commit adultery with her; in this case I may use fantasy as a way of thinking imaginatively about the situation, and that may show me that it would be a bad thing to do. Or I may be an actor or a priest or some sympathetic person trying to understand what it is like to be in such a position.

The inside of the cup

Lurking behind many of the views I have criticized in the preceding pages is the mistaken use of the distinction between the internal and the external, as if there were two different theatres of action – the common space in which we live, move and have our being, and the private theatre of the imagination or the heart. Allied to this is the assumption that Jesus works with the same distinction when he talks about the heart. I have tried to show that both these ideas are mistaken. Grisez, Boyle, Finnis and May perform a service in that they make explicit the distinction Jesus actually is making. They say, 'The New Testament makes it abundantly clear, against false, legalistic conceptions, that morality is in the heart.' This is right. Jesus is not opposing the heart or the internal to behaviour, the merely external. He is opposing the heart to what might be called a legalistic view of morality. What is meant by this?

When Jesus says of the Pharisees and others that their service does not come from the heart, he does not mean that they are concerned to uphold the Law of Moses, or that their thinking is centred on the Law. Jesus himself is just as concerned as any Pharisee that the Law be obeyed. The very passage in Matthew we have been discussing at such great length comes from a part of the Sermon on the Mount that is in effect a rigorist commentary on the Law. Only a few verses earlier Jesus tells his audience:

> Truly, I say to you, till heaven and earth pass away, not an iota, not a dot, will pass from the law until all is accomplished. Whoever then relaxes one of the least of these commandments and teaches men so, shall be called least in the kingdom of heaven; but he who does them and teaches them shall be called great in the kingdom of heaven. For ¹ tell you, unless your righteousness exceeds that of the scribes and Pharisees, you will never enter the kingdom of heaven (Matt. 5.18f.).

As part of his concern for the integrity of the Law he criticizes the Pharisees for not being, in this sense, legalistic enough. When he complains that the Pharisees' service does not come from the heart, he means that when they do obey the prescriptions of the Law their heart is not in it, and this is shown by the fact that their religious observances do not cohere with the rest of their behaviour in the right way. They tithe scrupulously, but they do not help others; they fast, but they despise others (Luke 18.10–15); they say long prayers, but they cheat old people out of their property (Mark 12.40); they preach 'Honour your father and mother', but they make up rules which encourage people not to provide for their parents (Mark 7.10–13). That is why their religion may be said to be legalistic.¹⁸ The Pharisees are legalistic not in that they are concerned for the law, but in that they are concerned in the wrong way, losing sight of the purpose of the law, and so disobeying its central commandments and being wrongheaded about the laws they most insist upon. Jesus' concern is with the rest of what people do, not with what goes on inside their heads – except in so far as this affects what they do.

' We keep on returning to this point. But there is something missing in this treatment, for surely there is something in human action that is hidden and that is important. People deceive by their actions; they hide a rotten interior with fair actions. They may speak fine-sounding words or do fine-looking deeds while at heart they are evil. This also is a well-attested aspect of New Testament teaching, as well as an obvious fact of human existence. And surely, we may think, when Jesus criticizes the Pharisees and others for their hypocrisy his stress is on what is internal. But not so. It is true that when you see a single action of somebody, you do not see their heart. Their action may look generous, but it may really be self-seeking or full of hatred. But what you do not see when you do not see their heart is not something inaccessible inside them; it is how they behave on other occasions, their wider pattern of behaviour. What you cannot now see is not inaccessible; it is simply that you have not yet accessed it. Seeing somebody's heart is seeing a pattern. That is why you can get to know what is in somebody's heart by living with them, or being with them over an extended period; it is then that you can see the full range of what they do and organize it into a coherent pattern. (But however long you are with somebody you can never get at what is inaccessibly interior.) So when Jesus criticizes the hypocrisy of the Pharisees he does so by contrasting their fine words and fine-looking deeds with other things they do, not with anything that is interior to them, such as the sentences that run through their heads. When he implies that morality is a matter of the heart (not in the heart, as if concerned with what goes on in some private theatre) he is indeed combatting a legalism of sorts, as Grisez, Boyle, Finnis and May say; but he is opposing to it an integrated way of behaving, not a concentration on what goes on inside them.

Conclusion

I have dwelt on this passage from the Sermon on the Mount for so long not only for its importance in helping to establish the basically social character of Jesus' teaching, but because it raises several other issues that will be important in later discussion. First, the way Lawler, Boyle and May treat this text is an example of how theological and anthropological presuppositions inhibit the clear understanding of a text, even at a superficial level. They, like others before them, treat it as a matter of course as being about thoughts, while a plain reading of the text shows that it is about what people do, in the first instance how they look at other people. This misreading of texts is a particularly common feature of Christian use of scripture in the field of sexual ethics, where the idea seems more often to be to use passages of scripture to support predetermined positions than to look and see what they are actually saying.

Second, this tendency is sometimes made worse by a very faulty appreciation of the ways in which we talk about human beings and their behaviour, such as a misuse of the division we sometimes want to make between the internal and the external. It is going to be important to get clear about some problems concerning human activity if we are going to get a proper understanding of Christian ethics.

Third, the allusion in this passage to marriage and the way it was regarded in the time of Jesus is an indication that wider social institutions are of importance in any understanding of sex. Here we find marriage and sex bound up with particular notions of possession, and therefore rights and authority, as well as with a particular idea of the significance of gender difference. The teaching that Jesus gives here depends for its significance on there being in Jewish society well-developed ideas of personal property and property rights which allowed for extension to people, so that people, in particular wives, could for certain purposes be regarded as analogous to property. In addition, it tacitly presupposes ideas of male superiority in virtue of which a man could standardly have a kind of authority over a woman which a woman could not have over a man; there is no talk here of the injustice done to a woman by looking at her husband so as to covet him. We can only properly understand the teaching of Jesus if we see it in its wider social context, and we shall find that in examining other parts of scripture, as well as tradition, we cannot understand what they have to say about sex in isolation. We have to look at the social institutions and structures they presuppose, or indeed seek to undermine. This will become clearer as we examine the second of the texts I mentioned at the end of chapter 1, that from Leviticus 18.

3

The Treatment of Men

In the previous chapter I suggested that the way to understand sexual ethics was to look at the social significance of our sexual and sex-related behaviour. We should look not to some laws putatively specially set up to cope with private sexual relations, but to whether sexual behaviour, like the rest of our behaviour, is loving – whether it is respectful, considerate, generous, and so on, and not only to our current sexual partner, but to others with whom we have to do. Thus the reason why Jesus tells us not to look lustfully at a woman is not because it is important to keep our 'inner life' pure but because this kind of behaviour is one that threatens to disrupt an important social relationship, that between husband and wife. More specifically, it infringes the rights of the husband over his wife. It is inconsiderate. So it is against that love which we are to have for our neighbour, which includes respecting his rights. However, the rights and status enjoyed by people in any particular society are not above criticism.

Leviticus and gender distinction

In this chapter I want to make another series of points about the way sexual behaviour is connected with society, to try to show that we have to be sensitive to the social context of laws governing sexual behaviour, to say not only what is obvious – that sexual norms and customs vary from society to society – but also that even to understand what a particular norm or law means, what it is for, we have to look at the structure of the society whose norm it is. I want to do that by looking at the context of the other apparently difficult text I mentioned in the first chapter, Lev. 18.22: 'You shall not lie with a man as with a woman: it is an abomination.' The problem with this text, in relation to the point of view I have been putting forward, is that the behaviour it refers to appears to have no social significance, to affect nobody apart from the two partners in the activity. It looks as if it is being condemned simply because it is wrong in itself, without considering any wider social ramifications, since there are none to consider; it's a private act. Perhaps it is being condemned because, as many Christian writers have said, it is 'against nature'. However, if we look more closely we shall see that there is indeed a wide and deeply important social aspect to this prohibition.

We should note first of all that this piece of legislation comes from the so-called priestly writer (or school of writers), whose influence on the final form of the Pentateuch is great. The epithet 'priestly' comes from the concern which this writer characteristically shows with the cult; much of his legislation, particularly in Leviticus, is concerned with various sacrifices and festivals and with the ordination and life of priests. But an equally important characteristic of this writer is his concern, almost obsession, with division and distinction. Much of this is encapsulated in a couple of verses from Leviticus:

> I am the Lord your God, who have separated (root *bdl*) you from the peoples. You shall therefore make a distinction (root *bdl*) between the clean beast and the unclean, and between the unclean bird and the clean; you shall not make yourselves abominable by beast or by bird or by anything with which the ground teems, which I have set apart (root *bdl*) for you to hold unclean. You shall be holy to me; for I the Lord your God am holy, and have separated (root *bdl*) you from the peoples, that you should be mine (Lev. 20.24–26).

The regular recurrence here of the verbal root *bdl*, which can be variously translated according to context as 'divide', 'separate' or 'distinguish', makes the writer's concern inescapable. We can also see from this passage how closely it is bound up with his conceptions of holiness, cleanness and uncleanness, and election. Israel, as the nation chosen by God, is thereby made separate from the rest of the peoples of the earth. That separation is also part of its holiness; from elsewhere in the priestly writings it is evident that the holy is primarily that which is separated from the everyday, from the profane.[1] Unclean foods are those which God has separated off to be held unclean. And the point of all this division is not merely that the separated things are to be put in separate places, but that they are to be treated differently. Holy things are to be used in special ways, and not used in the same way as ordinary, profane things.[2] Israel, as a separated, holy people, is to live differently from all the nations.[3] Animals that God has separated for Israel to hold unclean are ones that are not to be eaten in the way that clean ones are. No doubt physical separation is of some importance here: both functionally, as it is easier to distinguish things and treat them differently if they are in different places; and also symbolically, since putting things in separate places is itself a way of treating them differently and expressing a commitment to treat them differently.

But the major point is that this making of distinctions between things is not just a game or a matter of noting distinctions that occur naturally. It has an important social function, and indeed dominates the way life is ordered. The things that are distinguished play different parts in the life of Israel, and the proper ordering of life consists in making and observing these distinctions.

Genesis 1 and gender distinction

The creation narrative at the beginning of the book of Genesis is also by the priestly writer. We can note the same emphasis on division and separation. God distinguishes (root *bdl*) the light from the darkness (1.4); he commands that there be a firmament to separate (root *bdl*) the waters from the waters (1.6f.); he creates the great luminaries to mark the distinction (root *bdl*) between the light and the darkness (1.14–18). Further, the period of creation is carefully marked off into days, separated by evenings and mornings; the world is compartmentalized neatly into dry land, sea and air; and plants and animals are created as members of definite and separate species, not haphazardly, as individuals, but 'according to their kind' (1.11f., 21, 24f.). Finally, God hallows (root *qdš*) the seventh day (2.3) and remember that making holy is a kind of separation. This distinction between the seventh day and the rest is not just a matter of recording how things were in the beginning, it is not mentioned as a matter of casual interest. It will later be one of the most important distinctions in the life of Israel. The Israelites will treat the sabbath differently from all other days, live differently on the sabbath.[4]

All this is vital for understanding the account of the creation of people that forms one of the climaxes of this narrative:

> Then God said: 'Let us make man in our image, after our likeness; and let them have dominion over the birds of the air, and over the cattle, and over all the earth, and over every creeping thing that creeps upon the earth.' So God created man in his own image, in the image of God he created him; male and female he created them (Gen. 1.26f.).

Many theologians find the basis for Christian sexual ethics in these verses. An obvious reason for this is that it does mention sexual difference, but there is a further and ultimately more important reason. Since in this narrative we are at the beginning of the human story, indeed at the beginning of the world, the story can be viewed as being about people before the advent of different human societies in all their particularity and contingency. What we are presented with here it is tempting to call 'natural humanity'. Here are people as they were made by God, before they started making themselves, before they moulded themselves by habit and custom, before different races and civilizations developed. Here we appear to be at a stage in which the nature of people is primarily biological rather than social, where people are fleshy atoms who only later on have to be fitted into a social context. So the biological division between the sexes is the natural, that is God-given, division. For example, the Catholic theologian Bernard Häring, under the heading 'male and female he created them', writes:

> Sexuality is a relational concept; it points particularly to the bipolarity between

men and women ... God's word is solemn: 'So God created Man in his own image; in the image of God he created him; male and female he created them' (Gen. 1.27). It is not my intention to give the impression that this text points only to sexuality; it speaks also about the image of God in man's and woman's vocation to be co-creators in ordering the world around them. But sexuality cannot be excluded from the concept of 'image of God'.[5]

Again, the Protestant writer Eric Fuchs asserts:

> Sexual differentiation has something to do with God's very intention to make man in his own image. The experience of otherness which is made possible through sexual differentiation refers to and finds its meaning in the experience of the otherness of God.[6]

But it is, I believe, a mistake to use these verses as a basis for sexual ethics if they are seen in isolation, partly because that is to misunderstand the verses themselves. Although the setting of the story is prehistoric and perhaps presocial, it is written by an author with a definite historical place and time, who lives in a particular society with a definite structure. And similarly it is written for people living at a definite time and place, with particular concerns, and it addresses those concerns. Though it is holy writ, we cannot with any integrity read it as if it were not a historical document. If we are to understand it we have to ask what it meant in the thought-world in which it was written. We should ask first why the division of people into two sexes appears here. There are plenty of ways people can be divided – say, into left-handed and right-handed. If the writer had written that God made people left-handed and right-handed it would have been just as true. Granted that division and distinction are important to the priestly writer, why does he make just this distinction here? It must be one of particular importance for him. As we have seen, there are a host of distinctions important to the priestly writer, for whom proper living consists in making proper distinctions. The reason why this one is such an important distinction is the same as the reason why the other distinctions are important: it affects the social life of Israel because the people who are thereby distinguished from each other are to be treated differently; they have different places in that society. 'Male' and 'female' are not just biological terms here, and the distinction between them is not just a biological one. Rather is the biological difference made the basis of a fundamental social one. That is why this particular division figures in the creation narrative, in a way that the distinction between left-handed and right-handed or between the fair-haired and the dark-haired does not. These divisions are not made the basis of primary social distinctions, as is the distinction between the sexes. While being male or female may be a biological fact about people, being a man or a woman is a matter of belonging to a social category, having a particular social identity.

To say that God made them male and female is not just to point to the fact of sexual differentiation (perhaps with a view to going on to talk about sexual reproduction); it is to underpin a division of adult human beings into two great social classes.

Gender role and social identity

It needs only a very cursory look at the Old Testament to see what a hugely important social distinction that between male and female is. And the distinction is a vertical one. Men are in a number of ways superior to women. To begin with, there is a huge preponderance of men and their concerns in the narrative sections of the Old Testament. Though there are stories, and important ones, about women in the Old Testament, it is much more common for women to enter into the narrative as part of the story of a man. It is true that there is the story of Ruth, and of Esther and of Judith, but there is no story of Bathsheba; she is a character in the story of David. There is no story of Delilah; she is a character in the story of Samson. And the same is true of most of the appearances of women in the Old Testament. The men are active in public life; the importance of women in the life of men is clear enough, but the influence of women is largely confined to the home.[7] In general, men are dominant, women submissive. Public power is in the hands of men, and this is mirrored within the home. In marriage men have all the authority; the husband is always the head of the family. Men may divorce their wives (Deut. 24.1–4), but not women their husbands. Judah is able to order the burning of his daughter-in-law Tamar when it appears she is guilty of harlotry; there is no suggestion that he has done any wrong in himself going with one he believed to be a prostitute (Gen. 28). In the wider society, it is almost always men who lead tribes and rule over nations and empires, and who administer justice. The priests are men. It has to be stressed again that the division is a social one, even though it may be based on a biological difference. Many of the ways men and women are distinguished have nothing at all to do with the biological differences between them. There is no biological reason why the ability to bear children should disbar somebody from being a priest or from having a position of authority in the city.

None of this can be very surprising to us; we are familiar with the same kind of thing from the workings of modern societies throughout the world as well as of our own society, today as well as in the past. As in ancient Hebrew society, we and others have made quite small biological differences the basis of great and important social distinctions. Our sexual identity as men or women, boys or girls, is a social construct; it is a social identity. It is built on biological differences, but is dependent too on our giving those differences a significance which is crucial for the way we see ourselves as individuals and the place we occupy in the society around us. The biological differences between men and women are actually quite small in comparison to the similarities. Yet those differences can be enormously important to us, and it appears that most societies have made those differences the basis for a division that runs through their entire structure.

If the differences between men and women are slight, those between male and female babies are even slighter. But when a baby is born we observe what there is between its legs. This is not just casual observation, idle curiosity about the physical features of this individual. What might be found there is never very much, but on it can depend the broad outlines and even some of the details of the future life of the child. It will determine in the first place the range of names that can be given it. It can determine what kind of education, if any, the child will have, what kind of presents it is given, which of its interests will be fostered and which discouraged, what freedom it will have to move about as an older child, what kind of clothes it will wear, what way its hair will be styled, whether as an adult it will play a dominant or submissive role, whether it will command or obey, what kind of work it will do, the degree of sexual licence that will be accorded it, the way it will spend its free time and with whom, the places it will be allowed to go, the range of its responsibilities, the extent of its rights and opportunities, the ceremonies it will be allowed or obliged to perform, and so on.

And here we are not just talking about 'primitive' societies. Most societies, primitive or modern, make much of the biological distinction between the sexes. Even in England, until not many years ago, if when you were born one thing was discovered between your legs you would as a small child be dressed in pink; if another thing, in blue. What was found there would determine whether you would later wear a skirt or trousers, a blouse or a shirt and tie; it would determine what styles of shoes you might wear, what length of hair you might have, the parts of your body you had to keep covered, what school you might go to, what subjects you might study there, what kind of job you would be likely to get on leaving school, even whether you would get a job at all, whether you could wear makeup and jewellery, what clubs you would be allowed into, etc.

Even today, while we appear much more relaxed about gender distinctions in many ways,[8] they are still very important to us, especially as they touch on the body. Women may be able to wear (suitably modified) trousers, but men may not wear skirts or lipstick, except as a joke. A man cannot normally walk or move his hands in a way that is considered feminine. Any man who did that as a normal, matter of course way of presenting himself would be considered an abnormal man. Many people would genuinely feel not just that he was doing something unconventional or even wrong, but that there was something wrong with him; he would be doing something unnatural, and would perhaps *be* unnatural. For many people, perhaps most, this feeling would be difficult to articulate, and more difficult to justify by logical argument. They just 'feel that way'; or 'that's just how it is'. But these attitudes nevertheless have identifiable origins, which we can investigate. We did not acquire such opinions out of thin air. And that we cannot give adequate reasons for them, or even feel that no reasons can be given, that 'it's just obvious', means that we did not work them out for ourselves. We largely inherit them when we are trained into the conventions that underlie them. This shows how 'nature' can be a social construct, dependent on conventions about clothing, make-up, etc; for it is conventions that a man who behaves in a feminine way is transgressing.

This is not to belittle our feelings about what is natural and what is not, to make them a matter of mere convention. It is to show that conventions, particularly conventions concerning the body, are extremely important to us and shape our way of seeing things, our conception of what is natural. It in no way lessens their importance to know that such conventions differ widely from society to society. Conventions of this kind are never 'mere'. This is testified to in the Old Testament as well, as we might expect. The book of Deuteronomy contains this law: 'A woman shall not wear anything that pertains to a man, nor shall a man put on a woman's garment; for whoever does these things is an abomination to the Lord your God' (22.5).

Gender role, nature and sexual behaviour

An important part of learning gender role is learning what kinds of sexual behaviour are considered appropriate to your sex, as well as to your state in life. Whatever the biological facts, biology is never allowed to take its course, but is channelled by ceaseless social pressures: boys are actually trained (or acculturated) into finding girls – the girls of their society – attractive. And vice versa. Advertisements, the assumptions of parents and teachers, the gossip, encouragement and threat of peer groups, as well as many other factors, all teach young people whom they are to find attractive. They also teach them what they are expected to do with them. Boys are expected to show sexual desire and to be glad when it is responded to, but they are not supposed to feel comfortable with being the objects of sexual desire. Friends in class lie to each other about their sexual successes, and after a while it becomes embarrassing if you have nothing to say. Even if you don't do what they say they do, still you learn what counts as success. Mothers start to get worried after a while if their boy is still not showing any interest in girls, and start talking subtly about what nice girls there are in the neighbourhood, and how all the boys who were in your class are engaged or married now, except that funny one; and so on. All this socialization can fail, for the material is sometimes recalcitrant, but its central importance in shaping people's sexual attitudes is undeniable.

An important point to note here is that these socially learnt attitudes, in moulding our view of what dress or style of talking or sexual behaviour belongs to us as men and women, form also our sense of what is natural. If you do not live up to the expectations that others have of you, and which you may be taught to have of yourself, you are not just different, there is something wrong with you. You may be thought, and think yourself, unnatural. This is particularly clear if your behaviour actually contradicts the gender role that belongs to you. If, for instance, you behave towards members of your own sex as you are expected to behave towards members of the other sex, your behaviour is likely to be branded unnatural; and similarly if you act in any other markedly deviant way, like wanting to be beaten as part of your sexual activity. If you behave in ways that differ significantly from the norm – and what behaviour is normal and what deviation from it is significant varies much from society to society – then you are not just different, you are abnormal. You do not occupy some further socially accepted position; you do not fit into the classification at all, but cross it. Societies do not note the varieties of human behaviour and leave it at that; they classify and then try to fit everybody into the classification. Those who do not fit are simply anomalies.

Social divisions are generally more rigid than biological divisions. This can be illustrated even in the case of the division into two sexes. Though the way we classify people is based upon observed physical differences, it is still a distinction that we make, not nature. There are hermaphrodites, people who unite in their one body the characteristics we use to distinguish the sexes. They are as much a natural biological product as everybody else, but they cut across the strict binary classification that we set up. We might be inclined to say that with such people something has gone wrong, they are anomalous. But that only means that the classification that we make and that we insist on allows for only two possibilities, male and female. We do not make room for a third possibility, even though nature does. As a result, hermaphrodites do not have their social niche, a place where they belong, a social identity, a role they are expected to play. They have no place, no role, no identity. They are merely 'abnormalities'.[9] We insist on binary opposition here as we do not in many other places. And we insist on it because it is fundamental to our social organization. Anything that cuts across it threatens the neat organization of the world, threatens a sense of place.

By way of analogy, imagine that we insisted that people were either blonde or dark-haired. Such an insistence would make people with middling brown hair or dark hair with blond streaks anomalous. Something would have to be done about them, or they would have to be quietly ignored.[10] This may seem a bad analogy, for surely a distinction between the blonde and the dark-haired is a quite unimportant one. We wouldn't bother to classify people in this way, because hair colour just doesn't matter. That is true, but the insignificance of hair colour is not something that we read off from the book of nature. In our society we *treat* it as insignificant. Things might easily have been different. It could have been that anybody with blond hair was classified as a free citizen while anybody with dark hair was made into a slave. Then it would make a very great difference what colour hair you had; it would make a great difference to your place in society, your freedoms and responsibilities, who you could marry, what clothes you could wear, where you could live, your social identity. It would then be an important question what to do with somebody who had streaky hair. If this sounds a bit far-fetched, remember that similar social distinctions have been made and are still made on the basis of skin colour. And not so long ago it could be a matter of life or death whether you were classified as Jewish or non-Jewish.[11]

Where such binary classification is important it becomes necessary also to establish clear boundaries between the two classes, to make it obvious to which class a person belongs. This means making it visually obvious, if it isn't already, as in the case of skin colour. A Jew may actually look like anybody else, so Jews are made to wear special badges to show their identity. It also means making sure that anomalies, cases that cut across the classification and cause confusion, are minimized. That means forbidding marriages between Jews and non-Jews so that there will be no children who cannot be easily placed in one category or the other. Ways of classifying people that we in our still fairly liberal Western society would not dream of using have been and are now elsewhere extremely important. Socially important: physical, biological differences have been made to bear an enormous social weight.

The biological differences are made to bear this weight by dominant social groups. It was not Jews who insisted they wear badges, be driven from their homes, be starved, tortured and murdered. It was not blacks who insisted they be treated as servants, be badly housed, be denied any say in the running of their country, be kept off beaches. (Neither, by the way, do the 'anomalies' insist they be treated as such. If German Jews did not ask to be carted off to concentration camps, neither did the German homosexuals. If members of socially inferior racial groups have a bad time, so do the half-castes.) What people might do with differences of hair colour, what they have done with differences of skin colour, we and many other societies have done and still do with differences of sexual organs. When I say 'we', I mean the publicly dominant group, the males. It is not women who have insisted that they be paid lower wages than men, be virtually excluded from prestigious jobs, do all the housework and be left in sole charge of the kids, be expected to be dependent on a man, to obey their husbands and occasionally get beaten by them.

The two bodies

Our learnt sexual behaviour and attitudes are particularly important for our place in society, for the same reason as the way we dress has a peculiar importance: they concern the body. Our life involves two bodies: the physical body which we are as individuals and the social body in which we live and move and have our humanity. Mary Douglas has shown how there is a symbolic interaction between these two bodies, so that we organize our bodily behaviour in such a way as to reflect the organization of society. As she puts it:

> The social body constrains the way the physical body is perceived. The physical experience of the body, always modified by the social categories through which it is known, sustains a particular view of society. There is a continual exchange of meanings between the two kinds of bodily experience so that each reinforces the categories of the other. As a result of this interaction the body itself is a highly restricted medium of expression. The forms it adopts in movement and repose express social pressures in manifold ways.[12]

To give a simple example, in the essay 'Do Dogs Laugh?' Douglas points out how laughter varies from culture to culture:

> We know that some tribes are said to be dour and unlaughing. Others laugh easily. Pygmies lie on the ground and kick their legs in the air, panting and shaking in paroxysms of laughter.[13]

She relates these differences to variations in the degree of social control. Where a society has a highly organized and disciplined structure, laughter will be rarer and more subdued. Where the society is free and easy, laughter will be more frequent, louder and longer, and involve more extreme bodily movements. For genuine laughter is not deliberate; laughter is one of the ways the body gets out of control. And highly organized societies demand a high degree of bodily control from their members, while loose societies allow more bodily freedom. If the social body is disciplined, so must be the physical body, for the way the body behaves is more significant; it is the bearer of more social meanings.[14] We can see this principle at work in a slightly different way in familiar situations in our own society. You can yawn while at home chatting with your friends, but not if you are having an audience with the queen; you can guffaw in the pub, but not during Mass. The more formal, the more rule-governed a situation, the more you have to control your body.

'Active' and 'passive'

We may think of sex as the most informal kind of bodily behaviour, but
when we go to bed with our partners we do not divest ourselves of our social
identity as male and female, we do not set aside the distinctions made
between us by the society in which we live. Rather do we play them out.
This is evident from the way we talk unreflectively about sex. Men are
typically projected in society as the leaders, active, dominant. Women are
followers, passive, submissive. And so it is in sex that men are said to be
active, women passive; men take women, women are taken. 'Active' and
'passive' are in fact now standard terms for the roles taken by men and
women respectively in sexual intercourse. But in fact they are terms
belonging principally to power relationships; the active leads, and so
determines what happens, while the passive follows, has his activity
determined for him. If we think about it, the words 'active' and 'passive',
when we link them to gender roles, are not terribly appropriate terms for
describing what usually happens in sexual intercourse. Certainly
dominance and subordination occur in sexual activity, but there is not the
distinction between activity and passivity that people might unreflectively
think there is. It is not normally the case in sexual relations between men
and women that the man is active and the woman passive, that the man does
and the woman has things done to her. Rather are both active; they
undertake a joint sexual activity, in which they have complementary roles.
It is only in rape that the woman may be said not to take part in an activity,
to be genuinely passive. A penetrated woman is normally just as active in sex
(if the sex is any good) as the man who penetrates her. (There may in fact be
cases where she is a good deal more active. Consider the case where she sits
astride the man. In this position it is she who has the major share in
determining when penetration will take place, to what depth, and how long
it will last. In other cases, such as oral sex, it is impossible to speak
standardly of either partner as active or passive. And whether the sex is
vaginal or oral, the degree of activity and passivity of both partners may vary
during the act.) Since they may both be equally (if differently) active, both
partners may have a kind of equality. But this has been ignored. The
activity of the supposedly 'passive' partner has officially been completely
overlooked in the interest of making sexual relations symbolic of social
relations, of seeing one partner as subordinate to another. Of course,
because when a man and a woman have sex one partner is subordinate to the
other: the woman is really, that is socially, inferior to the man.

Even the physical position of the partners has been at times made
expressive of their social relations. As the man is superior to the woman, so
it has been held that there is a 'natural' position for lovemaking, with the
man above the woman.[15] Given the close connexion between the physical

body and the social body this is not surprising, even if nature is not invoked. The social inferiority of women, their relative passivity, may also induce a woman to be correspondingly inferior and passive sexually, not to be as energetic or even dominant in her sexual activity as she might otherwise wish to be. Similarly, a man may wish just to lie there quite inactively and let his female partner do all the work, but feel obliged to be the one who takes initiatives and works on her.

We can note in passing that other societies have been equally concerned with this distinction between the 'active' and 'passive' or dominant and submissive roles in sex, though for them the biological difference between the sexes has not always been the socially important one. For example, in Rome, at least for a while, little significance seems to have been attached to the sex of the adult male's sexual partners. Martial testifies to the readiness of men to have sex with anybody, male or female.[16] Catullus, too, whose passion for Lesbia is famous, writes of the love of two brothers, one for a girl, Aufilena, and one for her brother Aufilenus, without seeing anything remarkable in this, and indeed going out of his way to wish success to him who loves Aufilenus.[17] He also writes with amusement of an occasion on which he thrust himself on a boy who was already sexually engaged.[18] On the other hand, it was considered bad for a grown man to be treated, or to allow himself to be treated, in the same way. A free adult male was expected to take a role in his sexual relations which expressed power and dominance. Hence the opprobrium in which the conquering Julius Caesar was held for letting Nicomedes of Bithynia 'conquer' him sexually, the strong taking the part of the weak, the male of the female.[19]

As in the case of Caesar, the active/passive dichotomy was sometimes related to the distinction between masculine and feminine, a distinction of power. Though sometimes related to sexual activity, it was equally important in people's wider behaviour, according to Veyne. Indeed, the passive homosexual's sexual behaviour was seen as a function of a wider femininity, rather than its cause:

> The passive homosexual was not rejected for his homosexuality but for his passivity, a very serious moral, or rather political infirmity. The passive individual's effeminacy was not the result of his perversion, far from it: it was simply one of the results of his lack of virility, and this was still a vice, even where no homosexuality was present. Roman society never bothered to ask if people were homosexual or not, but it devoted an excessive scrutiny to tiny details of dress, speech, gesture, and deportment in furthering its contempt for those who showed a lack of virility, whatever their sexual tastes.[20]

Michel Foucault, in volume 2 of his *History of Sexuality*, has shown that similar considerations of the relative social status of men were important in classical Greece. He sums up his findings thus:

Sexual relations – always conceived in terms of the model act of penetration, assuming a polarity that opposed activity and passivity – were seen as being of the same type as the relationship between a superior and a subordinate, an individual who dominates and one who is dominated, one who commands and one who complies, one who vanquishes and one who is vanquished. Pleasure practices were conceptualized using the same categories as those in the field of social rivalries and hierarchies: an analogous agonistic structure, analogous oppositions and differentiations, analogous values attributed to the respective roles of the partners. And this suggests that in sexual behaviour there was one role that was intrinsically honourable and valorized without question: the one that consisted in being active, in dominating, in penetrating, in asserting one's superiority.[21]

Leviticus revisited

Suppose we were in a society where difference of hair colour was terribly important; where, say, the fair were free and the dark slaves. The position of the fair must then be protected and the division between them and the dark strictly preserved. There would then of course be great penalties for those dark ones who tried to pass themselves off as blond, who dyed or bleached their hair. But, equally importantly, movement in the other direction must be prevented. For a fair-haired man to dye his hair black would not just be a sign that he had got bored with having had the same coloured hair for so long. It would be a gesture with a grave social meaning. It would be the abandonment of one class, his own, for another, alien and despised class, the rejection of his superior social identity, a sign therefore that he rejected the values of the dominant class and did not value belonging to it. In the eyes of the dominant group it would be to take degradation upon himself and to say that that degradation was preferable to the honour and privilege he previously enjoyed. That is, it would be to demean and degrade the status of being fair-haired in general; it would be an attack on the dignity of his own class, a betrayal. Further, to prefer degradation to honour is perverse, unnatural, and it shows a lack of self-respect.

It should be fairly clear by now that the law in Leviticus forbidding a man to lie with another man as with a woman is no mere proscription of an unusual form of enjoyment for those men who occasionally get bored having sex with women. We do not here have only a transgression of learned and customary sexual behaviour. If one man lies with another as with a woman he puts that other man in the position of a woman, and that other man takes on the position of a woman. And for a man willingly to take a woman's role is for him to dye his hair black, to take on the identity of an inferior and so to demean himself and all others of his own dominant social group. And the other, by putting him in that role, actively humiliates the male, reduces to submissiveness what should be dominant. Together they collude in attack-

ing a distinction fundamental to Israelite life and enshrining male superiority. We need have no doubt that this law was formulated by a man.

It is interesting to note that there is no corresponding law forbidding
sexual relations between women. This would be surprising if the law were
concerned to condemn homosexual acts as such. If the horror were of
homosexuality, then the homosexuality of women ought to be just as
important and abominable as the homosexuality of men. It is not as if the
law generally speaks in the masculine and expects us to generalize to include
women. Not only would this be an odd procedure where laws about sexual
behaviour are concerned, where one might think it important to mention
gender, but in fact there are laws relating explicitly to women as well as to
men. Indeed, the very next verse does contain a law which is applied
explicitly to both sexes:

> You shall not lie with any beast and defile yourself with it, neither shall any
> woman give herself to a beast to lie with it: it is perversion... If a man lies with a
> beast, he shall be put to death; and you shall kill the beast. If a woman approaches
> any beast and lies with it, you shall kill the woman and the beast; they shall be put
> to death, their blood is upon them (Lev. 18.23.).

Similarly, 20.15f., which prescribes the punishment for bestiality, again
mentions both sexes explicitly. On the other hand, 20.13, which prescribes
the punishment for supposed homosexuality, is like 18.22 in that it
concerns only a man lying with a man as with a woman; there is no mention
of women lying together.

But if we see the laws as taking into account social status, it does become
intelligible why there is no law against a woman lying with a woman. There
is no demeaning of anybody involved in this case. Since a woman is
naturally inferior, she cannot be reduced to inferiority, and whatever
relations of superiority and inferiority may be established or expressed
sexually between women have no bearing on the inferiority of all women to
men.

The understanding of this law that sees it as forbidding homosexual
relations, just like that, is oversimple and misses the point. People may
nowadays object to sex between two men, or between two women, because
they believe it is somehow in the nature of sex to require sexual complementarity, a male and a female partner, to demand difference rather than
sameness, or because they believe that God's law forbids homosexuality as
such. These are lines of thought we will have to look at later, but it is far
from the meaning of the law of Leviticus we are discussing. This does not
forbid sex between men, between people of the same sex (who as it happens
are both male), but it forbids a man lying with a man *as with a woman*. Sex
between two men is conceived on the model of sex between man and
woman, which is itself conceived in a stereotyped way; it is assumed that

there will be one taking the man's role – the 'active' – and another taking the woman's 'passive' role. Such activity is forbidden as a crossing of gender roles, doing to or with a man what should be done to or with a woman, treating a man as a woman, putting him into the 'passive', subordinate role that belongs to a woman. A man is active; that is his nature. To treat him as a woman is to pervert the natural order of things, because it is a symbolic disruption of the social order.[22] So the law forbidding such behaviour depends for its sense on that social order.

Christian thinking on sex has largely failed to give due weight to the significance of the symbolic interaction between the physical body and the social body for an understanding of the law of Leviticus 18.22. For example, the recent *Letter to the Bishops of the Catholic Church on the Pastoral Care of Homosexual Persons* of 1986 rightly places much emphasis on the importance for Catholic thought of a proper understanding of the biblical texts relating to sex. One of the texts it picks out as important for a biblical understanding of sex, again surely rightly, is this verse of Leviticus. In the light of this it is disappointing that in discussing this text the *Letter* notes only that 'in the course of describing the condition necessary for belonging to the Chosen People, the author excludes from the People of God those who behave in a homosexual fashion' (§6). This stands in need of considerable expansion and modification. We need to ask how the biblical author conceives the people of God, how it is divided from other peoples and what are its internal divisions. And, as I have argued, it is not 'behaving in a homosexual fashion', as we would naturally understand that phrase today, that is important for the author, but treating a man as a woman.

Leviticus and Christianity

Though this levitical law seems at first glance to be just about sex, it is in fact to do with social structure, especially power relations, in particular the socially superior status of the male over the female. Take away that set of social relationships, lift it from its context, and you destroy its sense and render it unintelligible. This point applies generally to the use of scripture, but is particularly important in the field of sexual ethics, where the temptation to proof-texting is so apparent. We cannot have an attitude to this law and others like it without having an attitude to the social organization it presupposes. The significance of all this discussion from a Christian point of view is this: Christians have very definite views about social organization, particularly as it involves relations between the sexes. I want to go into Jesus' attitude on this point in a later chapter, but Paul's is clear: 'As many of you as were baptized into Christ have put on Christ. There is neither Jew nor Greek, there is neither slave nor free, there is neither male nor female; for you are all one in Christ Jesus' (Gal. 3.27f.). Whereas for the priestly writer and the Jewish tradition that followed him the making of distinctions was vital, to Paul it is the breaking down of divisions that is of the essence: not denying differences, but refusing to recognize those differences as principles of division between people. Whereas for the priestly writer the Jew was set apart from the Greek by God, for Paul they are united by God in Christ. Similarly, slave and free, male and female have a fundamental unity that goes beyond their differences.[23]

Beyond relations between the sexes, it is clear that for Christians society cannot be based on the dominance of any group over another; Christian society is rather to be based on service: 'You know that the rulers of the Gentiles lord it over them, and their great men exercise authority over them. It shall not be so among you; but whoever would be great among you must be your servant, and whoever would be first among you must be your slave' (Matt. 20.25–27).

Social organization has sexual consequences. Because we want a different kind of society from that in and for which the law of Leviticus 18.22 was framed, we cannot uncritically take over that law or any other from the same source into our sexual ethic. There are many kinds of sexual behaviour forbidden in Leviticus, as well as in other Old Testament books that come out of a similarly structured society and express the same outlook. We cannot take it for granted that we will want to dissuade people from the same kinds of behaviour, or that we should. We need to discourage those kinds of behaviour that conflict with the kind of social structures that we, as Christians, want and believe ourselves commanded to build up, not those that conflict with another kind of society.

For example, if we believe, in the sense that Paul believed it, that there is neither Jew nor gentile, neither Greek nor barbarian, but all are one in Christ, then we shall not encourage division between races; we shall not, as Ezra and his followers did, forbid marriage between people of some putatively special race and outsiders.[24]

If we believe with Paul that there is neither male nor female, then we believe in a certain equality between the sexes; we will not try to build a society in which there is structural inequality, in which women are made inferior to men. We cannot take over laws on adultery which are based on the idea that wives are inferior to or even the property of their husbands. There may well be reasons why we should discourage adultery, but they cannot include the simple fact that adultery is forbidden in the Old Testament. Again, in a Christian society to treat somebody as a woman is not to treat that person as an inferior. If that person is in fact a man, there may an error involved, but it is not an error which threatens social status, as it would have been in the society from which Leviticus emerged. In a Christian society, if a man lies with a man as with a woman, and so treats him as a woman, he does not thereby demean him; neither does the other demean himself. There may well be reasons why Christians should want to discourage sexual relationships between men; but if there are, the simple fact that such relationships are forbidden in Leviticus 18.22 is not one of them.

4

The Pleasures of the Flesh

Suspicious pleasures

Almost from the beginning, there has been in Christian thought a suspicion of sexual pleasure. This suspicion classically found expression in a contrast and opposition between sexual activity for the sake of pleasure and sexual activity performed for the sake of children. For example, Augustine, like the entire official Jewish and Christian tradition before him, saw marriage as the only fit and proper place for any sexual activity. But for Augustine sex, even within marriage, had a very restricted place: 'Intercourse which is necessary for the purpose of generation is blameless, and only this kind belongs to marriage. But that which goes beyond this necessity follows not reason but lust.'[1] And its being a matter of desire, *libido*, is a bad thing. He discusses in one place the morality of the fact that the patriarchs sometimes had more than one wife. This was all right, for it was for the sake of children. Why could not a woman have had more than one husband?

> If a woman had done this, what would compel her to have more husbands but the baseness of concupiscence, when by this licence she would not have more children? ... So, if one woman lies with several men, because she derives no increase of offspring from it, but frequency of lust, she cannot be a wife, but only a harlot.[2]

In Augustine's mind, there is a straight dichotomy between sex for the sake of children and sex to which one is impelled by sheer lust and concupiscence. There is no innocent enjoyment of sex for its own sake. Though in many cases within marriage pardonable, all sex without a procreative purpose is sinful. He complains that in all the conversations he has had with his friends who either are or have been married, he has never heard one say that he never sought intercourse except in the hope of children.[3]

Augustine's position is an extreme one, but the dislike of sex for pleasure – 'lust' – apart from procreative purpose is a common theme throughout Christian history. Its roots, though, are entirely non-Christian. Nowhere in scripture is it said that procreative purpose is the only legitimate reason for having sex, or that having sex for the sake of sexual pleasure is a bad thing.[4] The source of the dislike of sexual pleasure and its being placed in opposition to procreative intent is to be found rather in pagan philosophy, particularly stoicism.[5] This pagan influence was absorbed consciously by the early Christian fathers.[6] We have seen to what lengths it is carried by Augustine. His position is greatly softened by some later writers, and some also attack it from the later Middle Ages on. But it remained a strong current in Catholic thought, at least. In 1679 Innocent XI condemned the proposition that 'a marriage act carried out solely for pleasure is entirely devoid of blame or venial defect'.[7] As late as 1966 Bernard Häring, commenting on this condemnation, seems to take for granted the dichotomy and opposition between sex for pleasure and sex for the purposes of reproduction:

> If the act, however, still retains its basic character as service to life despite the intention 'for mere pleasure' it is only a venial sin, for the fault is ultimately a defect of integral motivation and as an individual act is not mortal sin. But our judgment would be far more severe if there were question of a general attitude rather than of an individual or isolated act. An attitude of mind which is governed by indulgence of venereal pleasure as the sole motivation for marital union divorces the sheer sexual instinct from authentic marital love and the reverential spirit of service to life. Such an approach to marital relations is one of the most dangerous sources of impurity. It is totally and utterly unchaste.[8]

It is plainly possible to make some kind of distinction between sex for the purpose of procreation and sex for pleasure; and some such distinction may well be necessary if we are to think straight about sex. But we have to be careful here. The concept of pleasure is a very variegated one. It would be unfair to church teaching to say that it condemns sex for pleasure. The last two of the quotations above are importantly more nuanced than the others. Here it is not sex for pleasure that is condemned, but sex for *mere* pleasure, or having sex *solely* for pleasure. There is a real question to be asked about when a pleasure is a mere pleasure. I do not want to attempt to answer that question here. For my purposes it is sufficient to note that we would not naturally count all pleasures as mere. We might speak of the pleasure of sipping gin in a bath of ass's milk as mere pleasure; here words like 'self-indulgence' and 'hedonism' come to mind. On the other hand, the psalmist writes of the great pleasure he gets from the commandments of God.[9] That people might get pleasure from both is surely intelligible, but the kind of pleasure is quite different. We might want to say that somebody bathes in ass's milk for mere pleasure, but surely not that somebody would do the commandments of God for mere pleasure. It would be paradoxical, at the least, to say that somebody who does the commandments of God because he delights in them is being self-indulgent or hedonistic.

Pleasure, then, is a fluid concept. The difference in our attitude to doing the commandments of God and bathing in ass's milk points up an important difference among pleasures. Pleasures extend over time in different ways.

Some are highly confined and delimited in time, like the pleasure of eating an ice cream or the pleasure of bathing in ass's milk. Others are more diffuse and extended. A person may get great pleasure from his job over a number of years. Here pleasure shades over into happiness; somebody who says his job gives him great pleasure is likely to be a happy, contented person. Somebody who enjoys such large tracts of his life is, other things being equal, a joyful person. The pleasure of doing the commandments of God is such a pleasure; it shapes a life, and turns it into a happy life. Sharing your life with somebody in friendship can also be a pleasure which extends over a long time. To seek such pleasures is not to be a self-indulgent pleasure-seeker, but to seek to live well, and therefore happily. Sharply delimited pleasures may bear little relation to overall happiness and fulfilment; you can eat ice cream with pleasure and yet be generally miserable. Indeed, people often turn to such pleasures for consolation, because they are miserable, and as a distraction from their misery. But the more diffuse, longer-term pleasures of life are closely related to happiness, to not being miserable, and so not standing in need of distraction and consolation.

I want in this chapter to examine the dislike or suspicion of sexual pleasure that surfaces from time to time in pagan and Christian tradition and in popular attitudes to sex. I want to suggest that, apart from the stress on procreation, it has two major roots: a particular social model of what a human being is, and a too narrow and therefore mistaken view of the nature of sexual pleasure, a view which tends to see it as necessarily and only *mere* pleasure. Further, and this is the more important part of what I want to say, if we look at the elements of sexual pleasure more accurately, we shall find that pleasure is more friend than foe of central Christian views on sex.

The body politic

First, the fathers inherited from the surrounding culture a complex of ideas according to which human beings are some kind of combination or composite of soul and body, the soul itself sometimes being seen as composite. The exact nature of this combination varied from thinker to thinker, but a common element is that the whole is seen as a quasi-political entity, with relations of authority between the parts. The proper state of things was that the rational part of the soul should command and the rest obey. The conception of the individual as a micropolis goes back at least to Plato. In the *Republic*, there is a strict correspondence between types of city and types of individual. Just as the citizens are enslaved in a political tyranny, so the 'tyrannous' man is the one enslaved by his desires, his rational part being subject to the irrational:

If therefore ... the man resembles the city, must not the same order be also in him, and his soul be full of servility and lack of freedom, and those parts of it be enslaved which are the most reasonable while a small part, the most worthless and frenzied, has mastery?[10]

One of the fathers who was most importantly influenced by this political metaphor was Augustine. We can see it at work in his version of the story of the Fall, which he tells in *The City of God*. In the garden, he says, there was only one tiny prohibition which was not difficult to observe, and in general it was very easy to obey God, because desire was not yet in opposition to reason. The crime of eating the apple was therefore very great. The due social order which existed between man and God was subverted: man, the servant, failed to obey God, the master.[11] The punishment was made to fit the crime. The due order within man himself was upset: 'Man was handed over to himself, because he forsook God by pleasing himself; and not being obedient to God, neither could he obey himself.'[12]

This talk of inability to do what we want sounds not dissimilar to what St Paul says in chapter 7 of Romans, and in *De Nuptiis et Concupiscentia* Augustine uses language like that of Paul. But he gives it a much more specific reference than Paul's:

> When the first man transgressed the law of God, he began to have another law in his members which was repugnant to his mind, and he felt the evil of his disobedience when he discovered himself most justly punished by the disobedience of his flesh ... For it was unjust that obedience should be given by his servant, that is his body, to him, who had not obeyed his Lord. For how is it that the eyes, lips, tongue, hands, feet, and the bending of back, and neck, and sides, are all placed in his power to be moved in ways suitable to perform their work ... but when it comes to children being generated, the members created for this purpose do not obey the will, but lust has to be waited for to set these members in motion, as having rights over them, and sometimes it will not act when the mind is willing, while sometimes it even acts against the mind's will! Does the freedom of the human will not blush at this, that through despising God when he commanded, it has lost all proper command even over its own members? Where, then, could be better demonstrated that human nature has been justly depraved through its disobedience, than in those disobedient parts whence that nature itself survives by succession?[13]

One of the principal effects of the Fall, then, is that there is a problem about erections. This part of a man's body will not obey his will. Already we can see that for Augustine the problem of sex is very much a male one, principally of getting erections independently of your control, mostly getting them when you don't want them, though occasionally not getting them when you do want them.[14] This part of a man's body is not under his authority, but is under the control of lust, as if it were its own private property, and it is this lack of control that makes sexual activity and the sexual organs shameful.[15] Augustine's views on other aspects of sexual desire and experience are also expressed in terms of the political metaphor. With the problem of sexual desire goes that of sexual pleasure. Just as a man's penis is not subject to his control, so the pleasure of sex disturbs his mind:

> When lust is mentioned without its being said what it is lust for, normally nothing occurs to the mind but that it is that by which the indecent parts of the body are excited. This appropriates not only the whole body, and not only from outside, but also internally; and it disturbs the whole man, the mental emotion being joined to and mixed with the fleshly appetite, so that a pleasure follows greater than all bodily pleasures. It is such that at the moment when it reaches its climax almost all awareness and as it were the guards of thought are overwhelmed. Which friend of wisdom and of holy joys, living a married life ... would not prefer, if he could, to beget children without this lust?[16]

Notice how the language here is that of power. Lust assumes power over the whole body. The pleasure – clearly of orgasm – is so great that it overwhelms reason, overwhelms that which controls, so that in intercourse the whole man 'can be said to become flesh' and 'the pleasure of his body makes him a slave and holds him captive'.[17] So great is the pleasure that it becomes impossible to think while it is going on:

> I feel that nothing more casts down the masculine mind from the heights than female allurements and that contact of bodies without which a wife cannot be had.[18]

Note too that the problem is that the *man* goes out of control, the *man* is brought down from the heights. There is no problem about the woman here. This is understandable if we remember that it is the man who is supposed to be superior, to be in the heights, and to be in control.

Here, I think, is the basic reason why sexual desire is so extremely suspect, and also why it is so wrong, for Augustine and for the later tradition, to seek sexual pleasure, that is to say, to want to take part in sexual activity for the sake of pleasure. At first sight, it looks a very curious idea. There is surely nothing wrong with the idea that we might simply seek pleasure in what we do, do things simply because they are pleasurable. We do this all the time: watching football, drinking, listening to music, playing games, etc. All these might, if we are pushed, be said to serve a purpose, yet we do not need to justify them on that account. It is enough that we take pleasure in them. Doing pleasurable things just because they are pleasurable is an ordinary human good. Why not look upon sexual activity in the same way? Why not have sex just because you enjoy it? The answer, for Augustine, lies in the kind of enjoyment it is. Sexual desire is not, for him, sinful in itself; it is something we suffer from, a hangover from the Fall. But we all too readily turn it into desire for sexual pleasure, and to desire sexual pleasure is to desire the overwhelming of reason and the body's escape from the control of reason; and that is to desire the subversion of the due order of things, to desire an evil. In addition, reason is what is distinctively human, and to abandon it is to abandon humanity, become a mere animal, which is again an evil. But to desire evil is a sin. So the desire for sexual pleasure is gravely sinful. Hence sexual desire leads us to sin.

Here also we can see why the opposition between sex for pleasure and sex for the purpose of procreation was so important for Augustine. It could not be denied that sex was, at least potentially, a good, for it was necessary if the human race was to survive, which was a desirable thing. It was the necessity of procreation, then, that justified sex. That alone justified the terrible loss of control and loss of reason that sexual activity involved for a man.[19] Hence sexual activity could only be justified if it was undertaken for the purpose of procreation. This position went largely unchallenged for a thousand years. In the thirteenth century, Thomas Aquinas repudiated the position that sexual pleasure in itself was a bad thing; for him, sex would have been even more pleasurable before the Fall, since our nature would then have been purer and therefore our body more sensitive.[20] However, even given this positive view of sexual pleasure, Aquinas still held to the Augustinian view that sex for the purpose of pleasure was sinful. And much of later tradition followed him.

Pleasure and control

Not only is this view of the rebelliousness of the body and of sexual desire limited to males but it is possible only if we have a model of a human being which is basically a social, political one, of a specific dualist type, which explains action in terms of the command of the will and the obedience of the body, a model which is very deficient. Much of Augustine's language may well be metaphorical, but if it is a metaphor it is one he takes very seriously. Metaphorical or not, the way he writes here fosters a serious misunderstanding of the relationship between mind and body. For, put shortly, the body does not in fact either obey or disobey the mind; it is neither rebellious nor obedient.

One way to see how misleading his particular social model of the relation between mind and body is is to observe how it enables him to make an important mistake when thinking about control. His idea that normally the will commands and the limbs of the body, its 'servants',[21] obey implies that when there is no supervision by the 'higher faculties' the body is out of control, like a plane without a pilot. But there are at least three things wrong with this.

First, there are in fact occasions when the body is not being controlled by anything else but is obviously not out of control. A good dancer may not have to control the movements of his body, but his body is anything but out of control. It does not need to be controlled. The movements may be so well rehearsed, and the body so well trained, that it performs them almost automatically.

Second, in any normal sexual activity nobody is out of control. They know what is happening, what they are doing and what they are likely to do; they decide to do some things rather than others; and so on. They may get excited, they may let themselves go, but when they do that they do not in general get out of control. I am not denying that it is possible to lose control of ourselves in sexual activity, to get carried away and do things we would not normally do and of which we may later be ashamed or for which we might reproach ourselves. But when we do that, it is not a matter of the body escaping from the control of the mind. It is not the mind that loses control of the body, or that the mind loses control of itself or is controlled by the body; simply, we lose control of ourselves. And the notion of control that comes into play here has a large social component, and raises again the social dimension of sexual activity. People sometimes talk about others being out of control in their sexual behaviour, and plainly they feel insecure about this. Perhaps the important point is that these other people are thought to be out of *social* control. They are said to be out of control when they do things that are forbidden by the section of society to which the speaker belongs. They are out of our control; we do not know what they might do, sexually. And their sexual behaviour is held to be symptomatic of them as a whole. If they can do that, what might they not do? – Unless people are controlled, they are dangerous. Thus people whose sexual behaviour is unorthodox are often for that reason held to be a danger to society.

Third, neither is it true that sexual pleasure is so great that when it is at its height one cannot think. It is not that we might be trying to think of God during intercourse, can do it but are finally unable to continue thinking of God at the point of orgasm. If we do not think of God (or anything else) at the climax it is because we do not want to think. To use Augustine's terms, the mind is not dragged down from the heights; it does not want to be in the heights, but comes down of its own accord. His talk of being dragged down, overpowered, and so on, gives the impression that all this is happening against one's will, whereas the reverse is true. If you are in any sense held by this pleasure, it is not against your will. Sexual pleasure is often intense, and it belongs to the notion of intense enjoyment that you are fully engrossed in what you intensely enjoy; you do not want to tear yourself away from it, are not easily distracted, and maybe want more of it. We would only 'be able' to think (i.e. want to think) at the climax if the pleasure were less intense. This applies not only to sex but to all pleasures which may be intense, such as listening to music. It is a criterion of finding a Bartók string quartet intensely enjoyable that you are absorbed in it and don't think about God or anything else while listening to it.

Aquinas is very sensible on this point. In reply to an objection to sexual pleasure on the ground that it is so great that it offends against the Aristotelian doctrine of the mean, he says:

> The mean of virtue is not according to quantity but according to its conformity to right reason. Therefore the abundance of pleasure which is in a sexual act ordered in accordance with reason is not contrary to the mean of virtue. . . Neither, if the reason cannot freely think of spiritual things at the same time as that pleasure, does that show that that act is contrary to virtue. For it is not contrary to reason if the act of thinking is sometimes interrupted by something which is done in accordance with reason; otherwise it would be contrary to reason for somebody to give himself up to sleep.[22]

Sexual pleasure and the soul

If we examine the nature of sexual pleasure a little more closely, I believe we will see that far from being a threat to Christian living the desire of sex for the pleasure it gives can actually be used as one of the bases of a Christian sexual ethic, an ethic which embodies recognizably Christian values and which, moreover, is recognizably related to traditional Christian attitudes to sex. Christians have always said that the proper place for sex is within the context of a relation of friendship, normally that kind of close friendship which is called marriage. I don't think you can get as far as establishing the rightness of that traditional stance just by thinking about sexual pleasure independently of Christian doctrine, but it gives us a definite start. Sexual pleasure is the friend of Christian thought, rather than its enemy. We can see Christianity not as seeking to limit pleasure but to enhance it, so that we can actually offer ourselves and others a Christian ethic, rather than feel we have to impose it on ourselves and them. This is because to have sexual pleasure with another is largely to take pleasure in a person; it is to enjoy a soul.

The pleasure of sex is almost universally talked about by theologians either as the pleasure of orgasm or at least as essentially related to it; and it is almost invariably the male orgasm that is meant.[23] This is a grossly inadequate view of sexual pleasure; it will not do even for an activity like masturbation. In fact, especially in a normal sexual encounter with somebody else, there is a much wider pleasure or range of pleasures, one that is often seen as more important than orgasm – the pleasures of touching and being touched, movement of one's own body with and against another's, of sight, smell, taste, of exploration and being explored,[24] of experiment, of play, the pleasure of giving pleasure in all these ways.[25] These are not merely pleasures preliminary and subordinate to the ultimate pleasure, things one can enjoy while waiting for orgasm. Much pleasurable sex does not involve orgasm at all, and is not considered defectively pleasurable for that reason. A woman engaged in vaginal intercourse with her husband may not experience orgasm, but may nevertheless enjoy the intercourse without regretting the lack of orgasm, as may her husband. If the penetration is oral or anal she cannot thereby have an orgasm, yet she may again derive great pleasure from the activity. Further, when there is orgasm, it may sometimes not be welcomed as the longed-for ultimate pleasure, but almost regretted as that which brings the other pleasures of sex to an end.

Pleasant activities

These other pleasures are not just a matter of bodily sensations; they are primarily the pleasures of doing things. In this they are like most, if not all, of our pleasures. As Aristotle points out,[26] what gives us pleasure is to *do* things. Pleasure comes from the free exercise of our faculties. We get pleasure from doing things we want to do, and it is because we want to do them that we find them pleasant. There has in the modern period been a certain tendency to associate pleasure with pleasant sensations, in the sense of pleasant sense impressions, such as having pleasant sensations on one's skin from contact, or hearing nice sounds. Certainly, there are many pleasures which have pleasant sensations as one of their important elements. Here the pleasures of eating, drinking, sex and music come readily to mind. But these are also all pleasures of doing something. In our pleasures we are not just the passive recipients of sensations, but are engaged in an activity, and the activity is pleasant to us. It is the activity which is generally the more important element. There are in fact activities which people regard as pleasant and which yet involve little or nothing in the way of pleasant sensation. Think of playing rugby. There are no good sensations to be had here. Rugby players get kicked, crushed, wet, muddy, freezing and exhausted; and they think it's marvellous. Of course playing rugby may be exciting and exhilarating, and the players may enjoy it, may feel good; but their feeling good is not a matter of their having pleasant sensations. The pleasure comes rather from the competitive and strenuous nature of the activity itself. Again, it may give a conference chairman great pleasure to introduce a guest speaker, but that is not because introducing him gives him pleasant sensations.

Further, our pleasures are defined by the activity that gives us pleasure. The pleasure of going for a walk round the park is a different pleasure from the pleasure of drinking gin in the bath, because the two activities are different. They may be equally pleasurable activities, but they are not the same pleasure. Having the pleasure that a particular activity gives you is not detachable from performing that activity. You can't have the pleasure of doing something without doing that thing, even though you may be able to have some of the same sensations by doing something else. This is not an unfortunate limitation. It would make no sense to say: 'How I wish I could have the pleasure of walking round the park without having to go to all the trouble of actually walking round the park.' If you got pleasure in any other way it would be a different pleasure. And its being a pleasure to walk round the park means that it is not a trouble to do it. Doing just this is what makes it *this* pleasure. To have the pleasure of doing something is simply to do the pleasurable thing. In general, then, we do not desire pleasure so much as to do things.

This is true also when we get pleasure from those of our activities which consist in having things done to us or for us. To have my hair cut is itself to do something, though I may not move a muscle while it is going on. (An indication that this is an action is that I might be praised or blamed for having my hair cut.) The hairdresser's snipping away involves us both in activity. It is because I am doing something here that I can enjoy it, find it pleasurable. My hair's being cut is not my passively undergoing its being cut, normally; it is not something inflicted on me; and if it is, if it is not something I have done, then it is not a pleasure.

Suppose I *must* have my hair cut, that am having a haircut inflicted on me (I am a conscript newly arrived in the army, or have been sent unwilling to the barber by my mother). In so far as it is inflicted on me I will not like it, not find it a pleasure. But while it is going on it might begin to strike me as not so bad, even as enjoyable. I then 'throw myself into it'. I may even urge the barber to carry on when he stops. Then my having my hair cut has become my activity, or rather our activity, a joint activity of myself and the barber. So it is too in sex. Even somebody who wants the most 'passive' or inactive sex wants *to have something done* to him or her. A person has so-called passive sex as part of a joint *activity*, unless he or she is being raped, in which case it gives no pleasure. In that case, the sensations may be in a certain sense the same, but the context is different; above all, the person does not want this to happen, so that the sensations are not enjoyable.

This becomes clear if it is remembered that it is even possible for two people to play at rape. If Andrew actually rapes Jane, Andrew will enjoy it because he is acting in a way that he wants to. Jane will not, for she is not acting at all and so has no activity to enjoy; she is also being imposed on and invaded. She is a passive victim who is rather liable to be distressed by what is going on. If they play at rape the scene may be indistinguishable to an onlooker from a real rape scene, but this time Andrew and Jane are both doing something. Their play is a joint activity which, in so far as they both want to do it, they both enjoy. (And it will perhaps be part of Jane's enjoyable activity that she pretends not to enjoy what is happening.)

Sex and sensations

We must not put the emphasis exclusively on activity and forget the place of sensations in sex. In sex we do not just have pleasure from what we do, but also from what we feel. Those many varied bodily sensations – as of orgasm, or of hand or tongue gentle or rough upon skin – come largely from what our partners do to and with us; and even when they come from what we ourselves do, still the sensations are not activities, and the pleasurability of those sensations is not the pleasure of doing something. Nevertheless, though there are pleasurable sensations involved in sex, just as there are in many other of our activities, they are not free-floating pleasures. They are pleasant largely because we have them in the context of a pleasurable activity. This contextual element is a vital component in our appreciation of our sensations. We do not just feel our own sensations; we do not live imprisoned by the bounds of our body. On the contrary, our body and our sensations are already ours as *in the world*. We are not just aware of a sound – we hear the doorbell or a car accelerating or a friend calling; we do not just smell a smell – we smell a rose, or something cooking.[27] And so also we do not just have sensations in or on the surface of our bodies. For example, we are not just confined to having more or less painful sensations in various bits of our bodies; we feel a stone in our shoe or a hand on our shoulder.[28]

So in sex we do not just have sensations. Or rather, our having sensations is largely a matter of feeling ourselves or others doing things; and our enjoyment of those sensations is bound up with our perception of what we or our partners are doing. We enjoy the sensation of penetrating or being penetrated, the feeling of our partner stroking or biting us, etc. So it is that if in the course of sex we have an unusual sensation, and if part of its strangeness is that we cannot work out what our partner is doing to produce it – what it is a sensation of – we can be not at all sure that it is pleasant; learning what they are doing may settle for us whether it is pleasant or not.

Once again, context is very important here. To feel a hand stroking your thigh in the tube in the rush hour, an anonymous and unseen hand grasping at you, is an unpleasant experience. What is in an obvious sense the same sensation can be very pleasant if you know who is doing it and if it is somebody whose attentions you appreciate. In the former case the sensation is the sign of an invasion of your intimate space; in the latter it marks the presence of a welcome guest. That is because of the difference in your understanding of what is happening, your knowledge of context, in particular of who is doing this to you. And if it is somebody you like and you want them to do it to you, then you are doing something together, are engaged in a joint activity, a joint pleasure.

The pleasure of orgasm, which bulks so large in theological writings on sex, is no exception to this. The quality of orgasms varies in any case, but one important factor is whether the orgasm is experienced during or as the climax of an activity which is itself felt to be pleasurable. If you have an orgasm during a sex act you feel you have been forced to take part in, or at the end of it,[29] or if you do not want to have an orgasm, it will hardly be experienced as very pleasant. Sheer knowledge of what is going on is also important. For one who is inexperienced in sex, who does not know what is going on, the first orgasm may well be bewildering rather than supremely pleasurable.

Sex and friendship

Whether an activity is pleasurable very often depends on who you do it with; it is the pleasure of doing something together with somebody you like, as is the pleasure of eating or drinking or playing together. This notion of a joint activity is rather important for our subject. If Andrew and Jane are playing chess together, they are joint agents in a single activity. They are not merely playing chess in the same place, but playing together. They are making different contributions to one shared activity. Similarly, if Andrew and Jane are having sex together, they are joint agents in a single shared activity, each contributing to that activity in different, complementary ways. They are not performing two separate activities, so that Andrew or Jane might be doing exactly the same thing if their partner were not there. Thus even if they are simply masturbating, which each could perfectly well do alone, but they are doing it in each other's presence as a form of sexual engagement, they are not merely doing it in the same place; it is an essential characteristic of what they are doing that they are doing it together. It obscures an important aspect of sexual activity, as of all human activity, to say that people can do the same thing 'alone or with others'.

Thus also the pleasures of doing such things together are essentially joint, common pleasures. If I am playing chess with a friend and we enjoy doing this together, then there are not two separate, individual and private enjoyments, but one common one, just as there are not two activities but one common activity. The common activity creates a shared space between us in which we enjoy the activity together. So if I am aware that he has ceased to enjoy what we are doing, I no longer enjoy it; or if I do, my enjoyment is a different kind of enjoyment. The different context makes it a different pleasure. It may be the pleasure of subjecting him to this activity. The pleasure of a shared activity is logically different from the pleasure of a solitary activity.[30] It is interpersonal, and has as one of its elements the pleasure of doing something with somebody else.

Doing things together is often a way of being together, and the pleasure of doing things together a form of the pleasure of being together.[31] It is a mistake to talk in these cases of pleasure as separate from people. To seek sexual pleasure is here at least partly a matter of seeking to be with somebody in a particular way. But this is of the essence of friendship. We want to be with friends, to do things with them. We get pleasure from being with them, and the pleasure just is the being with them, doing whatever it is that we do with them. If, in wanting to be with friends, it is that pleasure that we seek, it is nonsense to speak of 'seeking only pleasure' here, as if seeking pleasure were just a matter of seeking certain sensations. To seek the pleasure is to seek the friend. I cannot seek the pleasure of being with a friend without seeking him or her. When the Christian tradition condemns sex for pleasure alone, this is not well understood as a condemnation of friends doing something pleasurable together because it is pleasurable. Rather, it is a way of stressing the interpersonal nature of shared sexual activity and of reminding us that the pleasures of sex cannot be reduced to having a range of sensations; they are, at the very least, the pleasures of doing pleasant things together with a friend. A sexual encounter that neglects the importance of friendship is therefore defective, as is the pleasure that is derived from it.

There are plenty of anonymous sexual encounters, where the pleasure of sex is not the pleasure of being with and therefore doing something with a friend; but there are important pleasures denied to people in such an encounter. Nigel is a gay man and goes a bar to pick up a complete stranger for half an hour or so of casual sex, with the intention of parting for ever afterwards. Nigel cannot take the same kind of delight, for instance, in exploring this stranger's body as he can in exploring that of a friend, because he does not want to know it as he can want to know the body of a friend. He cannot delight in his body just because it is *his* body, the body of this particular person, as opposed to that of anybody else who might have been available. He cannot delight in being touched by *him*, enjoy being with *him*, doing this with *him*. There may be other pleasures open to Nigel, like the pleasure of doing this precisely with somebody he does not know and does not want to know, or the thrill of making himself vulnerable to a stranger. (Note that though this is what may make the activity pleasurable, again it has nothing to do with sensations. It is contextual, to do with Nigel's knowledge of the circumstances, here consisting in the lack of any relation of importance, lack of friendship,[32] the excitement of doing it with somebody new, or of risk.)

It is no doubt possible to maintain quite a pleasant sex-life if you have such an approach to sex. (Though the pleasure of newness is liable to be short-lived. Get somebody new often enough, and the newness ceases to be exciting; it is the same old newness.) But in so far as it is bound up with a search for excitement it is defective simply in terms of pleasure, let alone morally. Specifically, it manifests too narrow a view of pleasure. Such excitement may not be available to a long-married couple, but their sexual activity may still be very pleasurable. A walk round the park is not normally exciting, but can nonetheless be very pleasant. It is simply a mistake, normally, to go for a walk round the park in search of excitement. Pleasure is much wider than excitement, and one who seeks sex for the excitement it gives deprives himself or herself of much that sex has to offer in the way of other pleasures.[33] Those other pleasures depend on a context of friendship. Here we see Christian ideas beginning to come in, not as a way of putting a curb on pleasure, but on the contrary as a way of recognizing how wide and how contextualized a thing pleasure is and of seeking to increase pleasure.

Note here how far it is from being true that the pleasure of sex turns us into animals by overwhelming our rational faculties. On the contrary, sex being pleasurable, when it is pleasurable, actually depends on our 'cognitive faculty', on our knowing what the context is, who we are doing things with, and it depends a great deal on our knowing *them*.

The person and the flesh

It may seem as if all this is rarefying sex, almost making of it a matter of enjoying a 'personal communion' with another to which the body is all but irrelevant, or something similar, a matter of paying attention to the person, as opposed to mere flesh. But this is a false impression: there can be no such opposition. Enjoying sex is to a large extent a contextual enjoying of flesh: enjoying fondling flesh, touching flesh, stroking it, kissing it, licking it, twining yourself round bits of it, playing your fingers very lightly down an arm or round a shoulder, etc. It is also enjoying your own flesh, enjoying being fondled, stroked, kissed, etc., and enjoying the sensations you get from all this. Why is this, particularly doing things with somebody else's flesh, enjoyable? It is not that flesh is an intrinsically delightful thing. Most of us would think twice about fondling a piece of cod or running our tongue playfully along a side of pork. It is different with human flesh, of course. People can and often do just enjoy other people's flesh. It makes sense to say that anonymous or fleeting sexual encounters can be simple enjoyment of the flesh. But there is no reason to say that married couples, even those who have been married a long time, enjoy each other's flesh any less than partners in one-night stands do. If they enjoy their sex together, then they do enjoy each other's flesh, for that is what sexual enjoyment largely is.

Andrew and Jane are a happily married couple, and neither would dream of having sex with anybody else. Andrew may enjoy Jane's flesh very much, but there is a sense in which his enjoying Jane's flesh is also his enjoying Jane. It matters very much to him that the arm he is licking is Jane's arm, that the leg he is twining his leg round is Jane's leg. It is precisely because these bits are Jane's bits that he is doing all this licking and twining. He wouldn't dream of doing it with Mary's bits or Peter's bits, that is to say with Mary or Peter. It is because this flesh *is* Jane that it is such enjoyable flesh, that doing all this is such an enjoyable activity. This kind of sexual activity is just as much an enjoyment of the flesh as any other, only it is highly specific: it matters very much that it is just this flesh. The flesh is specified by being the flesh of just this particular human being. Similarly, it matters to him that it is these hands, this mouth, this person, that is doing various things with his body. And the same goes for Jane.

Here, a passing remark about masturbation. The importance of the identity of the flesh, of the person, in sex is a reason why, for most people, masturbation, if done for pleasure, is a substitute and inferior pleasure. Unless Peter is genuinely autosexual, though he may get pleasure from masturbating, it cannot be a pleasure for him that just this person – Peter – is doing this to him. Woody Allen (in the film *Annie Hall*) said of masturbation: 'Don't knock it, it's sex with someone you love.' This is witty, but false. The most obvious fact about masturbation is that it is not sex with anybody, let alone with someone you love; this means that it has limited possibilities for pleasure. Part of the pleasure of sex with someone you love is the pleasure you take in the fact that it is the loved one who is doing this with and to you. But if Peter masturbates, however much he loves himself, he does not normally delight that it is just *this* hand that is grasping his penis, precisely *he* who is doing it with or to himself. It might just as well be another hand, somebody else, and indeed he would likely prefer if it was. And though he can have the pleasure of an orgasm, he cannot have the pleasure of giving pleasure to just this person. The identity of the partners in a sexual relationship is part of what gives the pleasure, whereas in masturbation the identity of the sexual agent is irrelevant.

Soulful sex

In kissing Jane's shoulder Andrew kisses Jane. For him, what he is with is not just an agglomeration of bits. It has a unity; this is what is meant by saying that he is with a person, that the flesh he is enjoying has or is a soul. And a soul is always the soul of a particular person. If Nigel wanders into a bar a few minutes before closing time, picks up somebody he has never seen before and goes for an anonymous grope round the back, that might in its way be very enjoyable, and an enjoyment of the flesh, only this time it is irrelevant to him what flesh this is that he is enjoying; though it is important that this is live human flesh, a human being, it is irrelevant to him which human being it is. Indeed, he does not even know which human being he has here (and it might be important to him not to know). Whoever he is holding might just as well be somebody else. In this sense, his enjoyment of this flesh is enjoyment of flesh in general, as opposed to Andrew's highly specific enjoyment of Jane's flesh. Andrew has chosen her to do this with, and she has chosen him, in a way in which Nigel has not chosen his anonymous partner. Of course Nigel has picked out this person rather than others, but it might just as well have been somebody else, and tomorrow night, with a bit of luck, it will be: but nobody else in particular. There is a particular person whom Andrew will choose tomorrow night and a particular person that Jane will choose. Andrew and Jane are each concerned with a soul, whereas Nigel is not.[34]

This is an aspect of what is meant by saying that their sexual relationship is a personal relationship, whereas Nigel's anonymous encounter is not. To be concerned with a person's body (rather than with a load of bits of flesh) is to be concerned with him or her. Not every concern with somebody is concern with their body, but concern with their body is concern with them.[35]

This is to do with what in the Middle Ages was called the unity of the soul. The question was raised whether human beings had not just one but three separate souls: the vegetable soul, which they shared with plants and animals, in virtue of which they were alive and grew; the animal soul, in virtue of which they could sense things, were conscious; and the rational soul, in virtue of which they could think, and which makes us distinctively human. Aquinas rejected this view, claiming that there is only one soul, the rational, our properly human soul.[36] This is surely right. In being concerned with human beings you are always concerned with them as people. There is no separate animal soul, so that you can be concerned with Jane *qua* live flesh, as you might be able to regard a fish or a pig as live flesh. The unity of the soul means that you cannot relate to somebody as animal without relating to him or her as human. This flesh cannot be alive without being human flesh, and it cannot be alive without being the flesh of this particular person. To regard Jane as live flesh and without being concerned with her as human being, as person, is not a way of being concerned with her but a failure to be concerned with her. This is what is meant by the Christian insistence that what is important in sexual relationships is that they should be relationships between people.

For example, a surgeon may be concerned in a very direct way with Jane's flesh if he is operating on her. But in the Christian view it is important that his operating on her is an operating on *her*, so that he deals with her in accordance with the general principles of Christian ethics. It is important that his work on her be efficient, but important too that it be loving, that he care for her sake whether the operation is successful or not. He may not know her, and he may not be thinking about her while operating; indeed in a certain sense he should not be thinking about her, for all his attention should be given to what he has to do to help her. But his attitude will be ascertained from a general picture of his life: Is he in medicine because he wants to help people or because that is where he can make the most money or have the most brilliant career? Is he generally considerate of other people? Etc.

In this respect sex is no different from any other way of interacting with people. Human sexual activity is essentially personal. Not that there should be no sheer enjoyment of the flesh, of your own body and somebody else's, but that the enjoyment should be as of people's bodies. Sex is largely a matter of enjoying and being enjoyed. People enjoy being enjoyed, if they like the one who is enjoying them. But on the whole we enjoy being enjoyed fairly specifically, that is, if the one who is enjoying us might not just as well be enjoying somebody else. If Andrew, climaxing with Jane, moans 'Oh, Daphne,' Jane is going to be disappointed. It is not her specifically that Andrew has been enjoying. While she has been furnishing Andrew with pleasure by allowing him to enjoy her body, he has not recognized this body for what it is, as her. This means not only that she will not have enjoyed the experience, but that he does not get any pleasure from the context of his sexual activity; he would rather have been doing this with Daphne. Both partners lose out.

Jane particularly will feel aggrieved; she is liable to feel that she has been used. This use of 'used' is perhaps part of what lies behind the idea that in justice one can never treat people as means but only as ends. But to say that can give the wrong impression. Enjoying somebody, enjoying their body, may indeed be thought of as using them. That is no objection to it. There is a sense in which it is perfectly all right to use people. We all use each other all the time; we get other people to do things for us, and get them to behave in ways which suit us. We also use each other for sexual pleasure; and in that sense we like to be used, to be of use to people. But it matters to Jane that the one who uses her for his sexual pleasure wants to use her in particular. Then she will not ordinarily complain of being used. But if he feels he might just as well use somebody else, and shows that in what he says and does, then Jane may complain of being used. She will want to say something like: in his enjoyment of me, I am not there for him.

There is a further element of injustice in our current example: Because people like to be enjoyed as themselves, Andrew's failure to cater for Jane's enjoyment is a failure of friendship, to do as he would be done by; it is a failure of love.

These considerations are relevant to the Christian attitude to prostitution. Even in making a transaction, two people meet each other as people, and respect for each other as people requires that they behave in appropriate ways; e.g. that people buying and selling in shops address each other courteously according to local custom, deal honestly, do not insult or hit each other, etc. But buying and selling is not a personal relationship in the way sex can be. If I buy a packet of cigarettes, it is not normally important to me that I buy from just this person. Why then, in Christian ethics, cannot sex properly be a transaction, like buying a packet of cigarettes? Why not just exchange pleasure for money, or pleasure for pleasure? Why, in Christian thought, does it have to be a personal relationship in some deeper sense? Because, though I can want a person's body without wanting him or her, I cannot get this body without getting him or her. A human being is his or her body. I cannot get the flesh without getting the person. A sexual relationship, precisely because it is an engagement with a human body, with live human flesh, is an engagement with a human being. Whether the people involved realize it or not, a sexual relationship is a meeting of particular persons in the way that transactions are not, and the Christian talk of sex as personal is simply a recognition of that. So, at a minimum, Christians generally ask that it be important to Andrew that it is Jane that he is doing this with, and important to Jane that it is Andrew that she is doing this with. Jane's body cannot, unlike a packet of cigarettes, be an element of a transaction between Jane and Andrew. It is always one of the parties to the transaction, because Jane's body is Jane, and she is one of the parties to the transaction.

Seeing people

What is it to be concerned with somebody as a person, to see somebody as having a human soul, so that it becomes possible to treat them lovingly in sexual relationships and elsewhere? What makes flesh human flesh? There are several aspects to this. I will touch briefly on just two. First, human flesh is the flesh of somebody with a history, and who is therefore social and linguistic. A person's soul is historical. It is not just what holds the bits of his body together or keeps it breathing. For somebody to have a soul is for him to live, and it is central to human life that it is viewable as story. A human being is an animal with a story or a potential for story. Our view of ourselves is a matter of the story we tell of ourselves. And since a story is told, having a story means also being social and linguistic. When somebody says: 'Tell me about yourself,' a large part of our response will be to tell part of a life story, perhaps a very sketchy one. It will not and cannot be a catalogue of everything we have done and everything that has happened to us. It will be highly selective and shaped; and what we put in and what we leave out, the terms in which we tell the things we do put in, in general the way we shape the story we tell, is an expression of how we view ourselves, how we identify ourselves. And similarly, when others say what they think of us they do it often in a narrative form, giving their version of our story, which will sometimes amount to saying how we figure as characters in their own story. We give form to our lives and to bits of our lives by turning them into narrative. To see somebody as a person is to see them as having a history and a future (a possibility of history), and as having a story which they can tell.

Nigel's groping partner of the back alley cannot be a person for him because he is not for him somebody with a story. In the same way Nigel cannot be a person for his partner. A human relationship is never just a matter of the here and now. If I have a human relationship with somebody, sexual or not, I cannot ignore my past and future or his or her past and future if I am to treat the two of us as what we are, as human beings. Here we can see the beginnings of a foundation of the common idea (not just a Christian one) that a proper sexual relationship between two people presupposes the context of a wider relationship between them, a shared story. This begins to relate the pleasure of sex to the longer-term pleasure of friendship, one of those pleasures which constitute living well. This is much developed in the Christian concept of marriage. I shall have more to say on it in chapter 6.

Soulful eyes

The second aspect I want to mention is more directly physical. It concerns what people might actually do together sexually. The soul, the person, is very much associated in our culture with the face, and particularly the eyes.[37] This is part of what is involved in regarding a person as having a soul, seeing him or her as one, rather than as an assemblage of bits. Compare the remark of Wittgenstein:

> What sort of issue is: Is it the *body* that feels pain? – How is it to be decided? What makes it plausible to say that it is *not* the body? – Well, something like this: if someone has a pain in his hand, then the hand does not say so (unless it writes it) and one does not comfort the hand, but the sufferer: one looks into his face. How am I filled with pity *for this man*? How does it come out what the object of my pity is?[38]

Looking into somebody's face, and that mostly means their eyes, is looking at that person in a way that looking at their hand is not. So that one would respond to the command 'Look at me' by looking into the speaker's face, not at his hand or chest or leg.

A human being looks *at* you, comes out to you through the eyes. To be with somebody and engaged with them as a human being normally, unless it is prevented, involves eye contact. This is well expressed in Donne's poem *The Extasie*:

> Where, like a pillow on a bed,
> A pregnant banke swel'd up, to rest
> The violets reclining head,
> Sat we two, one anothers best.
> Our hands were firmly cimented
> With a fast balme, which thence did spring,

Our eye-beames twisted, and did thred
Our eyes, upon one double string;
So to'entergraft our hands, as yet
Was all the meanes to make us one,
And pictures in our eyes to get
Was all our propagation.
As 'twixt two equal Armies, Fate
Suspends uncertaine victorie,
Our soules, (which to advance their state,
Were gone out,) hung 'twixt her, and mee.

Less poetically, the following remarks of Wittgenstein make allied points:

The face is the soul of the body.[39]

We do not see the human eye as a receiver, it appears not to let anything in, but to send something out. The ear receives; the eye looks. (It casts glances, it flashes, radiates, gleams.) One can terrify with one's eyes, not with one's ear or nose. When you see the eye you see something going out from it. You see the look in the eye.[40]

One can add that, if somebody has a penetrating gaze, it is your eyes that his gaze penetrates. In personal contact, you look into somebody's eyes, not just at them.

So we will expect two people having sex, if they are concerned with each other as people, however much they may be interested in other bits of each other, to look into each other's face and eyes. If Andrew does not look at Jane's knees, it means only that he is not interested in her knees, but if he does not look into her face, into her eyes, it does not mean that he is not interested in her eyes or in her face; it means that he is not interested in her.[41]

The pleasures of sex, to sum up, are largely personal. Sex has more possibilities for pleasure and enjoyment if entered into as part of a relationship between people who mean something to each other. Those who want to treat sex purely as a matter of bodily sensations or as activities in which the identity of the partners is irrelevant or of little significance are actually missing out on a good deal of the pleasure that sex has to offer. They are also making a mistake about the nature of human activity and what it is to be a human being. They fail to see that a meeting of flesh in sex is a meeting of souls. In stressing the importance of personal relationship as a context for sexual activity, Christians have simply latched on to a truth about things. And they are not being strict, but trying to open themselves and others up to greater truth and greater enjoyment.

It will be seen that the considerations I have been talking about apply to the activities of both heterosexual and homosexual men and women, both within and outside marriage. For everybody, sex is better if it is a genuine being with somebody, a genuine doing something with them. And even the most conservative Christian thinker, who thinks that no sex is ever right outside marriage, and certainly no sex between people of the same sex, will acknowledge that sex within the context of a wider personal relationship is better than, say, a series of fleeting anonymous encounters. But the very fact that what I have been saying applies to everybody is perhaps an indication that an examination of pleasure alone will not suffice as a basis for the traditional Christian doctrine that the only proper context for sex is marriage.

5

Sexual Purposes

Purpose and pleasure

In the last chapter I began to examine the traditional opposition between purpose and pleasure in sex, and I tried to show that we could make a beginning towards a more soundly based Christian sexual ethic by taking seriously the importance of pleasure in human life and by obtaining a better understanding of the concept of pleasure. In this chapter I will concentrate on the other half of the opposition. Apart from a suspicion of pleasure, the tradition has relied heavily on the idea of the purpose of sex in order to establish norms of sexual behaviour. Briefly, certain activities are ruled out, it is said, because they conflict with the Creator's design for sex; they do not accord with the purpose of sex. I want now to examine how far this is true: How far can the traditional Christian norms of sexual morality, or for that matter any sexual norms, be based on the idea that sex has a purpose? What is meant by saying that sex has a purpose?

As I said in the last chapter, the early Christian fathers adopted from the pagan philosophers around them, particularly the Stoics, the idea that sexual intercourse was only legitimate if it was done in order to generate children. So too for Augustine, the only thing that could justify sexual activity was the purpose of procreation, that is to say that people should have sexual intercourse with the intent, or at least the hope, of generating a child. I shall call this the strong form of the procreative purpose theory. This idea was modified in later centuries. The more common view then was that sexual intercourse was sinful if it was done in such a way that procreation was purposefully prevented, or was of a kind such that children could not result. This I shall call the weak form of the procreative purpose theory. This weak form persists till today, especially in Catholic circles. For example, the contemporary Catholic theologian Henry Peschke writes:

> Sexual love has as its purpose the propagation of mankind through procreation of children. Any unprejudiced evaluation of sexuality will have to agree with traditional sexual ethics in this affirmation. Procreation of children is the innate, ultimate purpose of man's sexual faculties. The whole sexual structure and inclination indicates the child as its aim. The Creator's ultimate intention in providing man with the sexual faculties is the propagation of mankind. The urge

for sexual union and the sexual organs themselves would not exist without the necessity of procreation.[1]

What are we to make of this idea? We have to say first that, even if we accept it fully, the notion that God gave us sexual organs so that we might reproduce cannot be the end of the story. If somebody wants to say that this is how God has arranged things, then it may be replied that God could have arranged them differently. We could, for instance, have been created in such a way that we reproduced asexually. Our sexual organs and activity are not necessary for us to reproduce, but only to reproduce in the way we in fact do. If God had arranged things differently, so that we increased and multiplied without any sexual activity, then what would be lost to us would just be this particular way of doing things, this kind of activity. That means that this kind of activity may well have a value which is independent of the purpose it is said to serve, perhaps serving another purpose, or having a value in itself, independent of any purpose. So to say that the purpose of sex is procreation is not to preclude there being other reasons why we might want to have sex, or why God might want us to have sex. And indeed, on the whole the Christian tradition has allowed that there might be such other reasons, such as to give expression to and foster love. And we saw another possible reason in the last chapter: pleasure. Sex is a pleasurable activity, and remember that the pleasure we get from an activity is absolutely tied to that activity. You cannot have the pleasure of doing something without doing that thing. You cannot have the pleasure of sipping gin without actually sipping gin. If there were no gin to sip, then there might be all sorts of other pleasures open to us, but the one pleasure we could never have would be the pleasure of sipping gin. And so if we reproduced in another way, if there were no sexual organs and therefore no possibility of sexual activity, then, though we might have all sorts of other pleasures, the one pleasure we could never have would be the pleasure that we get from sex.

However, though the church has in general allowed the legitimacy of sexual activity for purposes other than procreation – and we might want to count sheer enjoyment as such a purpose – yet it has commonly set itself against any sexual activity which deliberately made conception impossible – contraception – or sexual use of the genitals which was not in itself apt to lead to generation – masturbation, bestiality, homosexual relations and heterosexual activities which involved the deposition of semen elsewhere than in the vagina. I want to talk about contraception and homosexual acts specifically in later chapters, but here I will talk in general about the procreative purpose of sex.

That the purpose of sex is procreation – that is, that God's purpose in making us sexual is that we might reproduce – has often been taken to imply that our purpose in having sex has to be bound up with having children. Not just that our sexual activity has to be open to the possibility of procreation, but that such a purpose has positively to lie behind the activity. This idea has made it difficult to explain theologically the potential of sex for giving pleasure. We are naturally attracted to pleasant activities; finding an activity pleasant just is one way of being attracted to it. We often do things without purpose, just because it is pleasant to do them, and their being pleasant counts as a reason for doing them. So if sexual activity is pleasant, it is natural for us to have sex without any reference to procreative purpose. But to insist on a procreative purpose in sex is to say that doing it for pleasure is illegitimate: it may be pleasant, but to want to do it because it is pleasant sinfully neglects the divine purpose.

But in that case the problem arises: why is sex a pleasure at all? A traditional answer to this has been: so that we may be induced to procreate. The pleasure is there as a bait to get us to perform this activity so necessary to the survival of the species. Thus Henry Peschke writes:

> The sex instinct incites man to maintain the human race in the same way as the instinct of self-preservation impels him to maintain his life as individual by taking food. The Creator has attached pleasure to the satisfying of these instincts in order to bring them into play and to reach the goal. But pleasure is not the purpose and aim of their functioning. It is rather the divinely instituted allurement of human beings to use these powers and thereby to maintain and to propagate life.[2]

There are several things wrong with this account of why sex is pleasurable. First, we do not need pleasure in order to be induced to do those things that are necessary; we merely need to be convinced of their necessity for our ends, and then we will do them whether they are pleasant or not, if the end is important enough to us. That is why most people perform the work they do, not because it gives them pleasure but because it is necessary for their survival and that of their loved ones. Secondly, and this is a connected point, work is also essential to the survival of the race, as well as of individuals, and God did not ensure that planting rice or going down coal-mines is intensely pleasurable. Thirdly, if God has made the act of procreation pleasurable so as to induce us to do it, that means the induce-ment to perform this activity must, in God's design, be pleasure. There cannot be anything wrong with doing it just for the pleasure it gives. To do it for pleasure is to be induced to do it in just the way that God intends. And the pleasure that we do it for must be that of the sexual activity itself, not the pleasure of procreating, of begetting or conceiving. Begetting and conceiv-ing are not activities but achievements, results of activities, akin to winning a race rather than to running it. Since procreating is not an activity, it is not a pleasurable activity, one that God induces us to perform by making it pleasurable. To take pleasure in procreation is to be pleased at having begotten or conceived, to rejoice in the news that your sexual activity has resulted in pregnancy. But this is different from enjoying the sexual activity by which a child is begotten or conceived, and it is this that God wishes us to perform.

It is fully in conformity with God's purpose, then, that we recognize sexual pleasure as a value in itself and pursue it as a good. In other words, to say that God's purpose for sex is that we should propagate cannot be held to imply that it must in any way be our purpose in having sex. There will of course be right and wrong ways to seek sexual pleasure, just as there are right and wrong ways to seek anything, and ordinary Christian values must be our guide here. But one thing that cannot be wrong is to seek pleasure from sexual intercourse without procreative purpose. So the stronger form of the idea that the purpose of sex is procreation – that procreation has to be the end that we pursue in doing it – cannot be held.

Before leaving this topic one more remark is in order about the relation between pleasure and procreative purpose. Lurking behind some of the discussion has been the idea that pleasure and procreation might be opposed purposes of sexual activity. Such an idea was expressed in the second century BC by the neo-Pythagorean pseudo-Ocellus Lucanus who claimed that:

> It is particularly well established that we have intercourse not for pleasure but for the purpose of procreation... The sexual organs are given man not for pleasure, but for the maintenance of the species.[3]

This is a false opposition. To have sex for pleasure is not to have sex for the end of obtaining pleasure as opposed to the end of having children. Reproducing can be the end or purpose of an activity, what you seek to achieve by that activity. But activity is not similarly related to pleasure as means to an end. Doing something is not what we have to go through in order to get the pleasure, not the means we have to go through to achieve the end. Pleasure is not what is sought after as the end of the activity, but what is experienced in performing the activity. So to seek a particular pleasure, the pleasure of doing a particular thing, is just to seek to do that thing. To desire to do something 'for the sake of pleasure' is simply to desire to do it. To do it 'for pleasure' is not to do it for that 'end', but to do it without end, or without reference to an end. So it is not to do it for the wrong end, either. Neither, therefore, can it be an end of sexual activity in competition with procreative purpose.

The necessity of sex

Peschke draws an analogy between sex and food and drink. The analogy is an old one, going back among Christians at least to Augustine.[4] Just as food is necessary to the survival of the individual, so, it is said, sex is necessary to the survival of the species. There is an obvious truth in this analogy. However, it cannot be used properly unless we take care to avoid a mistake concerning food itself. It is easy to slip from the truth that because of our nature food is necessary to our survival to the erroneous idea that we naturally eat in order to survive. From here in turn it is but a small step to go on to say that it is against nature to eat except for the sake of self-preservation and therefore that, in conformity with nature, we ought to eat only that we might survive. Human life does not consist only in survival, but in enjoying a certain happiness or well-being. Many of the things that go towards making up our happiness are things that we do not do because we have to do them (even if we do have to do them). Though we need to eat to survive, we hardly ever actually eat to survive; to eat in order to survive we would have to be in a bad way, threatened with starvation if we did not eat. Most of us, if we are lucky, actually eat because we are hungry or because it is time to eat or because we fancy something to eat. The best eating is often unnecessary; it is a treat, something that we do over and above what we need, just because it is delightful. We also recognize a value in positively feasting, in self-indulgence, occasionally eating beyond, even far beyond, our needs as a form of celebration. To eat beyond necessity contributes to human well-being, as does most going beyond need.[5]

This is a value which scripture attests is recognized by God, and feasting is proposed as a picture of the fullness we are to look forward to. For example, Isaiah promises Israel: 'On this mountain the Lord of hosts will make for all peoples a feast of fat things, a feast of wine on the lees, of fat things full of marrow, of wine on the lees well refined' (25.6). In the New Testament, the messianic or heavenly banquet is a standard image of the well-being promised to the followers of Jesus.

Going beyond need allows us to enjoy eating in its own right, not as what is necessary for survival but as one of the things that make survival worthwhile, and that is a good thing. And so with walks in the country, listening to Bach, dancing, playing football, singing, lying in the garden on a hot summer's afternoon sipping a long, cool drink and reading a favourite novel; etc. Doing things because we delight in them – i.e. for no particular reason at all – is central to human living. And it is essential to it; if we do not do it, we languish. Think here of the difference between doing a job that you enjoy and doing one that you don't, one that you do only because you need the money to survive, or for some other purpose. The time when you cease to do it just for the money is the time you actually start enjoying it, when it contributes something to the quality of your life. And that is when you start flourishing. We need occasionally to do things we do not need to do.

From the fact that food and drink are necessary to the survival of the individual it does not follow, then, that our eating and drinking should be limited to what will enable us as individuals to survive. Similarly, though sex is necessary for the survival of the species, that is no reason to say that sexual activity should be limited to what is necessary for the species to survive. To have sex beyond necessity is to appreciate it as a good in itself, one of the things that contribute to the festal quality of human life and make it a desirable thing that the species survive.

It is also worth noting that if sex is necessary for the survival of the species, this is not to say that there is no sense in which individuals can need sex. We do in fact speak of individuals needing sex; we say e.g. that some need more than others. This way of speaking is not to be dismissed. It may be true that we do not need sex in the same way that we sometimes, if we are unfortunate enough, need food. We do not die if we don't get it. But then it is false that a need is something you absolutely cannot do without, that you would die without. Needs are relative to purposes and well-being, and there are essential needs and less important ones. It makes perfect sense to say, for example, 'If you are going to make that you will need this tool'; that means that you will not easily or efficiently or at all manage what you want to do without it. A person may not need to go for a stroll on the moors, but still it is quite in order to say to him or her: 'If you are going to walk there you will need a pair of strong waterproof boots' – if you don't wear them your feet will get sore, cold, wet and generally uncomfortable, and you will have a miserable afternoon. So too it makes sense to say that people may need sex, for their own sake and not for that of the species; and it may actually be true of some individuals. They may need it for all sorts of reasons, such as to relieve sexual tension so as to be able to get on with their work, or to get some comfort after an unpleasant day at work, or so as to try to satisfy their desire to have a child. Though this is not, of course, to say that such needs are in all cases important to the well-being of the individual; nor is it to imply that it is always or ever right for such people to satisfy their needs. It may be right that in certain circumstances some needs, even important ones, remain unsatisfied.

As I tried to show in the last chapter, what lies behind the kind of reasoning we find in Peschke is a traditional dislike of doing things, especially things sexual, for pleasure. But once we realize that doing things for pleasure is a natural human good, important for our well-being, then, if we want to talk about the purposes of God here, we might better say: The purpose of sex is to be a pleasurable activity, so that we might get enjoyment from our own bodies and the bodies of others, and God has so arranged it that our desire for this particular pleasure serves also to ensure the propagation of the species.

'Be fruitful and multiply'

I turn now to the weaker form of the procreative purpose idea, that our sexual activity ought at least to be open to procreation. Despite the early

importance and persistence of the stronger form, it is this weaker version
that has proved more popular with Christian thinkers. Historically the
concern of most theologians has not been to ensure that people have sex for
the purpose of having children, or even to stop them doing it just because
they like it, but to find reasons that will justify a ban on kinds of sexual
activity which have nothing much to do with procreation. What arguments
can be brought in favour of such a position? Use has sometimes been made
of scriptural texts, particularly Genesis 1. Verse 27 shows God creating
people: 'So God created man in his own image, in the image of God he
created him; male and female he created them.' That is followed immediately, in verse 28, by these words:

> And God blessed them, and God said to them: 'Be fruitful and multiply, and fill
> the earth and subdue it; and have dominion over the fish of the sea and over the
> birds of the air and over every living thing that moves upon the earth.'

For some authors this is the basis of the teaching that the purpose of sex is
procreation. The sexual differentiation of man and woman finds its
rationale in the following command to be fruitful and multiply. Thus
Lawler, Boyle and May say:

> The Priestly account [of creation] explicitly brings into focus the procreative
> dimension of human sexuality. The couple, whose sexual complementarity is
> seen as being 'very good' (Genesis 1.31), is blessed by God and instructed to 'be
> fruitful and multiply'.[6]

So the point of human sexual complementarity, according to this view, is to
enable God's instruction to be carried out. The reason we have sexual
organs is to be able to use them for the production of children. That is God's
purpose for sexual activity.

However, the matter is more complicated than that. First, we have
already seen, in chapter 3, how inadequate it is to treat the sexual differentiation which is so important for the priestly writer as a matter of biological
difference. It is a social distinction, to which the roles of men and women in
the generation of children are largely irrelevant. Secondly, the words of God
'increase and multiply' are not straightforwardly to be interpreted as an
instruction or command; they are a blessing. This is stated explicitly, and is
in any case plain from the context; here people are being given good things,
that is things that they will see as goods, like dominion and an abundance of
food: 'Behold, I have given you every plant yielding seed which is upon the
face of all the earth, and every tree with seed in its fruit; you shall have them
for food.' All of this reflects a Hebrew vision of well-being which is amply
attested elsewhere in the Old Testament. For abundance of food, think of
Isaiah's promise of a feast of fat things. As for dominion, Psalm 8 speaks of
the wonderful position God has put man in:

Thou hast made him little less than God,
and dost crown him with glory and honour.
Thou hast given him dominion over the works of thy hands;
thou hast put all things under his feet,
all sheep and oxen,
and also the beasts of the field,
the birds of the air, and the fish of the sea,
whatever passes along the paths of the sea.

Almost everywhere in the Old Testament, one of the great blessings is to have many children. In Genesis, the promise of God to Abraham is above all that he will have a multitude of descendants. In chapter 15 God says to him:

Fear not, Abram, I am your shield; your reward shall be very great... Look toward heaven, and number the stars, if you are able to number them... So shall your descendants be.[7]

So in saying 'Be fruitful and multiply' God is not laying down instructions which people have to follow; he is blessing them with ordinary human goods as recognized in Israelite society. So there is no question here of obedience to or failure to conform to the divine purpose. What is at the centre here is not divine purpose, but human well-being. Or rather, if we wish to speak of divine purpose here, the divine purpose is not that people should have children, be powerful and eat cereals and vegetables whether they want to or not, but to bring about human well-being by satisfying human wants. So neither can there be any question, on the basis of this passage, of sexual activity which goes against the purpose of God, unless by that is meant sexual activity which militates against human well-being.

The appeal to nature

Another important line of argument is in terms of nature, what it is natural for human beings to do. The idea is that nature by its very constitution lays down certain laws of behaviour: look at how you are made and look around you, and you will see what we ought and ought not to do. In the realm of sex, nature sets a standard in two ways, through the behaviour of animals and through the constitution of the human body. Once again, this line of argument is not Christian in origin, but pagan. The argument from the behaviour of animals goes back at least as far as the time of Plato. In the *Laws* he mentions one such argument:

If anybody, following nature, enacted the law in force before the time of Laius, saying that one may have sexual intercourse with a woman but not with men or boys, and adducing the nature of animals, pointing out that among them males do not touch males, since this is unnatural, he would probably be using an unconvincing argument.[8]

This kind of appeal to nature is indeed fraught with difficulties. We can note to begin with that we found in chapter 3 just how socially controlled notions of what is natural are; we do not read off the concept of the natural from the world. 'Nature' is something that we construct. We do not just observe; we classify some things as natural and others as unnatural, for various purposes. What we find natural and unnatural depends very largely on what our society teaches us to find natural or unnatural, and that will reflect other values of dominant social groups. Indeed, the above passage from Plato's *Laws* is an illustration of that. The appeal to nature comes in the context of asking how a legislator might deal with socially disruptive passions; and it continues:

> How far would it [sex between man and man or man and boy] contribute to virtue? Will it engender a courageous character in the soul of him who is seduced, or temperance in that of the seducer?... Everyone will blame the weakness of him who yields to pleasures and cannot contain himself, and will they not censure the one who imitates the female for his likeness to a woman?[9]

Here we meet once again the importance of sexual activity as part of gender role and symbolic of social relations. This kind of sex is regarded as unnatural not because it is seen by observation of nature not to happen but because it goes against socially established behaviour patterns.[10]

The idea of acting according to nature, following 'natural law', was developed most in the Middle Ages. For Aquinas, natural law for human beings could mean two things. It could mean first simply being rational, doing that which reason showed to be right. In this sense all sin, because it is against reason, is also unnatural, a failure to conform to natural law.[11] But there is another sense of natural law, as something that can be more or less read off from the natural world around us and of which we are a part. He says:

> There is in man an inclination to certain things... according to the nature which he shares with other animals. Because of this these things are said to belong to the natural law which nature has taught all animals, and such is the union of male and female, the education of children, and similar things.[12]

As we can see from this passage, Aquinas held that there was a kind of sexual intercourse that is natural for people: the union of man and woman. This was what nature taught. And it was also natural that this intercourse be such as to be able sometimes to lead to the generation of children: sexual activity is naturally ordered to procreation. But what this meant was that any other kind of sexual activity, sex which excluded the possibility of procreation, was not natural; it was a 'sin against nature'. Unnatural sex included masturbation, homosexual activity, and so on.[13]

This idea, that our behaviour should conform to 'what nature teaches all animals', is a somewhat curious one, and indeed there are a number of well-known difficulties surrounding it. First, it is not a self-evident principle, but stands in need of justification. Nature does not in any significant sense teach anything to any animals, or to us. The personification of nature in this way is misleading. We simply see animals doing various things. From what we see we may, if we wish, extract a pattern of behaviour that we would like to follow, and some people may even feel impelled to do so. But there is no apparent reason why we should. We could, and often do, completely disregard animal behaviour, and if we do not we might just as well look at how animals behave and take that as a model of how we should *not* behave.

Second, this is in fact what is done, inconsistently, by Aquinas and others. Some forms of behaviour are part of the natural law because they are practised by animals, like the union of male and female; but it turns out that intercourse in unusual positions or positions like those adopted by other animals is against the natural law.[14] That is because different species have different kinds of behaviour proper to them. It is against nature to adopt a mode of behaviour proper to another species or to abandon that which is proper to one's own. But the obvious question is how it is to be decided whether a particular kind of behaviour is naturally common to all animals, including people, and therefore legitimate (not to say compulsory), or proper to a particular species. Plato observes that in other species males do not mate with males, and that such behaviour is therefore unnatural in humans. But, regardless of whether he is actually right in his claim about animal behaviour, we could equally argue that since such behaviour is observed in humans and not in other animals it is not unnatural but proper to human beings and therefore legitimate.

What appears to be going on in arguments of this kind is not that a lesson in human behaviour is read off from nature, but that examples from nature are used to illustrate or reinforce positions which are held independently. This is rather in the manner of scripture. 'Go to the ant, thou sluggard', says Solomon in the book of Proverbs. But why not 'Go to the three-toed sloth'? Because Solomon, like Aquinas and Plato, already knows, without reference to nature, the moral teaching he wishes to inculcate. To suit his rather different teaching, Jesus told his hearers instead to take idle birds and flowers for their model. Nature is not the source of our moral opinions.

A third difficulty is that observation of animal behaviour just will not yield the results that proponents of natural law want. There is in fact all sorts of sexual behaviour among animals, including behaviour that is not ordered to procreation. There is male and female homosexual behaviour, masturbation, and so on.[15]

This difficulty is compounded if it is desired to draw an analogy between human and animal behaviour in terms of purpose. Suppose somebody said, in support of Augustine's position that sexual activity must have a procreative purpose: 'Animals only have sex in order to reproduce.' Now we have to ask: what could give us the idea that animals have sex to reproduce *at all*? We know that in fact, causally, many animals do reproduce that way, particularly animals to which we are closely related. But this is a statement about an efficient cause, not a final cause or purpose. It tells us the results of what animals do, but says nothing about their intentions or purposes in doing the things they do.

How then is purpose displayed in behaviour, how might we see purpose in animals? It is a feature of behaviour that we are normally prepared to call purposive that it is adaptive. A lion gets downwind of a gazelle as part of its attempt to achieve its purpose of catching it; if the wind shifts direction, the lion also shifts position. When a cat leaps in the direction of a mouse, we can see that this is purposive, and what the purpose is, if, having missed, it leaps again in the direction of the scurrying mouse. How does this apply to sex? Do we see animals adapting their sexual behaviour in order to reproduce? If two lions mate and the female does not conceive, do they try it again at a different time of the month, or use a different position? Do they change their sexual behaviour at all? Apparently not.

Further, purposive behaviour is either successful, or it fails. There are typical expressions of success – looking pleased, excited, satisfied; and there are typical expressions too of failure – looking gloomy, being disappointed, frustrated. Does a lioness looked pleased when she gets pregnant after mating? (How does a lioness look pleased?) Does she look disappointed and frustrated when she does not? We have no reason to think so. There does not appear to be any room for the use of purpose-language when it comes to animal sexual behaviour. There is nothing here to invoke as a guide to how humans should understand their sexual behaviour and purposes.

A fourth difficulty with the appeal to nature is that a norm for behaviour cannot be established from observation of behaviour, enjoining some kinds of behaviour and banning others. A norm would rule out some behaviour as unnatural, but no observed behaviour can count as unnatural, since it is observed behaviour that establishes what is to count as natural; if masturbation is observed as a feature of human sexual behaviour then it will *ipso facto* count as natural.

Fifth, the application of so-called 'laws of nature' to human behaviour neglects the fact that it is part of people's make-up to play, be inventive and to use the things of nature in an artificial way – to chop down trees, dam rivers, plant trees, build canals, use nature for our own ends. We do not just let things go their natural course but intervene in nature, and doing that is essential to being human. We also mould ourselves, forming habits, subjecting ourselves to disciplines, cultivating some attitudes and getting rid of others. We make ourselves fat or thin according to taste; we tattoo or scar or paint ourselves; and so on. How much of this is to be called 'natural' behaviour and how much 'unnatural'? In human beings the concepts 'natural' and 'unnatural' cannot get a proper hold; if we have a taste for the paradoxical we might say that it is natural for people to be unnatural. But that is only to say that we will only get into a hopeless muddle if we try to apply this kind of natural law theory to people's sexual behaviour, if we try to say that some forms of sex are natural while others are against nature. The idea of nature that lies behind the kind of argument we have been considering appears to be of little value in helping to determine norms of sexual ethics; on the contrary, views of what is natural are themselves partly shaped by pre-existing ethical norms.

Aquinas on semen

It is true that Aquinas is not open to quite all these objections, as others are. He does have a separate criterion for what is to count as natural for people, apart from how they are observed to behave: their good, both as individuals and as a species. He says:

> God cares for each thing according to what is good for it. But it is good for each thing that it purpose its end, and it is bad for it to swerve from its proper end. As in the whole, so in the parts: each part of a man and all his acts should be allotted to its due end. But semen, even if it is superfluous to conserving the individual, is still necessary to the propagation of the species. Other superfluous things, like faeces, urine, sweat etc., are not needed for anything, so the good of a man requires only that they be emitted. But semen is needed to be emitted for the purpose of generation, to which coitus is ordered. From which it is obvious that every emission of semen in such a way that generation cannot follow is against the good of man. And if this is done on purpose, it must be a sin. But I mean a way such that generation cannot follow in itself (*secundum se*), such as any emission of semen without the natural conjunction of male and female; that is why such acts are called sins *against nature*. But if generation cannot follow an emission of seed *per accidens*, it is not therefore against nature, nor a sin – as when the woman happens to be sterile.[16]

God is the author of nature, and he orders everything for the good of his creatures. That is why it is worth our while to follow nature, and why it is good for us. To go against the natural order that God has established in human action and desire is to work against the good of his human creatures. Here we see something close to the picture in Genesis 1, where it is human well-being, not the independent commands of God, that is in question. What is good is what is good for people. This is surely right. It reminds us of something that is easy to forget in these arguments over what is natural: that the question we should be asking about our actions is how they affect people. Nature is only relevant to us as Christians in so far as it helps us determine what is the loving thing to do.

But now, if particular activities are to be shown to be wrong, arguments or evidence have to be produced to show that they are bad for human beings; and Aquinas does indeed produce an argument, one which would rule out most kinds of sexual activity as sins against nature. However, it is not a very good argument. Semen, he says, is not just superfluous, like other bodily excretions; it is necessary for the propagation of the species. Therefore every emission of semen which cannot result in procreation is, if deliberate, a sin, and a sin against nature. But the argument trades on an ambiguity about the necessity of semen. Semen is indeed necessary to the propagation of the species, if by that is meant that the species cannot be propagated without some semen (not yet, anyway: scientific discoveries may one day take us to the stage where that is possible). But the conclusion that every deliberate emission of semen which does not serve this end is sinful requires the stronger premise that the propagation of the species requires all the semen that there is; and that is plainly false. It is an argument from scarcity of resources. Nobody would argue that since water is necessary to life all deliberate wastage of water is a sin against nature, except where water is in short supply; that is, where all water is necessary to life. It may be sinful to throw away water in the Sahara, but not in the Amazon basin. In fact, not all semen is necessary for the propagation of the species. There is plenty of semen around; there is no shortage at all. It is a renewable resource, and all the non-procreative emissions of semen that go on threaten to produce no shortage. People have tried to produce all sorts of arguments to show that things like masturbation, homosexual activities, bestiality, and so on, are against nature in the sense that they run counter to human well-being. Whether or not any such argument can be sustained, it is clear that if any harm does come to human beings through such activities, it does not come from their failure to serve a procreative purpose, in the way that Aquinas alleges.[17]

Aquinas' starting position here, that what is natural is what conduces to human well-being, is surely a reasonable one. But what is conducive to our well-being is an empirical matter; we can tell by looking whether people are doing well or not, and then investigate the causes. There is also, as we saw, great difficulty with establishing anything as natural or unnatural without using some such criterion as human well-being. The obvious conclusion from these considerations is that it we cannot determine *a priori* what is natural. If we want to retain the concept of the natural, we have to establish what is natural to human beings by looking and seeing what allows people to flourish; what is called unnatural will be what is found to be harmful to human beings. Aquinas uses the language of purpose: it is good for a creature to purpose its proper end, and bad for it to swerve from that end. But again, that means that what counts as the proper end of a creature is not to be determined *a priori*, but from actual examination or experience of how it acts and how it fares. If it is bad for a creature to swerve from its proper end, then a creature cannot swerve from its end and still flourish; if a creature is flourishing, then it is purposing its proper end. So we find out what is the proper end of a creature by seeing what makes it flourish.

This is relevant to another argument which Aquinas produces. This second argument depends on the notion of an activity being ordered towards an end. In the *De Malo* 15.1c he says:

> Sometimes, along with disorder of concupiscence, there is also a disorder of the external act in itself, as happens in every use of the genital organs outside the marriage act. And that every such act is disordered in itself is apparent from the fact that every human act is said to be disordered which is not proportioned to its due end, just as eating is disordered if it is not proportioned to the health of the body, to which it is ordered as to an end. But the end of the use of the genital organs is the generation and education of offspring, and therefore every use of the aforementioned organs which is not proportioned to the generation of offspring and its due education is disordered in itself. Every act of the aforementioned organs apart from the intercourse of male and female is manifestly not fitted for the generation of offspring.

And so the conclusion follows that all such acts are disordered. But what makes the generation and education of offspring the end of the use of the genital organs can only be the good of human beings. There may be several ways in which the use of the genital organs contributes to the good of human beings (e.g. expressing love, making us feel relaxed, etc.), so Aquinas has no right to talk of *the* end of their use. We may say that sexual activity is 'ordered' to any number of ends. In any case, it will be human well-being that determines what are the natural uses of the genitals, the uses to which they may properly be put.

In the following question Aquinas does use the criterion of human good to rule out non-procreative sex. Objection 4 to the thesis that every act of lechery is a mortal sin runs as follows:

> Every mortal sin is contrary to charity... But simple fornication is against neither the love of God, as it is not a sin against God, nor the love of neighbour, because it does no injury to a neighbour.

Aquinas replies:

> All the vices of lechery, which are beyond the legitimate use of marriage, are sins against a neighbour, inasmuch as they are against the good of the offspring to be generated and educated (*De Malo* 15.2).

I commented in chapter 1 on the way in this passage Aquinas relates sexual morality to love of neighbour. But the question now is whether he is correct in the way he argues from love of neighbour to the sinfulness of all the forms of lechery. His argument is unconvincing for several reasons. First, a neighbour is somebody living; it is only to a living being that one can do good or ill. And the offspring to be generated and educated is not a yet living being. Second, even if we made sense of harming one who does not yet exist, the argument here would only work if there is a child who is going to be generated and educated. But from Aquinas' point of view the objectionable feature of some lecherous practices, such as masturbation and anal inter-course, is precisely that no child is going to be, or can be, generated and educated. Third, there is no identifiable individual to be harmed, and you can only harm an identifiable individual. The argument of the objection is correct. Fourth, even if an individual could be identified, it is not clear that anything harmful is done to him or her through lechery.

Nature and pleasure

Does this mean that we can do nothing fruitfully with the idea of nature in our thinking about sex? It may appear so. Yet this conclusion would be impoverishing. We do after all have the concept of the natural, however it is unpacked, and it is important in some of our sexual attitudes. In one straightforward sense what is natural is what is observed in nature. In this sense whatever people do is natural. Our observation of what people do contributes to our idea of human nature. But we also speak of what is natural and unnatural. As I argued earlier, much of our conception of what is natural is a social construct and an insecure basis for Christian sexual teaching. Nevertheless, there does appear to be another sense in which we can properly speak of human nature, and of the natural and the unnatural. Aquinas points the way forward in the texts we have just been examining. Though the particular arguments he deploys are defective, yet his insistence that the natural be understood in terms of what is conducive to human well-being is an important insight. We do as human beings have common physical characteristics, as well as social and psychological ones. We do know that, because of our nature, certain things are good for us and other things are bad for us. Breathing water is bad for us; it leads to our rapid extinction. The right kind and amount of food and drink is good for us and necessary to us. A moderate amount of exercise is good for us; it makes us stronger and healthier. Having the conditions to live in accord with our nature means not only being able to survive physically, but having the opportunity to flourish, to live happily. So, because we are constituted as we are, confinement is bad for us; unless we have the freedom of a reasonable space to move about in we languish. That is one reason why imprisonment can be used as punishment, just as being forced to breathe water can. And it is not good for us, not natural for us, to be alone for long periods; other people are good for us. We are deprived and unhappy, lonely and diminished if we are without the company of friends for too long. We need friends and freedom, just as we need to breathe air. This relates to one of the themes of chapter 1. Because we are by nature social animals it is essential to happy human living that we cultivate, and encourage others to cultivate, those qualities that enable us to live together as friends. Seen in this light, the Christian insistence on the centrality of the virtue of love can be understood simply as a recognition of human nature.

This approach also ties in well with what I said earlier about pleasure. We flourish, live happily, if we are able to do at least some of the things we want to do; the more deeply we want to do something, the more central to our happiness is our ability to do it. But doing what we want to do gives us pleasure. In some cases, if our desire is transient and trivial, like the desire to eat a cream cake, so also will be the pleasure of our doing; if the desire is deep and lasting, like the desire to spend our life with one we love or to devote ourselves to the spread of the gospel, so will be the pleasure in the satisfaction of that desire. So there is a close and obvious connexion between pleasure and happiness: we live happily if we do things that give us pleasure. This can be put by saying that it belongs to our nature that we flourish when we do what we want to do, and hence get pleasure out of the things we do.

However, notoriously, we can want to do, and get pleasure from doing, things that are bad for us. We can perform activities which give us pleasure in the short term but which in the longer term make our lives miserable or bring it to an end. For example, drug abusers may very much enjoy the activity of taking their favourite drug, but they can also reduce their lives, curtailing their possibility of enjoying other things through their preoccupation with and dependence on drugs; and they may ruin their health, perhaps to the point of killing themselves. It makes sense to say of such people that their desires and activities are unnatural, or against nature. They do, and want to do, things which, given their constitution, are bad for them. Given the importance to human beings both of doing what they want to do and of not doing things which are bad for them or against their nature, it follows that it is important that they not have unnatural desires, that they not want to do things which are bad for them. If, as a matter of fact, some individuals do want to do something which is bad for them, then the right, the sensible, course of action for them, the one which will lead to their flourishing, their happiness and lasting pleasure, is not to fulfil their desire, but to unlearn it and to learn to desire instead to do what is good for them, what accords with nature.

By this I do not mean that it is morally wrong for people to engage in unnatural activity, wrong to do what is bad for them. I have been stressing love of neighbour as the fundamental principle of Christian ethics. If I am correct in this, then Christians must reject any behaviour which is contrary to love of neighbour, such as deliberately seeking his or her harm. But on this same principle it also looks doubtful whether any convincing line of reasoning can be generated to show it to be a moral law that people should not do what is bad only for themselves. However, even if this is so, that does not mean it is a matter of indifference to the church if people do what is bad for them. The church is not merely a moral policeman, seeking to enforce moral laws or a particular conception of nature; it is a people and an organization with a divine commission to love. But it is an aspect of love that it seeks the good of the one loved. The church, like all those committed to love, seeks the good of human beings. It is therefore committed to dissuading people from doing what is bad for them and persuading them to do what is good for them. If certain activities are shown to be unnatural, this is not to say that it is possible to show those who practise them that they are wrong to do so, but it is to give the church the responsibility of trying to persuade them away from such things. If we cannot show that the practises are wrong, that means only that one particular form of persuasion is not available to us. Persuasion will then rather take the form of showing that the practices are harmful, and fostering in their practitioners a sense of their own worth and goodness that will make them reluctant to harm themselves. It will also include encouraging them to seek solid joys and lasting pleasures.

If it is true of our actions and desires in general that they may be unnatural in the sense of being bad for us, so is it true of our sexual actions and desires. There is a wide range of sexual behaviour observable among human beings. In one sense, all this variety of activity is, just because it is observable, natural. Nevertheless, it may be true that some of the things people do sexually are unnatural, in the sense that it is actually bad for them to perform them. In which case, they may still be perfectly free to do such things; they may have no moral duty to uphold nature. But it is still the duty of the church, stemming from its love for people, to encourage people to abandon those activities and to behave sexually in a way that is better for them.

The vital question here, of course, is what sexual activities, if any, are actually bad for people and therefore against nature. As I have said before, this is not something to be decided *a priori*, by abstract argument. It is only from investigation and experience that we can tell whether, say, masturbation or fellatio have deleterious effects on those who practise them. We might be able to think of reasons why we might expect them to be injurious, and these might suggest lines of enquiry, but they cannot of themselves establish the fact, and render empirical investigation redundant.

What we can say from plain common sense is that these activities are not obviously harmful to their practitioners; people do not go mad if they masturbate, nor do they die of poisoning when they practise oral sex. If such things are bad for people, they are bad in quite subtle ways, ways that may need quite considerable investigation and experience to establish. However, if they are not obviously harmful, it does not follow that they are obviously not harmful. It is sometimes asserted by people outside the mainstream Christian tradition that such practices are harmless. But without a good deal of research the most that can be said is that they are apparently innocuous. However, if they are not plainly harmful, one needs a reason to stimulate the research; it appears to be incumbent on the church to show that it is at least reasonable to suspect that they might be bad for people.

Does sex have a purpose?

There is a further significant question lurking behind this discussion. An element of a number of the arguments considered above was the conception that our organs and activities have proper ends and purposes. What can we make of the idea that sex, in particular, has a purpose or end? The question itself needs a certain amount of clarifying. We can distinguish at least three things when we are talking about the purpose of sex. People have spoken of the purpose of our sexual organs, of sexual activities, and of our sexual faculties. There is in fact not much difference between these three. After all, the purpose of a thing, such as a sex organ, is nothing other than the purpose for which that thing is to be used, so discussion of the purpose of sexual organs comes down in the end to a discussion of the purpose of the activities in which they are used. (Though we should not forget that sexual activity is wider than activity in which the genitals are used: the play of limbs, biting earlobes, etc.) However, some remarks need to be made about these different ways of talking.

Some theologians and philosophers have preferred to talk in terms of faculties rather than actions, but such talk really comes down to talk about what people do. A faculty is an ability to do something. To use or exercise a faculty to do something is simply to do that thing: you exercise your pedestrian faculty by walking, your rational faculty by thinking, and so on. In these examples it is activities or ranges of activities that are involved. Our sexual faculties are faculties such as these; they are the abilities to act in a range of ways that we classify as sexual. As we often act for an end, to achieve something, so we may be said to exercise our faculties in order to achieve an end. Sometimes, however, in talking of faculties we are dealing rather with achievements. A pertinent example is the reproductive faculty, which we exercise by reproducing. As pointed out earlier, reproducing is not an activity but something that is achieved by an activity; it is akin to winning a race rather than running a race. So the reproductive faculty cannot be identified with sexual faculties; it is a logically different kind of faculty. And empirically, there are people with sexual faculties but without reproductive faculties, such as women who have undergone a hysterectomy, or sexually active but sterile men. So the sexual and the reproductive faculties can never be simply identified. In particular, questions of sexual ethics cannot be solved by re-labelling sexual faculties as the reproductive faculty; for example, non-reproductive kinds of sex, like masturbation or oral sex, cannot be thought of as defective uses of the reproductive faculty, and condemned as such.

In general, the exercise of one faculty is wrongly described as the defective use of another faculty. A faculty is the ability to do something. The faculty to do one thing, X, is a different faculty from the faculty to do another, Y. To do Y is to exercise not the faculty to do X but a different faculty. So to do Y is not a defective or abnormal exercise of the faculty to do X – unless Y is a defective form of X. The faculty to reproduce is exercised in reproducing. There are well-known ways of bringing this about, principally (and until recently solely) penetrative vaginal intercourse to the point of ejaculation between fertile partners in the fertile part of the woman's cycle. But we have sexual faculties other than this, that is abilities to perform activities we would classify as sexual which are not ways of reproducing. The reproductive faculty is simply not involved in such forms of sex. Here we are concerned only with logically different sexual faculties. It may remain a question whether such faculties are to be exercised for purposes other than reproduction, but the matter is not to be settled by talk of defective use of the reproductive faculty. Indeed it is difficult to see how one can speak of the defective use of the reproductive faculty. You can perform actions defectively, in the obvious sense of not doing them very well, and perhaps also in the moral sense of doing them in a morally defective way or in the wrong circumstances. But reproducing is an achievement, not an action. You cannot, in any relevant sense, reproduce defectively;[18] you can only fail to reproduce.

The purpose of organs

Though there is a large overlap between talk of the purpose of organs and the purpose of activities, there are a couple of preliminary points that can more easily be made in terms of the use of organs. The example I want to give reminds us too that it is not only sexual organs we have to be concerned with. I once heard it said in a discussion on anal sex: 'Use of the rectum for sexual purposes goes against its God-given function; God designed it for evacuation, not sex.' What is being complained of here is not the misuse of a sexual organ, but the sexual misuse of a non-sexual organ. While I do not want to dismiss that complaint, there are a number of questions to be asked about it.

First, why do we want to say that a function is God-given, that God designed a particular part of the body for a particular purpose? Though we may want to say that God created us, why should we say that he created bits of us to fulfil a certain purpose? One reason we might want to say such a thing is that the rectum, like the heart, has an obvious part to play in the functioning of the whole, in sustaining the life and efficient running of the person; it contributes in an evident way to human good. Since as Christians we believe that our life comes from God, it makes some sense to say that any organ that helps to sustain that life does so in fulfilment of a divine purpose. So then any use of it that prevents it from carrying out that function is to be avoided. But if we agree to say that the rectum has an important function as part of the digestive system, why should we not say that it also has a sexual function?

This is just one example of a more general question: We might want to say of an organ that it has a function, but why should we say that it has just one function? Why not lots? The penis is an example of a dual-purpose organ, having an important function both in reproduction and in the evacuation of waste. It could be countered that the rectum is not parallel to the penis in this respect, in that both the functions of the penis are important in sustaining life – the one in promoting the life of the species and the other in maintaining the life of the individual. There is some force in this, but even if an organ like the rectum has only one divinely-ordained function (because it only helps to sustain life in one way) why should it not also be given a human function, a function ordained by human beings – say, a sexual function? Human beings are after all inventive creatures, and it is common for people to discover or invent new uses for already existing things.

Again, if two people, say a married couple, decide to use the rectum of one of them for sexual purposes, how does that go against its God-given purpose? It does not prevent it from functioning in the normal way (except for the duration of the sex; but then, we would inhibit its normal excretory functioning in any case, even in the most ordinary forms of married sex). Clearly talk of 'going against a function', if it can be given any sense in this case, must mean something quite different from what it would mean in a normal case.

But suppose that sense can be given to it, that it makes sense to talk of anal sex going against a God-given function. The more radical question emerges: Why should we not go against a God-given function? We think nothing of going against a God-given shape and appearance. We are always doing things to alter the appearance and shape of our bodies, sometimes even by surgery. What is so sacred about function? Perhaps this is connected with our idea that God has purposes. And the purpose of an engineer is expressed, we might want to say, in the functions of the parts of his machine. But the purposes of a designer are not always functional ones; they are sometimes aesthetic. If the function of my rectum can show a purpose of God, why should not the shape of my nose likewise show a purpose of God?

Our earlier discussion of purpose does give us a pointer to why we should indeed not go against a God-given function or purpose for our organs. If we go against the proper purpose, it will be bad for us. But, once again, the divine purpose is not given us *a priori*; it is a matter of discoverable effect on human well-being. If people do things with an organ that are not bad for them or for other people, that means those things do not go against the divinely established purpose for that organ. This remains true however distasteful others may find such activities.

The point of these questions and remarks is to bring out some of the complexity of an apparently simple complaint, to indicate some of the issues it raises. I leave the questions unanswered and the issues unresolved, remarking only that I do not see how by unaided reason, without appealing to divine revelation, the traditional Catholic answers can be arrived at. Indeed it seems doubtful whether, even if we accept it as revealed that God gives us organs for certain purposes, any real sense can be given to the idea that certain forms of sex, like anal intercourse, run counter to the divinely-ordained purpose of our organs.

The purpose of sexual acts

Let us now move on to discussion of the purpose of sexual activities. The activities we regard as obviously sexual are very various, for example masturbation, vaginal intercourse between man and woman, anal inter-course between man and woman, oral intercourse between man and man. We may also want to include play of any number of kinds, such as dressing up, throwing cream buns, bondage, the administering and receiving of mild or even quite severe pain; and so on. What are we to say about the purpose of such varied activities? To begin with, we may say that these activities are so various that it is unlikely that we shall be able to talk of a single purpose for all of them. Some of these activities are ones the church would want to encourage in some circumstances; others it would be indifferent to or inclined to discourage. But we cannot yet at this stage distinguish between them by appealing to the one purpose of sexual activity, for we have not yet succeeded in showing that there is a single purpose, nor in making sense of the notion that there might be only one.

Now, in what circumstances do we normally ask the purpose of a particular activity or range of activities? Typically, we ask when we do not know or are unsure. And who do we ask? Those who take part in the activities; or, if they are doing it because they have been told to, we can ask those who ordain those activities. Given that these activities take place, where, by mutual agreement, there is more than one person involved, they are what we call voluntary activities, and we need not think anybody ordains them. We can find out the purpose of them by asking those who perform them. When people perform voluntary activities, the purpose of the activity is the purpose of those who perform it. If we interrupted people performing an obviously sexual activity and asked them why they were doing it, we might get all sorts of answers. They might be doing what they are doing to help them relax after a bad day, or to comfort a loved one or friend in distress, or to comfort themselves, or to earn some money, or to try to have a child, or to spite parents, or to confirm a negative self-image, or out of curiosity; or perhaps there is no purpose at all: they are doing what they are doing for its own sake, just because it is a familiar and enjoyable thing to do, or new and fun. Beyond any reference to the purposes of the participants, there would seem to be little scope for talking of *the* purpose of sex.

What might be said at this point is that God has a purpose for our sexual activities, including the case where those activities are voluntary. But can God be said to have a purpose for our voluntary activities? God might indeed have a rule, a law that if we perform this activity we may only do it in this way, in these and these circumstances, and not in others. He might even ordain that we may perform an activity only if we perform it for a particular purpose. In the field of sex, it is often claimed that the rules governing sexual behaviour in books like Leviticus are such rules of God. I have already, in chapter 3, discussed one of those rules, Lev. 18.22, forbidding any man from lying with another as with a woman, and found reason to doubt that it can be understood by Christians as a rule of God without more ado. But if I am mistaken, if it and others like it are really rules of God, can these rules be described as expressing his purpose in our acting sexually? Once again, the purpose of a voluntary activity is the purpose of the agents. The purpose of what I do is my purpose. If the laws of Leviticus are God's laws, then God may have a purpose in restricting my sexual activity or in guiding it in a certain direction; he might place such a restriction on me in order to safeguard some other purpose of his, e.g. to stop me getting more involved in the pursuit of pleasure than he intends me to be, or to encourage me to love and respect my neighbour. But if he has such a purpose, it is the purpose of what he does, of his laying down these laws; it is not the purpose of what I do, of my sexual activity.

There are other difficulties that raise themselves in this connexion, and that can be mentioned briefly. If I am wrong in what I have just argued and God can be said to have a purpose for our voluntary actions, and if it can be said, further, that God's purpose for our sexual activity is for us to reproduce, then it seems reasonable to say also that when we do not reproduce as a result of our sexual activity, God's purpose fails. Is this possible? Do we not often want to say rather that what happens shows God's purpose? Then, if pregnancy does not follow on intercourse, it seems to be God's purpose that it not follow. One can imagine a woman who has tried unsuccessfully to become pregnant being told by husband, neighbour or priest that she must resign herself to the will of God, or that her failure is in accordance with the purposes of God. And what was said earlier of animals can be said also of God: if his purpose fails, does God then feel disappointed? What is the typical expression of this? Does he adapt his behaviour (or ours) to ensure that we reproduce? Some of these questions raise problems for our understanding of the much more general question what it is for God to have purposes at all, or what we are doing when we use purpose-language in connexion with God.

But can we not after all make some sense of the idea of a purpose for sex, which is not the purpose of those who are actually doing it? We do sometimes talk of purposes which are not the purpose of anybody in particular. We certainly do this with the purposes of things. For example, if a child or somebody to whom our civilization is foreign sees a heavy hollow glass object on my table and is perplexed by it, he can ask: 'What is that for?', 'What purpose does that serve?' And he would not then be asking just what I am now using it for, but what purpose it has in general in people's lives. And so my answer will be: 'It's for drinking whisky out of' or 'It's a whisky tumbler.' The answer will not be in terms of what I am now using it for. I may indeed now be drinking whisky out of it, but I may be using it for another purpose, say as a paperweight; if I am using it as a paperweight, even if I never drink whisky from it, it still remains true that it is a whisky tumbler, that this kind of thing is in general used for drinking whisky out of. However, it is still the purposes of people that matter here. It does not seem possible to make any sense of the idea that there might be a purpose for whisky tumblers that could not be talked about in terms of what people use them for.[19]

But let us suppose that this is just my obtuseness. Suppose we can talk about the use of sexual activity, and establish that it has a God-given purpose, and only one, which we have to follow, and similarly that we can speak of a God-given purpose of our sexual organs and of sexual activity. Still it does not follow that sex cannot properly be used for any other purpose. We might say that the purpose of a whisky tumbler is to hold whisky in a satisfying way for us to drink from. But there is no reason why we should not also use a whisky tumbler as a paperweight or as a doorstop, until we need it for the purpose of drinking. To say that a thing has a particular purpose in no way indicates that it may not also be used by individuals or by everybody for some other purpose, so long as it is available and fit for its designated purpose when the time comes. If the God-given, sole purpose of whisky tumblers were to have whisky drunk from them, it would still be perfectly all right for me to use one as a doorstop provided I released it for its divinely-ordained purpose when somebody needed it to drink from. And an important point here is that this is true even though my using it as a doorstop is incompatible with anybody using it at the same time to drink from. What is needed is only that my using it as a doorstop not prevent anybody using it to drink from, that if somebody needed it to drink from it be released from its use as doorstop.

So with sex. Even if all the difficulties I have mentioned proved illusory and it could be established that God's sole purpose for sexual activity is procreation, still it would be perfectly all right for me to 'use' sexual activity for some other end, or for none, provided that I released it for its divinely-ordained end when required. This would be true even if the use to which I put such activity was known not to be procreative. My taking part in oral sex or masturbating would not be against the purpose of God; I would only have to ensure that if it were ever necessary for me to have sex for the purpose of procreation, that would not be prevented by my other uses of sex, my other sexual activities.

The gift of sex

However, that is not quite the end of the matter. I believe we can, after all, make some sense of the idea of the purpose of sex by appeal to the Christian view of our lives and our faculties as gifts of God. In the Christian view, all that we are and have comes to us from God, and that as his free gifts, tokens of his love for us. As I said right at the beginning of this book, one of the greatest goods for people is that they recognize the truth of that vision. A person who does not see that everything that he or she is and has is a gift of the loving God will not flourish properly. Somebody who does see this is a happy person, and the form of his or her happiness is gratitude.

It is possible to speak of the use and misuse of a gift. Using a whisky tumbler as a doorstop may not be in contradiction to the 'natural' use of a whisky tumbler, the use established by social convention, but it might be said to be an abuse if the tumbler is a gift. For, it could be said, to use it in such a way is to show disrespect for the one who gave it. Jane gave Andrew a whisky tumbler so that he might enjoy drinking whisky from it. If Andrew uses it for a different purpose, like putting it on the floor to use as a doorstop, he is insulting Jane and showing a lack of gratitude to her. Similarly, it could be claimed that God gave us our sexual faculties so that we might reproduce sexually and enjoyably. To use them for any other purpose is to insult God; it is not to show proper gratitude for his gift. Sexual activities which rule out reproduction are wrong, therefore, not because they are against nature, nor because they conflict with the divinely ordained purpose of sex, but because they abuse a gift of God.

Note first of all that this kind of argument is one that depends on a prior faith in God. It does not depend simply on thought or on reading the book of nature, but appeals to the idea that what we have is a gift of God; and this idea belongs in the realm of religion, of belief in God, not of unaided reason. Unlike some of the arguments I presented earlier, such as some of the natural law arguments or those deriving from the concept of pleasure, which are designed to have universal appeal, this one can appear cogent only to those who accept the Christian faith or something like it.[20]

For Christians, there is no doubt that the argument latches on to something important in our conception of life; that is why we make thanksgiving the central act of our worship. And so too with our attitude to sex. In this area of our lives, as in all others, if we live properly our behaviour will be informed with gratitude to God. But it is not clear that invoking the idea of gratitude is very productive when it comes to the question how we are to use our sexual faculties.

The argument as I sketched it depends on the premise that God gave us our sexual faculties so that we might reproduce, and this has not yet been established. It may seem clear to some that sex is for reproduction if by sex we mean vaginal intercourse between man and woman. But as I have said repeatedly, this is only one form of sexual activity, along with masturbation, sex play between women, etc. If we look upon sex as a gift, it is not clear that these other forms of sexual activity are abuses of the gift. They might be held, rather, to show the versatility of the gift. That these other uses are abuses could only be established if it were shown independently that vaginal sex between man and woman is the only proper use of the gift. In short, if appeal to the idea of gift is conceived as an argument to show that such vaginal sex is the only proper form of sexual activity, then the argument assumes what it sets out to show. We can use the idea of sex as a gift of God to give us an additional description, in Christian terms, of what it is to behave properly sexually: it is to respect an important gift of God. But it cannot be used to determine what proper sexual behaviour is.

Even if it were established independently that the use for which God gave us the gift of sex was procreation, that still would not show that non-procreative varieties of sexual activity constituted abuses of the gift. For not every use of a gift other than that for which it is given counts as a misuse. Andrew may be misusing Jane's gift if he uses his new whisky tumbler as a doorstop, but not if he uses it to drink water from. Probably not, either, if he uses it temporarily as a paperweight, though this use might be an abuse if it were permanent. A different use is an abuse only if that use is in some way unworthy of the gift. A doorstop, we might say, is a base thing, and to use something as a doorstop is to put it to base use. This is all right if the thing has actually been designed for that base use. For there is nothing wrong with being a doorstop, and doorstops perform useful service. But there is, we might say, something wrong with using a beautiful new crystal whisky tumbler for this service. Small things left on the floor get dirty, they get kicked, they are disregarded. If they are made of glass, they are also liable to get chipped, cracked or broken. It is not consonant with the nature of a whisky tumbler to use it as a doorstop. If Andrew has left his present on the floor accidentally or through negligence, Jane may be annoyed at his thoughtlessness. If he has put it there deliberately, she is liable to feel slighted. He has ignored the fact that the glass was a gift from her. Or worse, he may not have ignored it but in full consciousness of it performed a gesture designed to affront her; he may have deliberately abused the gift she has given him and shown his contempt for it, and thereby rejected her gesture of giving and shown his contempt for her.

If we accept that our sexual faculties are a gift from God, and if we accept further that they are given us for the purpose of reproduction, what can be said about other uses of them? What can we say about non-procreative sex? We might say that, in general, sexual activity which shows lack of gratitude, which shows contempt for the genitals or other parts of the body, and therefore for God, is to be avoided. But how is this to be cashed in concrete instances? Is to masturbate, for instance, to use one's genitals as a paperweight or as a doorstop? Is it simply to find another use for one's genitals, or is it to abuse them? Clearly, if we already regard masturbation as unacceptable behaviour, we will see it also as an abuse of the genitals and an affront to the God who gave them. But if we do not already know what to think of masturbation, it is hard to see how an argument can be developed on the basis of the above which will tell us.

Masturbation is quite an interesting case to consider in this connexion, since it is a form of sexual activity which is not dependent on the consent of anybody else. In so far as masturbation brings satisfaction, it is a satisfaction entirely within the power of the one who does it. Masturbation is not a cooperative, interpersonal exercise; if Andrew masturbates, his sexual satisfaction is not dependent on anybody else. So he has nobody else to be grateful to for any sexual cooperation. By its logical structure, masturbation seems to exclude gratitude, and hence to be an archetypal example of an ungrateful use of our sexual faculties. But this is not so. If Andrew masturbates he may not be grateful to any human being, but he does not necessarily lack gratitude to God. We can easily imagine that somebody might find in masturbation one of his few consolations in a life that is dreary and lonely, and quite sincerely thank God for that consolation. Thus, though he may have no human being to thank for his sexual pleasure (and he may regret this), he may be genuinely grateful to God for that pleasure, or for the organs which give him the power to give himself pleasure.

What is true of solitary masturbation looks true also of other kinds of sexual activity, at least at first glance. For surely we might be grateful to

God for all kinds of sexual pleasures, as for other pleasures. I might greatly enjoy raping young boys, their terrified whimpering only adding to the keenness of my pleasure. On each occasion I might thank God sincerely for that pleasure. Or might I? I can only thank God for something if I believe it is something he might have given me. Certainly it might be said that other people are among the most important of God's gifts to us. It might be said, further, that he gives us other people in order that we might love them. I argued earlier that to say that God gives us a gift for a purpose does not imply that it is improper to use that gift for another purpose. If that is right, then it appears that even if we are given other people to love, that is no reason why we should not instead terrify, assault and exploit them. If I rape them, this is simply to use them for a purpose other than what I was given them for; it is to use them as a paperweight.

But to rape people is not simply to use God's gift for a different purpose from that for which it was intended. Raping people is not just different from loving them; it is incompatible with loving them. This use of the gift actually contradicts the purpose of the gift, and is therefore fairly described as an abuse of the gift and an expression of contempt for God. Thus using the idea of gift can take us somewhere in our quest for sexual norms. But it is somewhere we have been before. We have moved away from talk of sex as a gift of God to speaking of people as gifts of God; and what makes it wrong to rape people on this account is that they are given us to love. But this comes down to saying that rape is forbidden because it is contrary to love. The appeal to the notion of gift is an unnecessary detour.

So it looks as if the idea of sex as gift gives us no guidance in trying to shape our sexual norms. Once we have established some norms it gives us a helpful way of articulating the connexion between those norms and faith in the God who gives us our sexual faculties. But for the norms themselves we have to look elsewhere. I believe I have also shown that talk of natural law and of the purposes of God cannot be used to establish such norms. Specifically, they do not show of themselves that forms of sex that do not lead to generation are illegitimate. A ban on using sex for other purposes does not follow from procreation's being God's sole purpose for our sexual behaviour – even if it can be shown, contrary to what I have argued, that the belief that God has a purpose for our sexual behaviour is tenable. Any ban is prior to and independent of such a belief, and has to be asserted and justified on independent grounds.

It is an important point to note that natural law has traditionally been invoked to rule out kinds of sex which the theologians and other Christians already find unacceptable. There has not been a dispassionate investigation of the law of nature with the result that extramarital sex, oral sex, masturbation, homosexuality and the rest have been found to be unnatural, and therefore wrong. The conviction that such things were wrong has generally been a presupposition of any thought about natural law. So even if appeal to natural law is put aside the bases of that presupposition remain to be investigated. However, it is an advance if we have discovered that one of the supposed pillars of Christian sexual morality has been found wanting. I repeat that I am not saying we cannot properly talk of nature. The fact is that we do speak of activities being natural or unnatural; only, the idea of nature cannot be used as it has traditionally been; it simply will not generate the appropriate conclusions, or any conclusions at all.

We do better to realize that the appeal to nature in its traditional forms always comes after it has been determined what may and what may not be done sexually, and that our perception of what is natural is shaped largely by pre-existing social norms. Doing this also allows us to appreciate better the function of purpose-language in our thought about sex. Such language appears to be used here, as sometimes elsewhere, not as a way of imparting information, as the answer to a question 'What is this for?', but as means of controlling behaviour. Think, for example, of the situation in which Jane might say to Andrew: 'Don't put that glass down there. It's for drinking out of, not keeping the door open.' Here 'it's for drinking out of' would not in normal circumstances be a sentence that gives any information; if you say that to someone you are not normally telling him something he doesn't know. You are, as Jane is doing here, expressing annoyance at his crossing boundaries, and trying to re-establish those boundaries. You want to keep the uses of things strongly compartmentalized. This is an important form of primitive reaction, but one to be distinguished from other uses of purpose-language. Similarly, in talking about the purpose of sexual organs or sexual activity – and also of God's purpose for them – Christians are not trying to impart information to people, telling them something they were unaware of; and nobody has asked them for such information. Rather are they attempting to reinforce certain patterns of sexual behaviour and to inhibit others, to re-establish boundaries which they believe are divinely ordained. Here we are close to the thought-world of the Old Testament priestly writer, and we touch upon some of the social dimensions of sex that concerned us in chapter 3.

6

Sexual Gestures

Meaningful sex

In the discussion of the last chapter there was one central aspect of human nature that I completely neglected. Much of our nature we share with other animals, but one thing that sets us apart is our rationality, signified by our use of language. For other creatures the world may consist of significant objects, and of instincts, appetites and urges. We human beings live in a world of meanings, given and articulated in and by means of the words we share. We try to understand what happens around us, and what we and others do, by gathering information, making connexions and divisions, grouping things and events into patterns, and so on; and we come to articulate our understanding, and share that understanding with others, by using language. That understanding also shapes our will. How we understand things determines how we act. If we cannot understand we are bewildered, and if we do not even try to understand we and our world are impoverished. We are animals for whom things – including our own actions and the actions of others – can be significant, and so also fail to be significant. This puts us apart from the other animals. So Pius XI, writing of marriage, says:

> The peculiar and unique character of this contract differentiates it totally from the unions which animals form among themselves under the impulse of a blind natural instinct, and in which reason and deliberation have no part; it also distinguishes marriage entirely from those irregular unions of human beings in which there is nothing of a true and honourable bond of will, and which are devoid of any legitimate domestic status.[1]

Sexual activity, as part of our world, and like other things we do, is, or fails to be, meaningful for us. To have sexual intercourse with somebody is, at least potentially, a significant thing to do with them.

Christianity gives sex a very specific significance. It was not always so in the tradition, but Christians nowadays find in sex a locus for the expression of the central Christian virtue, love. I tried to give some indication of the naturalness of this approach in the chapter on sexual pleasure. Sex is potentially more enjoyable if you enjoy the person you are doing it with.

One of the things that makes close encounters enjoyable is eye contact, and this is generally only sustainable at close quarters with somebody you like very much. And this is a large part of what love is, not a disinterested disposition to the good of the other, but actually liking them, being happy in their presence; it is a kind of friendship.[2] But we may want to go further than that; we may want to say not only that sex is more enjoyable if you do it with somebody else and actually like the person you are doing it with, but that this is what sex is actually about, that it has a kind of meaning that connects it with a close personal relationship. I want to examine this idea, and some related ones. In explaining why sex, as an act of love, is so important, some theologians have seen in it a peculiarly important kind of human fulfilment. All love involves a going beyond oneself through concern for another, somebody different. In sexual union people go beyond themselves in a special and specially fulfilling way; in sex, different and complementary halves, male and female, find their completion in each other. Sexual love is also, like all love, creative, but in a special, concrete way, in that it has children as its fruit. It is this complex of ideas, clustered round that of sex as an expression of love, that I want to examine, and to see what guidance we can obtain from them. In this chapter and the next I want to ask whether there is anything about the essential meaning of sex, its relation to difference and complementarity, and its creativity that confine its proper exercise to a loving relationship or more precisely, as in the Christian tradition, to a marriage.

We sometimes refer to sex as 'making love', and in the context of a relationship of love it can plainly function as one of the most important expressions of that love. It can be a way in which the partners communicate their love to each other as surely as saying to each other: 'I love you', and indeed the bodily and the linguistic behaviour often occur together. Letting somebody have the intimate freedom of our bodies, providing them with bodily pleasure as best we can, and being accorded a similar privilege by them, this is the sort of thing that belongs naturally in the context of friendship. We want to say that it is only with people to whom you are close that you can properly be physically that close. Sex is more than an enjoyable activity or range of activities. Having sex with somebody is not only a way of sharing a pleasure with them; it is doing something significant, making a gesture towards them, a gesture of friendship and intimacy.

But if we say that sexual intercourse belongs naturally in this intimate context, what is the force of this 'naturally'? And if sex can be a natural expression of a certain kind of friendship, why is it natural? Does it seem natural to us because of the ways we have been taught to think about sex, or is there something more biological about it? Is it a matter of our ideals, something given to us by our Christian faith, or of the constitution of our society; or is it to do with the physical constitution of our bodies and what

we do physically in sex, or with some other reality of the human animal? Is
there something about it that gives it a meaning, that makes it an expression
of love, regardless of how we actually think of it? Is there a kind of natural
language of the body apart from our conventional languages, a language
which has sexual activity as part of its vocabulary of love?

The body in context

I have already argued in chapter 3, following Mary Douglas, that our bodily
activity, including our sexual activity, is naturally expressive. But what I
argued for there was that it was expressive of the constitution of the social
body in which we live, that what we mean by what we do with our bodies
depends on the society in which we live. But what might also be suggested is
that what we do means something outside the particular social context in
which we are acting. Just being a human body, it can be argued, brings with
it the capacity to express particular things; the body is naturally com-
municative and has its own vocabulary. This seems obviously true in some
cases: whatever it might be among dogs or apes, a human smile is an
expression of pleasure, and to smile at somebody is to show pleasure with
them, to show approval, that you like them. To smile at somebody when
you are displeased with them or hate them is to deceive, even to lie. So, one
might say, to have sex with somebody just is to make love to them, to
express love, the kind of friendship which is deep, which commits you to
your partner fairly permanently.

I want to argue that this approach is broadly correct, but that we must be
careful in the way we articulate it. I will approach the argument by way of an
extract from the encyclical *Familiaris Consortio* of Pope John Paul II:

> Sexuality, by means of which man and woman give themselves to one another
> through the acts which are proper and exclusive to spouses, is by no means
> something purely biological, but concerns the innermost being of the human
> person as such. It is realized in a truly human way only if it is an integral part of
> the love by which a man and a woman commit themselves totally to one another
> until death. The total physical self-giving would be a lie if it were not the sign and
> fruit of a total personal self-giving, in which the whole person, including the
> temporal dimension, is present: if the person were to withhold something or
> reserve the possibility of deciding otherwise in the future, by this very fact he or
> she would not be giving totally.[3]

John Paul starts off from the fact that human sexual activity is not just a
matter of biology; it is not simply a fact of animal nature, but 'concerns the
innermost being of the human person'; it is part of the world of meaning
that is essentially and distinctively human. Sexual intercourse gets the

particular significance that it has from the fact that it takes place within, or rather is in itself, a personal relationship. The point here is, I think, similar to that for which I argued in chapter 3: a meeting of human bodies in a joint activity is necessarily a meeting of persons. But John Paul goes further than this. This particular kind of bodily meeting is a bodily total self-giving. Hence if the partners do not in fact have a relationship of total mutual self-gift, the relationship that we call marriage, then the sexual intercourse is a lie. To this extent, right sex is a matter of being truthful in relationships, and when sex is wrong, it is wrong because at least one of the partners is lying to the other.

John Paul's central concern here is to uphold the ancient and consistently affirmed Christian doctrine that the only proper place of sex is within marriage. My interest in it for the moment is in the argument he uses to support Christian doctrine. Though some of what he says touches on topics of previous chapters, the reasoning has aspects that I have not so far mentioned, and which deal with the meaning of human acts. Of particular interest is the idea that there is a kind of language of sex, that people as it were say things to each other in their sexual activity together. This line of thought is not confined to John Paul II; variants of it are to be found in a number of theological writers. I will mention three, all of whom raise questions which I will tackle later. The American writer Vincent Genovesi says:

> Just because two people admit to each other that they are in the relationship simply because of the fun or the pleasure involved, does not mean that they can, therefore, legitimately engage in genital expressions of their sexuality. The reason for this is that there is still a great discrepancy between their level of commitment and what the act of sexual intercourse itself says.[4]

Of course Genovesi is right when he says if two people admit they are in it for the fun that does not legitimate their sex together. But a further interest is that what he goes on to say actually differs significantly from our passage from *Familiaris Consortio*, in that it makes quite explicit and unambiguous the claim that sexual intercourse actually says something, and only one thing. However, unlike John Paul, Genovesi does not overtly locate the wrongness of sexual activity between uncommitted partners in their lying. There is simply a discrepancy between what their act says and what is actually the case. This leaves it open that they may not be lying but making a mistake, which needs to be corrected. For him, the morality of sex does not appear to be so closely tied to the moral injunction against lying. In one way, then, Genovesi's claim is weaker than John Paul's. But in another it is stronger, since for Genovesi the reason why uncommitted sex is wrong is this discrepancy between reality and what the sexual act says. For him, this aspect of sexual morality appears grounded entirely on the theory that our actions say things. This makes sexual morality very vulnerable, if it should turn out, as I believe it will, that such a theory is unsatisfactory.

A few pages later Genovesi approvingly quotes John Dedek writing in a similar vein:

> Sexual intercourse is a sign of total, unreserved giving of self. At the moment of orgasm, the individual's personality is lost in an interpenetration of the other self. Sexual intercourse is expressive of one's person. To be authentic and not a lie it must correspond to the existing relationship between the persons.[5]

Unlike Genovesi himself, Dedek does not commit himself to the thesis that in sex we actually say anything; rather is sexual intercourse for him a sign or expression of unreserved self-giving (though he does echo John Paul in speaking of inauthentic sex as a lie). As I will try to show later, this is a more fruitful approach. However, Dedek also makes it clear that there is another aspect of this whole approach that has to be clarified if it is to prove acceptable. If, with John Paul, he sees sexual intercourse as a sign of self-giving, the question arises just why it should be thought of in this way. Here Dedek goes further than John Paul in suggesting an answer in terms of what might be called a mysticism of the orgasm: at the moment of orgasm the selves of the partners interpenetrate. This seems to me to take us down the wrong road, and to produce needless additional difficulties. To begin with, it shifts the focus away from intercourse itself to orgasm, from a joint activity of two partners to what they feel and undergo; but it is only activity of some kind that we normally think of as expressive. And it only begins to seem plausible for partners who experience orgasm at the same time; this is not always the case, and we should not forget that in many cases one or both of the partners does not experience orgasm at all. Further, a human being's personality is something that shows itself over time, in a whole host of everyday dealings with people and things. It is not something that might be 'lost' at the moment of orgasm. The person may not be particularly conscious of his or her personality at the moment of orgasm, but then that is true of most of us most of the time. Dedek appears here only to be glorifying what so appalled Augustine: the fact that orgasms can be all-absorbing and that we do not think very much during them. It is not clear, either, what is meant by saying that the individual's personality is lost 'in an interpenetration of the other self'. We do not penetrate selves. Of course, males often physically penetrate their partners during sex, but not just at the moment of orgasm; and women do not penetrate their partners. It looks as if Dedek is inventing some mysterious reality of which sexual penetration can be the sign. And if he were right, it remains problematic what such a mysterious interpenetration has to do with the gift of self. Penetration, whether mysterious or physical, is not gift. These difficulties can be avoided and a more satisfactory view of the matter achieved if we eschew theorizing about what orgasm feels like and remain, as John Paul does, at the level of the objective bodily activity of the two partners. For it is, after all, with the significance of what they actually do that we are concerned.

In England, the Catholic psychiatrist Jack Dominian also, but in a different way, subjectivizes the significance of sex. He writes:

> In psychological terms when people make love they feel that the genital activity becomes a language which speaks of a personal dimension of love. Genital unity becomes the symbol of personal donation in which two people feel that they receive each other wholly and in a committed manner. They are saying with sex: 'I recognize you as the most important person in my life; I want you as the most important person in my life.' When these personal overtones are separated from coitus human integrity is distorted.[6]

Once again, as with Genovesi, the claim that people say things with sex is made quite explicit, and Dominian describes genital activity as a language. He actually tells us what sexual partners say in this language. However, this language is only something that people only sometimes feel is there, just as they only feel that they receive each other wholly and in a committed manner. But a language is something objective; feeling that we speak in our genital activity is not the same as actually doing so. Feeling guarantees neither that there is such a language of the body, nor that, if there is one, we are speaking it properly, or at all, in our sexual activity. We often think we are saying one thing when in fact, objectively, we are saying something quite different, or merely speaking gibberish. Further, to say that the meaning of the act is supplied by what the partners think about it leads us to a dangerous subjectivism, the belief that sex is all right if you feel good about it. As with Dedek's, we avoid the unnecessary difficulties of this approach if we hold to the objectivism of John Paul.

To return, then, to our passage from *Familiaris Consortio*, I want to begin by looking at the idea that the morality of sex is closely connected with or even reducible to the morality of speech, that sexual intercourse which takes place outside of marriage is wrong because it is a lie. In one respect, this line of thought is very congenial, since it supports one of the things I have been arguing for in the course of this book: it accords with the biblical view, echoed in the tradition, that sexual morality is a social morality. On this view, the rules that govern sex are those that also govern the rest of our social dealings. In particular, it is not good, in sex as in the rest of life, that people should lie to each other.

However, some difficulties with this approach to sexual morality surface immediately. Sexuality is described as a means by which people give themselves to one another, and as 'total physical self-giving'. But why should sexual activity be described in this way? It is easy to see how such a description might be appropriate in the context of a good marriage, in which two people have given their whole lives to each other. Then the sexual relationship between the two could easily be expressive of this total self-giving, and so might fittingly be called a total physical self-giving. As John Finnis writes:

> Granted an ideal of a profound, life-long, exclusive, loving union between man and woman, then intercourse between these spouses is to be regarded as a very apt expression of their union, their common and exclusive project.[7]

We might readily agree that this is how sex ought to be, that it is ideally an expression of deep love, of total self-giving and irrevocable commitment. But things are not always like this. What about an evening or half an hour of casual sex between people who are not so committed to each other? As John Paul points out, such people would not be giving themselves totally to each other. The conclusion we might expect is that their sexual activity is not properly called a total physical self-giving; it cannot express a deep commitment of the partners to each other, since there is no deep commitment to express. In such a context the act does not to appear to be an expressive gesture of self-giving. To quote Finnis again:

> To say that intercourse 'has' this expressive sense or force obscures the fact that often intercourse actually expresses no more than a mutual taste for diversion, or a mutual libido dominandi.[8]

But what John Paul says is that what any two people are doing when they have sexual intercourse just is, regardless of context, a total physical self-giving. In it the partners as it were say to each other: 'I love you and commit myself to you totally.' So in the case where the partners have no intention of being committed to each other, their activity constitutes a lie. It has a meaning independent of what they think they are doing, and independent of the context in which they are doing it. This idea is certainly attractive, in a way, for anybody who wants to find a connexion between sex and love, as Christians do, for it makes such a connexion intrinsic, not dependent on a special Christian morality but open for all to see, if they will. It would provide an objective basis for the modern Christian ethic that sees sex as an expression of love. But though I will argue that this ethic is fundamentally true (and this, I take it, is John Paul's essential point) I believe it is a mistake to assimilate human sexual activity to language in quite this way. First, our gestures have an affinity with language, in that we use both our body and our words to express ourselves. But one thing that gestures have in common with words is that their meanings, what they express, are not given absolutely, but are dependent on context. Second, though there is this affinity between gestures and language, it is a limited affinity. Human gestures do not constitute a kind of language; they 'speak' only metaphorically. Strictly, they say nothing, either true or false. I will try to substantiate these points before going on to contend that the central part of John Paul's teaching here is importantly correct.

Human action

I begin by saying something about human action. What is a human act? What is it for a human being to *do* something? We might at first glance think that it is a matter of moving, doing something with your body, like lifting an arm. So that if a child is told in an exercise class to raise her right arm sideways, and does so, we will say that she has *done* something. But human action is often much more complicated than that. Suppose somebody is going along the road on a bike and does what is in a sense the same thing, lifts his right arm sideways. Now it would be a quite inadequate description of what he has done to say that he has lifted his arm sideways. What he has done is to signal that he is going to turn right. That is what his act has been, and it is made into that by the context, the fact that he is riding on a bike on an English road, plus the various laws and conventions about signalling in England. The physical movement he has made is the same as the physical movement the girl makes in her exercise class, but the *acts* are different. His act has the status of a gesture, it is meaningful; hers is not. He signals indeed by or in lifting his arm, but lifting an arm and signalling are not the same acts. Here, as in so many cases, the question 'What is he doing?' is close to 'Why is he doing that?' Here, if we are asked 'Why is he doing that?' by somebody who sees him lifting his arm, we would probably answer by explaining what he is doing. And the question could equally have been 'What is he doing?' – to which we could not sensibly have answered 'He is lifting up his arm', for in this context that would not normally have been what was being asked. A proper answer would be something like 'He is signalling that he is going to turn', and we might have to supplement that with an explanation of English road signalling conventions. Here there lies part of the analogy with language: We speak, say words, by making noises with our mouths, but to make a noise is not the same as speaking a word. For a noise to be a word it has to have a regular use, be embedded in a context and in conventions. The girl too lifts her arm, but she is not thereby signalling that she is turning right. Her movement lacks the context which would give it meaning and thereby turn it into a different act. Bodily movements such as these are determined as the acts they are by the context in which they are performed.

I have tried in the case of the girl to reduce the significance of the context to a minimum by placing it in an exercise class, a situation which lays stress just on bodily movements. But it is not difficult even here to see a number of ways in which context might be important in determining the description of her movement as act. She lifts her arm because she has been told to; so she is also obeying the teacher, and obeying is a human act. Now let us suppose that this child has been having a feud with her teacher, refusing to do what she is told, and the teacher has threatened her with all kinds of grievous punishments if she does not do what she says. Now the girl's lifting her arm is an act of submission. Or, in this feud the teacher has not threatened the girl but has tried in all sorts of ways to get on friendly terms with her again. Now the girl's lifting her arm is an act of reconciliation. Or again, the girl and her teacher have been lounging around together smoking during lesson time. Hearing the head teacher approaching they begin to go through the motions of a lesson. Now the girl's raising her arm is collusion with her teacher in an act of deception. We cannot talk about what human acts such as these are independently of their context.

Signalling, submitting, colluding are fairly complicated forms of action: they are things we do by doing something else, like raising an arm. In this they are quite far removed from normal sexual acts. But context can be shown to be essential also for the understanding of very basic actions, even something as simple as a facial expression. Expressions are not just plays of facial muscle. Take the smile I mentioned earlier. A man is smiling. How would we describe this smile? All depends on what we know about the situation. Let us suppose he is giving an apple to a child; it is a benevolent, indulgent smile; he is happy to be with the child. He has injected cyanide into the apple; now his smile is malicious, evil. We could easily imagine pictures of such scenes, and the benevolent smile and the evil smile might actually look different – just as the same shade of green looks different in the context of different colours. Now we might say that, if the apple is poisoned, the smile is still a sign of friendship, and is being misused. He is lying to the child, or at least deceiving her, by putting on this facial expression. The expression in itself, regardless of context, is a sign of friendship. Does not this prove John Paul's point about the meaning of our actions? No. The reason why we think of a smile as a sign of friendship is because one of the standard contexts, and perhaps the most central one, in which we smile is when we are with people we like (and this may just be a brute fact about the human animal, that gazing on people we want to be with often makes us smile). The child is being deceived here, right enough, but about the context in which the smile happens. She is deceived by the offer of the apple; that it is poisoned has been hidden from her. We think of the smile as deceptive because in this particular context the child is being deceived. But a smile can express many other things apart from pleasure at seeing somebody or being with them. Think of the situation in which the man is torturing the child, smiling down at her as he pokes her with lighted cigarettes. Here his smile does not express his pleasure, even a feigned pleasure, at seeing the child; it expresses his pleasure at having the girl in his power, at hearing her scream, etc. Nobody is deceived, and there is no attempt at deception. All is made clear by the circumstances, which he is not concerned to conceal. In no sense is his smile a lie. In the case of the apple, too, we need not suppose that the smile is a deception. We will think it is only if we see it as feigned pleasure at being with the child. But it might equally be thought of as quite unfeigned pleasure at the fact that his plan is working, that the child is going all unsuspecting to its doom. Of course the child will misinterpret the smile, but not because what is going on behind it is hidden from her; she misunderstands it because she is unaware of what is going on around it, unaware of the situation in which the man's actions are set, the background against which they are properly to be understood. We all misinterpret gestures and other acts when we don't know what is going on, when we are unaware what chain of actions and events the gesture or act forms part of.

What is true of human acts in general is true of sexual acts in particular. It is possible for our sexual activity to be neither in pursuit of procreation, nor in pursuit of pleasure, but to have the status of a gesture. It can, and often does, *mean* something for us to act sexually. That is to say, performing this kind of activity together with somebody can be important to us, and it can express, for instance, the closeness of our relationship with that person. Such a meaning of the act immediately springs to mind because a loving relationship is one of the standard contexts for sex. That it is one of the standard contexts, even the standard one, may not be an accident but connected with human nature itself; indeed, I shall later argue for such a position. But sexual intercourse also takes place under other circumstances. This means that sex can mean many things. To understand the meaning of a particular sexual act, as to understand the raising of an arm or a smile, we have to look around it to see what else is happening.

That sexual behaviour signifies may be true at the level of the personal relationship between the partners, irrespective of any wider social context. Let us say that Andrew and Jane, a loving married couple, have had an argument and been estranged for a few days. Then an initiation by one partner of love-making can be an offer of reconciliation, the positive response of the other partner an acceptance of that offer and the rest of the act a celebration of reconciliation. Note that the activity's having this meaning depends once again on the context. It can only be reconciliation given that they are generally close to each other but there has been previous estrangement. Note too that its having this meaning makes it be the act it is. At one level, that of the physical movements of bodies, it is sexual intercourse, the coupling of man and woman. It is that regardless of context, whether there has been estrangement or not, whether the man and

woman even know each other or not. But because of the context, because
they do know each other and have had a row, it is also an act of reconciliation. They become reconciled by having sex together. If somebody saw
them doing this and asked 'What are they doing', we might say 'They are
having sexual intercourse', but only as part of an explanation of what sexual
intercourse is; we would be assuming that our questioner was ignorant of
the facts of sex. If the question is from one who obviously knows they are
having sex, the question is equivalent to 'Why are they doing that?' Our
answer would be to explain their actions as acts of reconciliation.

If the couple's reconciliation is dependent for its being what it is on the
recent history of the relationship, it is also dependent for its being what it is
on the immediate future of that relationship. If they have a great time
during the night but when they wake up the next day are at each other's
throat again, then clearly they have not been reconciled, even if it seemed to
them at the time that they were. So their sexual intercourse was not a
genuine act of reconciliation. It was just an insignificant, if enjoyable,
aberration from the current pattern of their relationship. So its being what it
is is dependent on its place in the non-sexual relations between the two that
surround it. Human action in general is not just a movement or series of
movements of a bodily limb or limbs, but it occupies a place in the human
life that surrounds it. And that is what gives it significance. This simple
example shows that sexual activity is no exception.

It is worth noting that, as in other areas of life, it is also possible to act here
without making any bodily movements at all, indeed *by* making no bodily
movements at all. Suppose that when Andrew and Jane make love, Jane
always makes the first move. She and Andrew have had a row, but there
have been slight indications from Andrew during the evening that he would
like to make it up. So here they are lying there, and she knows that Andrew
is hoping that she will start things off. But she is still mad at him, so just to
hurt him she doesn't move. At one level, the level of bodily movement, she
does nothing; but still, in context, she does do something: she refuses to
make it up and she hurts Andrew. She does something by doing nothing.

Sado-masochism

If sexual activity can be expressive of love and can also lack the power to
express love, according to context, it is important to realize that it can have
other meanings, again according to context. And it can have a meaning that
goes far beyond the relationship between the partners, reaching out to the
wider social context. Suppose the population of the country has been falling
recently and the government is rather worried about it. It has been urging
all married couples to have as many children as possible; it is their patriotic
duty. Though Jane and Andrew don't particularly want any more children

than they already have, they are patriotic types, so they do their best. Now their sexual activity is not an expression of lust or of love for each other or in a straightforward way of a desire to have more children. It expresses their commitment to the purposes of the state, or their love of country. On the other hand, suppose the population has risen to levels that alarm the government, which has urged on people the patriotic duty of not having any more children for the time being. Jane and Andrew do not particularly want any more children, and indeed have more or less given up sexual relations, but they really hate the government and resent its encroaching into family matters in this way, so they decide they will try to have another child. In this context their sexual activity is a private protest against the government, or an expression of contempt for it.

This is a fairly trivial and straightforward, if unlikely, example of how sexual activity can be used to express, not a deep personal commitment of the partners to each other, but a refusal to conform to social pressures. Such a meaning of sex can, however, go much deeper. Sexual activity of various kinds can express not just dislike of passing government policies but alienation from deep structures of society. Sex is peculiarly apt for this because, as I tried to show in chapter 3, the social body tends to load the physical body with such a heavy burden of significance. While sexual conformity can express social conformity, sexual nonconformity is a natural way of expressing social disaffection. One of the ways our society is most deeply structured, as I argued earlier, is through gender distinction. One of the things we are taught is most important about us is whether we are male or female; and we are taught what it means to be a woman or a man, we are trained into gender roles. If we are alienated from our society, for whatever reason, one of the most natural and effective ways of expressing this alienation is by breaking the rules of these gender roles. Jeffrey Weeks, in his book *Sexuality and its Discontents*, reports these words written by Pat Califia on her coming out as a lesbian sado-masochist:

> I like s/m because it is not lady-like. It is a kind of sex that really violates all the things I was taught about being a nice little girl and keeping my dress clean.[9]

The message from this is clear. This kind of sado-masochism is not just a perversion, nor are its practitioners ill or warped; they are in revolt. For one reason or another, rightly or wrongly, they see themselves as oppressed by the ways society is structured, and the kind of sex they go in for – bondage, humiliation and pain – expresses their suffering and alienation and is at the same time a self-affirmation, since it involves the free choice of sexual acts unacceptable to those who are seen as oppressors. Califia writes:

> s/m is ... a deliberate, premeditated, erotic blasphemy ... a form of sexual extremism and sexual dissent ... We select the most frightening, disgusting, or

unacceptable activities and transmute them into pleasure. We make use of all the
forbidden symbols and all the disowned emotions . . . The basic dynamic of s/m is
the power dichotomy, not pain. Handcuffs, dog collars, whips, kneeling, being
bound, tit clamps, hot wax, enemas, and giving sexual service are all metaphors
for the power imbalance.[10]

For there to be blasphemy and dissent there must be a prevailing dogma, a
prevailing ethos to be rebelled against, and sado-masochism (according to
this viewpoint) gets its meaning through being reactive. Clearly also the
pleasure of this type of sado-masochism derives partly from its significance,
not from the bodily sensations one might get during it. The same applies to
much other sexual behaviour which is publicly thought of as deviant. Part of
the attraction and meaning of homosexual activity for some gay men and
women is that it is a rejection of the gender roles into which they have been
educated and which they regard as oppressive, either in themselves or as
tokens of the power of a society which is oppressive in other ways.[11] (Not
necessarily, and only partially: of course homosexual people would say that
sex between two women or two men can express love as much as it can
between a man and a woman.)

This sexual expression of social alienation and revolt is natural, if
anything is, because of the social significance with which we load the body
and in particular our sexual activity. If Christians want to say that there is
something wrong with sado-masochism, because it is bad for people, we
have to be clear that at least some of it is a symptom or expression of
something that has gone wrong elsewhere: sexual disorder is often a sign of
social disorder. We cannot get rid of it by telling its practitioners to stop it,
maybe threatening them with punishment in this world or the next if they
don't. The Christian task is not to tell people not to find erotic delight in
being bound and beaten but to see why they are impelled to such dissent,
why they find conformity so oppressive. It may turn out that the structures
of society often are indeed deeply oppressive to numbers of people. Then it
will be the task of the church to work for a society that is not oppressive and
alienating, that enables us to be free and to be one, which is anyway what
Christians are supposed to be concerned about.

But it may well be, too, that some kind of alienation is inevitable whatever
kind of society we manage to build, that there will always be people who for
one reason or another feel they have been rejected or that they do not belong
and do not want to, people who do not fit. Given the way we naturally use
the body as an expressive medium, then, if we load sexual acts in particular
with significance, it may well be that such alienation will always be
expressed through deviant sexual behaviour. To make much of deviant sex
by strong insistence on a norm is to provide people with a ready-made way
of expressing dissent and alienation. Nobody is going to get rid of deviant

sex by preaching morals at people. It may not be eliminable at all. It is to be minimized by minimizing alienation, by working for a society to which as many people as possible can feel they belong.

Body language

The term 'body language' has come to be widely used, but it has to be recognized that this is a metaphorical usage. If two people love each other, they may say to each other: 'I love you.' They may also, in certain kinds of relationship, make love. Since the sex and the words hang together in this way, it is tempting to think that people *say* things to each other by their sexual activity together. In certain circumstances this may not be harmful, but it can be dangerously misleading. It can lead to the view that actions somehow have a meaning not only in the sense that they are important and expressive, but as having a lexical meaning, that there is quite literally a kind of language of the body, and in particular a sexual language. This is dangerous because it subordinates the bodily to the verbal, making our gestures into relatively inarticulate substitutes for words and thereby impoverishing our understanding of the expressive possibilities open to human beings (rather like the style of criticism which insists on asking what paintings or pieces of music are saying).

But our gestures and activities do not in fact constitute a language in any normal sense. Though we certainly express and convey attitudes through our bodily gestures, we do not convey messages, except by some arbitrary pre-arranged code. One of the important differences between so-called body language and a real language can be indicated in the following way. If I speak a German sentence I may discover that the one I am speaking to understands only English. I can give him the meaning of my German sentence by translating it, by speaking an equivalent English sentence. If I am with somebody who speaks both German and English it may be a matter of indifference whether I speak my sentence in English or German. Languages are to this extent alternatives, interchangeable. And they are independent: I can understand an English sentence even if I have no knowledge of German. Putting the meaning of our acts into words is rather different. It means something like explaining what we are doing or why we are doing it; it is not translating our acts into words. Acts and words are not substitutes for each other. Explaining what I have done is something I do after I have acted, not instead of acting.[12] Words and actions often belong together in the sense that they may both spring from a common background. If Andrew loves Jane he may, because of that, make love to her. He may also for the same reason say to her: 'I love you.' Now making love and saying this sentence are two things that he does in the same circumstances; but that does not make the one a translation of or substitute for the other, it does not make the one say what the other says. If Andrew says to Jane: 'I love you' and then makes love to her, he is not guilty of repeating himself. One will not do instead of the other. In this context, they are not alternatives; they simply belong together, and we may expect the one to lead to the other. They may both be described as expressions of Andrew's love for Jane; but they are two different expressions of that love. We express our emotions and our attitudes by doing a whole range of things; speaking in various ways is one of the things we do. Saying something is only one form of expression among many possible forms, one way of acting among many others. It is a mistake to think that all those other possibilities of acting, those other forms of expression, are ways of saying something. Our bodily gestures have importance in their own right, not merely as substitutes for words.

If it is a mistake to think of our actions as ways of literally saying something, it is similarly wrong to think that actions can be true or false, that we can lie with our actions, except metaphorically. It is sentences, what we say, that can be true or false, not our actions. We certainly can mislead others with our actions, give them a false impression. One of the ways we can deceive, that is to say deliberately mislead, people is by lying to them, by knowingly saying false things to them; but lying is only one way of acting deceitfully. If Andrew does not love Jane, he can deceive her into thinking that he does by taking her to bed. If his sex with her is deceitful, however, it will likely be only one element in a wider context, in a pattern of deception. He will probably have to deceive her in other ways as well – take her out to dinner, buy her expensive presents; principally, he may have to lie to her, by saying: 'I love you.' But that he will also lie to her does not make his deceitful sex with her into a lie. Just as our possibilities of expression are not confined to speaking, so the ways in which we deceive are wider than lying.

This perhaps does not matter very much in the present discussion. What *Familiaris Consortio* is insisting on, we might say, is truthfulness in sexual relationships, and lying and non-verbal deceit are both failures of truthfulness. But there is a further more substantial point to be made here. A central part of the concept of lying is that one who lies says something he knows to be false, and does so with the intention of deceiving. Novelists and storytellers are not lying, even though every word they say or write may be false, for they are not intending to deceive. In the context, listening to a story or reading a novel, everybody knows that the point is that the story be listened to or read, not believed. The same is true, *mutatis mutandis*, of non-verbal deceit. Deceiving implies the intention to deceive. Without such intent what we say or do may at most be unintentionally misleading. If we do mislead in this way, we may be guilty of carelessness, of not choosing our words and actions with sufficient attention, but we are not guilty of deceit. Two partners in casual sex, who have come together for the express purpose of enjoying a few minutes of pleasurable activity together and parting for ever afterwards, may be doing something that is not for their ultimate good, they may even be doing something reprehensible, but they are not lying to each other. They are not lying, both because actions do not lie and also because neither of them intends to deceive the other. In the context, both of them know that the point of the encounter is enjoyment, not commitment – even if it turns out that the physical intimacy leads to an unforeseen desire for personal intimacy, that as a result of the encounter one or both of them become committed to the other.

The result of all this is that John Paul is certainly right in the idea that seems to underlie much of what he says, that human sexual behaviour is capable of meaning, and not just in the sense that it can be important to us. It can have the status of gesture. Our non-verbal bodily activities are indeed connected with the ways we speak (and write) to each other. Only it is misleading to describe this by claiming that actions literally say things, or that we say things by what we do. It is also essential to recognize the great importance of context when assessing what people's actions might mean; actions do not have one fixed meaning which can be read off from them regardless of circumstances.

And so we have to modify what John Paul says about two people having sex. They do not thereby say anything to each other, so neither are they saying anything true or false. If they are committed to each other then their sexual activity is properly described as making love; it is a physical expression of their loving commitment. But the case is different for two people who are not committed to each other for life, or at all. Their sexual activity just does not express what that of a married or otherwise committed couple does, since it takes place in a different context. It is not a total physical self-giving that turns out to be a lie. It is not a total physical self-giving at all, because it lacks the context in which it can be that; the two people concerned are not saying or in some other way indicating to each other by what they are doing that they are committed to each other for life. So they are not saying it falsely, either (unless they do actually say it to each other); it is in no sense a lie. And also it is not a lie because nobody is attempting to deceive anybody, and nobody is being deceived. Their sexual activity does not express a deep love, and indeed, as Finnis says, it may express nothing more than a taste for diversion. So we cannot say that under certain conditions (say, if the partners are unmarried) sexual intercourse is immoral because it necessarily involves the partners in lying to each other. Sexual morality is not reducible to the moral need to tell the truth. We cannot derive norms for sexual behaviour from the injustice of lying. Of course truthfulness is important in sexual as in other relations, but it will not do as a foundation for restricting genital sexual relations either to married couples or to close friends. This is not to deny that, for instance, two unmarried people having sex together are acting immorally. But if they are it is not because they are lying to each other. We need to look elsewhere for the basis of a sexual ethic.

Natural metaphors

But we do not have to look very far. Although I have been at pains to argue against the idea that people literally say things, lie or tell the truth by what they do with their bodies, yet I believe this idea can be seen simply as an inaccurate way of putting a point that I myself have been constantly concerned to stress: that the human body is naturally expressive. Much of what we do has the status of gesture, it means something. In the right context, embracing somebody is a gesture of welcome. In such contexts you do not *say* 'Welcome' to somebody by embracing them, but you do welcome them. This involves expressing a welcoming attitude, an attitude that would also be expressed by saying 'Welcome'. The bodily gesture and the verbal gesture hang together. Part of what makes them go together is the context. In another context it might be equally appropriate to embrace somebody but completely wrong to say 'Welcome'; there the right thing to say might be 'Congratulations' or 'Goodbye'. But not just *any* words can go with an embrace. It is difficult to imagine a context in which an embrace might accompany the words 'I think you're dreadful and despicable, and I never want to see you again'; we would have to fill in quite an elaborate background story to make such a scene intelligible. The difficulty is that here the words are hostile, and an embrace is naturally affectionate. We cannot use an embrace to express hostility. We can of course embrace somebody if we are hostile to him, but then our embrace disguises our hostility and does not express it.

It may be that the particular significance or range of meanings we give the embrace is partly a matter of culture. In other cultures, perhaps, other gestures take its place. But where the gesture exists, it is hard to imagine it as a culturally determined expression of hostility. There appears to be something bodily significant about the embrace that goes beyond cultural convention. What is true of the embrace is true of many of our bodily dealings with each other. A punch in the face is a natural expression of hostility. To punch somebody in the face and say to him or her 'I love you' would normally be to produce bewilderment. Though we may occasionally punch those we love, it is despite our love for them, not an expression of our love. This too is not only a matter of culture; there may be cultures where people do not do this to each other; but where they do, they do it as a gesture of hostility. This has something to do with our brute physical nature. One aspect of hostility is the desire to hurt, and because of our bodily constitution we just are hurt by being punched in the face.

I want to argue that this natural expressiveness belongs to sexual inter-course also. To do this I need to say a little more about embracing. The embrace is normally a sign of affection. The gesture may become formal and conventionalized, as between political leaders. There may in fact be no real affection between them, but the convention is designed to give the impression that there is. When two people embrace they clasp each other close, and this is an expression and demonstration of the closeness of the people. Here the body serves as a metaphor for personal relations. It is because the people are friends, because they are close, that it is fitting that they share a certain bodily intimacy. Conversely, we do not expect people who do not like each other to embrace, unless, like politicians, they have an interest in simulating friendship. The fact that they hold their bodies apart is a natural metaphor for and an expression of the distance between them.

Physical proximity is not same as personal closeness. We often find ourselves physically close to complete strangers or even enemies, as in supermarkets, trains and lifts. But now a point I raised in chapter 4 becomes relevant again. Two strangers standing close to each other in the tube are engaged in separate activities as two unrelated individuals. The one is travelling and standing in the tube, and so is the other, and they merely happen to be standing close to each other. Two friends standing close to each other are, by contrast, standing together. It is not an accident that they are near to each other. They are engaged in a joint activity, travelling together. They are with each other in a way that two strangers are not. If the proximity of two strangers means nothing, the physical closeness of two friends expresses their personal closeness. We might say equally that the physical distance enemies put between themselves expresses the personal distance that separates them. The body acts as a kind of metaphor for personal relations. We often use physical closeness, distance etc., as a way of playing out social closeness or distance. While the physical closeness is plainly not the social closeness, we can say that it expresses it, in a way similar to that in which pain-behaviour – writhing, crying, etc. – which is not pain, expresses pain. Physical intimacy can be described as intimacy-behaviour. This use of the body, which is natural to human beings, is indicated by the ambiguity of words like 'close', 'intimacy' and 'distance'.

Friends attract each other and gravitate towards each other. It is part of the concept of friendship that friends, those who are close, want to do things together when occasion presents itself, and also that they want to be together physically. Close friends actively seek occasion to do things together and to be together. It is a pleasure for them to be close. They can engage in joint activities even at a distance, such as corresponding from opposite ends of the world. But if they are apart for any length of time, that is a misfortune, and the closer the friendship the greater the misfortune. It is a sign of the waning of a friendship if the two friends no longer create or even take opportunities to be close to each other. If they spend more and more time apart, it is a sign that they are drifting apart.

Conversely, people who do not like each other repel each other; they do not like doing things together, engaging in joint activities, and they are uncomfortable in each other's presence. They take or create opportunities to be physically apart from each other. The distance they keep between themselves is a natural sign of the distance between them.

Among the activities that friends undertake some have a special gestural character in that they embody or physically express the closeness of the relationship. Two friends may play chess or eat together or watch films together, and get pleasure from doing something together and being near each other. But they may also hold hands or embrace. Here the activity they take pleasure in is not only something they do together; it is an act of bringing themselves together. Here they show not their pleasure in their joint activities but their pleasure in each other, the pleasure that chiefly makes their joint activities pleasurable. The closeness of their relationship – their love for each other – may be seen in the other things they do together, such as that they often play chess or go for walks together. In the gestures of physical union that intimacy, that love, is expressed bodily.

Thus it is that these physical gestures have something that can properly be called a meaning. The meaning is not the result of the conventional use of an arbitrary sign, as in language, but belongs naturally to particular gestures. The embrace of two friends in which they physically draw themselves each to the other concretizes and expresses bodily the closeness of their relationship, a closeness which is a matter of the things they share, the things they do together because they like to be together. If in fact they share nothing, if they do nothing together, if they have no relationship, then they have nothing to express to each other by embracing. It is hard to see why two people would embrace in such circumstances, unless they wanted to simulate closeness, to give either others or themselves the impression that they have a close relationship. It is not natural to us to embrace those to whom we are not close. In such circumstances the embrace would be emptied of its natural significance; it would be meaningless. Because, as I have argued, an embrace has a natural significance, the meaninglessness of this particular embrace would not be the absence of an optional extra, but a loss of meaning; the embrace would be as it were denatured, dehumanized. And, because meaning is so central to our humanity, that in turn would mean that the embracers would suffer loss and be diminished. It would be as if they were using the sounds of human language to speak gibberish. Somebody who went round embracing people indiscriminately would be regarded as abnormal and defective, because he would be embracing senselessly; his embraces would no longer have the status of a genuine gesture, but would be pathological.

What is true of an embrace is true largely of sexual intercourse, which will in any case normally involve embraces. It is a gesture of personal closeness. A couple of close friends, standardly a married couple, having sex together are engaged in a joint activity, and one of a particularly intimate kind, one in which they not only do things together but in which they bring themselves together. In drawing themselves to each other they express to each other their personal closeness, the intimacy of their shared life, bodily. Sex is out of its natural place when it takes place between strangers or those who dislike each other. At the very least there seems to be something self-contradictory about being sexually intimate with somebody when you also want to express distance from them. It would, for example, not make sense to have sex with somebody and then to refuse, without particular reason, to lend them a small amount of money. You lend money to people you are in some degree close to. Refusal puts or expresses a distance between you. Sex is only appropriate where gestures of distance are out of place. And that means, at the very least, in the context of a close friendship.

The Christian tradition goes further than this in insisting that the friend-ship be of married partners. But for human beings in general, Christian or not, shared sex (not rape or masturbation) has a natural meaning. It naturally expresses personal intimacy, love, of one degree or another. When the sexual gestures include physical penetration of one friend by another, we regard this as a most intimate bodily closeness, naturally expressive of great personal intimacy, personal union. Two people out for casual sex, who are not close friends but meet for a few hours or minutes, to part for ever afterwards, express nothing to each other by their embraces, since they have nothing to express. If both of them know what they are doing, then there is no deceit involved in what they are doing, not even metaphorical lying. But their actions have lost their natural status as expressive gestures; they have become denatured, have suffered a loss of natural meaning. They are, in this sense, unnatural. We might say, if we favour that kind of terminology, that they constitute a breach of natural law. Those gestures now become less capable of the meaning that is native to them. Apart from any considera-tions of charity that may become apparent from looking at the wider context of the act, the partners themselves are both diminished, in that they become less able to express intimate friendship with another through sex.

There is of course another sense in which such actions are completely natural. Imagine that Andrew has left his wife Jane at home for the evening while he goes off to have a working dinner with Daphne, a passing female acquaintance at the office. During the course of the evening a little too much wine is drunk, she has dressed a little too comfortably, and the fact that they have to pore over tables of figures together brings them close together. Perfume and background music work on the senses. The hormones begin to flow, and mutual sexual desire mounts. This is just what might be expected to happen in these circumstances, and is to that extent natural. We are, in the right circumstances, susceptible to physical proximity and the attractions of the senses. That belongs to our nature as physical. Thus far there is little difference between the desire of a person and that of a dog. But if they actually go ahead and have intercourse, their act is meaningless, because it does not have the expressive character proper to it. It is natural only in a very impoverished sense of the term, one which neglects that reason is essential to our nature. If our nature is seen more adequately, then the act, pleasant though it may be, is unnatural. Apart from considerations of charity, such as Andrew's obligations to Jane, both partners are diminished by it.

That reason, meaning, is essential to our nature is connected with the fact that for human beings sex does not simply follow desire. Whatever our desires, and however difficult they may sometimes be to resist, intercourse is a human act, subject, since we are rational, to rational decision. Reason is served in this instance if Andrew and Daphne refrain from sex, since, apart from the demands of charity towards Jane, it is by refraining that Andrew and Daphne recognize that sexual intercourse involves gestures of intimacy and refrain from making bodily gestures of intimacy when there is no personal intimacy between them to express; they thereby retain the natural expressive capabilities of their sexual gestures. We might get an indication of the loss involved if they go ahead and have sex if we imagine Andrew going home to Jane afterwards. The natural thing to imagine is that they will not have sex together; at least, not on Andrew's initiative. The deception involved has put a distance between them which makes lovemaking inappropriate; and how could Andrew understand what he is doing with Jane in the light of what he has just done with Daphne?

As this example indicates, there is an important difference between sexual activity and a simple embrace. If it is difficult to see why two people who are not friends might want to embrace, it is very easy to understand why two strangers might want to have sex together. Quite apart from its expressive qualities, sex can be very pleasant even with a stranger, for reasons discussed in chapter 4. And pleasure is a genuine human good. Nevertheless, this particular pleasure, of sex devoid of meaning, is akin to the pleasures of drug abuse. It is not good for us, because it causes loss of meaning. It robs our body of an important element of its natural expressiveness. Metaphorically, it reduces us to speaking sexual gibberish. It thereby diminishes us. Alternatively, because sex normally has such great expressive power, it can give the illusion of intimacy where it does not exist. If the partners do not set out to deceive each other, one or the other may be deluding himself or herself. Either way, the practice, genuinely pleasurable as it is, is harmful. It belongs to all those who seek the good of human beings, and therefore also to the church, to discourage it, and to invite and assist people towards behaviour which allows their gestures the meaning that naturally belongs to them. Since shared sex naturally belongs within a context of an intimate personal relationship, of love, between two people, this means encouraging sexual restraint, urging people to refrain from seeking sexual pleasure outside such a context.

Friendship and time

A further aspect of personal intimacy, one to which John Paul II importantly draws attention, is that it has a temporal dimension. Human relationships are extended in time, sometimes considerable time. You cannot be close friends with somebody for an evening, or love them for a day. This is not to point to the familiar fact that close relationships take time to develop, that the familiar mutual knowledge on which intimacy depends takes time to acquire; and that, normally, love and friendship take time to decay. The point is rather a conceptual one. If two people are close, that means they are committed to each other, committed to stick by each other, to support each other in difficulty, to comfort each other in sorrow, to share their joys, their problems and, simply, their time. The more they are committed to share, the closer they are. There are some commitments that have a time limit. A soldier may bind himself to serve for three years, and the army to pay him and care for him during the same period; a volunteer charity worker may pledge himself to work for two years; and so on. To specify a time-span belongs to a temporary contract. But the mutual commitment of friends is not like that. Friendship is not contractual, but open-ended. One friend does not say to another: 'I'll share your joys and sorrows, go for walks with you, lend you money, drink your coffee, help you and seek your help – until next Tuesday.' To say that to somebody is to convey that your relationship with him or her is not one of friendship, that you do not actually like him or her, but are carrying on this relationship only out of a sense of obligation, from which you will be glad to be free next week. Friends are already free, and freely gravitate towards each other, because they like each other. Though we speak sometimes of the obligations of friendship, yet friendship is not constituted by obligations. On the contrary, the obligations are created by the friendship. You cannot set a deliberate term to a friendship, because you cannot make a decision to stop liking somebody by such and such a date. The bonds of friendship stretch into an indefinite future. There may be all kinds of limitations on a particular friendship; friends set limits on how much of themselves, their time, their money, etc., they are willing to give each other. What those limits are will determine whether we speak of it as a close friendship or not. But, however close or otherwise it may be, there can be no limit placed on its duration.

Further, friendship has a dynamic towards its own continuation. Because friends like each other, they want to be together. When two friends part, it cannot be a matter of indifference to them whether they will meet again or not. Friends may realize, from a review of their own history or because of circumstances or from a knowledge of the frailty of human relationships in general, that they may drift apart, that their friendship may cool and even end at some time in the future, but they necessarily realize it with regret, and may take steps to avoid it; to be indifferent to whether your friendship will continue is, *per impossibile*, to be indifferent to your friend. Still less is the end of a friendship something you can plan, for to plan to move apart is already not to be friends.

So if two people have a sexual encounter with the intention of being together only briefly, for an hour or a week, or if they are indifferent to whether they will meet again, they cannot be meeting as friends. Indeed, if they put any term to their relationship, be it a year or ten or twenty years, they do not come together as friends. Because they do not understand themselves as bound together indefinitely by any friendship, let alone the intimate friendship in which sex has its natural place, neither can they see their sexual activity together, their physical intimacy, as an expression of their unity as people. Their acts are deprived of their natural meaning.

There is an important distinction to be made at this point. If friendship is open-ended, it may in fact last a lifetime. But an open-ended commitment to each other is not the same as a commitment to be friends for life. If friends drift apart, or separate in bitterness, that is not because they have failed to honour their mutual commitment, but because that commitment has died or been destroyed. If, by the nature of friendship, friends cannot plan that their friendship should end, that is not the same as saying that they must plan that their friendship not end. To plan that a friendship not end is not just to be committed to the other, nor is it to become more committed; it is to make a commitment, and to make a further commitment. People do sometimes make such a further pledge, vowing to remain friends for life. They do not thereby necessarily become closer friends, but there is a certain dynamic in that direction. The vow commits them jointly to maintaining the mutual commitment they already have. That may not of itself make that commitment deeper. However, it does give them a joint project, something to do together, namely maintaining their relationship. And it is in doing things together that friends express and confirm their friendship. If they do what they are committed by their vow to do, their friendship may not become more intimate, but it will become stronger.

One form of such a vow, and one particularly important to Christians, is the promises a man and a woman make to each other when they marry. The marriage vows are not only an expression of mutual commitment, a sign of friendship; they also declare a joint commitment to maintain that friendship, for life. That joint commitment need not make them any closer, but the hope would be that they grow closer by sharing their life and activities together, including the project they have just committed themselves to by marrying.

If this is right, then those who are married are not thereby made closer. They are not necessarily made any more unified than close friends who are unmarried. The criterion for the appropriateness of sex that I have been developing in the course of this chapter has been in terms of intimacy of personal relationship. If the married are not necessarily closer than unmarried friends, that means that we cannot derive the restriction of sexual intercourse to spouses from this criterion. If personal closeness is thought of in terms of mutual commitment, as it seems natural to do, then the unmarried may be as committed to each other as the married. The physical intimacy of sex may therefore be just appropriate to some unmarried friends as to the married.

Such a conclusion is, of course, far from the fullness of the church's teaching. But, if I am right, the line of thought adumbrated by John Paul II and the other writers quoted above, natural and valuable as I have tried to show it to be, cannot get us any further. To do that we would have to look not to the mutual commitment of prospective sexual partners, but to their joint commitment to maintain their relationship and make it permanent. And such a shift in approach makes us ask why it is so important for a sexual relationship that it be permanent. The obvious answer is in terms of children and their need to be raised in a loving and stable environment, one in which they have set before them in the mutual love of their parents an example of the kind of relationship in which they too might find the lasting friendship in which they will flourish. But this takes us far from the thought of this chapter. It also raises questions about the place of sex where there are no children or can be no children. Two of the circumstances in which children are excluded are where the partners practice contraception, and where they are of the same sex. Here the argument for stability and joint commitment to lifelong friendship seems not to apply.

These two possibilities are important practically as well as theoretically. Sex shared between willing partners naturally expresses a close friendship we might call love. When the modern church teaches, as in the excerpt from *Familiaris Consortio* quoted above, that sex properly belongs in a context of loving mutual commitment, it is simply recognizing this fact.[13] But in insisting also that this loving mutual commitment be permanent, between married spouses, man and woman, ruling out contraception and homosexual partnerships, the church finds itself in disagreement with many others. There are many, both within the church and outside it, who, while agreeing that sex is essentially related to love, that it is realized in a truly human way only if it is an integral part of the love two people share, do not concede that a loving relationship, in order to be fittingly expressed in sexual gestures, has to be one of marriage, or even permanent. In such relationships, partly because they are not intended to be permanent, the use of contraception in intercourse is standard. There are those, too, who insist that two partners of the same sex may love each other as deeply and as lastingly as a man and a woman, and are therefore not impoverishing themselves or each other if they express their love sexually. One of the tasks of the succeeding chapters will be to try to shed light on some of these differences.

7

The Other Half

I want to go on now to talk about the aspects of sexual love that I mentioned at the beginning of the last chapter as being seen by some theologians as an important and indeed essential component of it as a meaningful human act: complementarity, and creativity or fecundity.

First, complementarity. What is meant by saying that the sexes are complementary? The idea, briefly, is that in love for and life with somebody of the other sex we find our completion or our fulfilment in an important way. Our love must not, of course, be confined to members of the other sex, since we are called to love all, without distinction of male and female. But the fact of sexual difference opens new possibilities for our life and our love, possibilities that normally call for realization. Male and female are different, but the nature of their differences makes them into two halves of a divided whole, who complete each other by their union. This union is primarily a union of lives shared in love, and the complementary qualities of a man and a woman in their life of love together balance and give point to each other, thereby enriching and fulfilling the life of both partners to the relationship, enabling both to flourish in ways that would be difficult or impossible to either man or woman in isolation. Without entering into such a relationship, men and women normally remain in a sense incomplete, one-sided. It is not good for man to be alone, or for woman. Those with a special vocation to celibacy or graced in other ways by God may be able to live satisfactorily and fruitfully without entering into such a partnership, but for most of us the way to become properly rounded human beings is by sharing life with one who complements us, and that means with one of the other sex.

Though this complementarity, it is said, embraces the whole life of a loving couple, it finds fitting and natural expression in the sexual union of the partners. This is partly because of the natural capacity of the body to function as an expressive medium, the personal physical intimacy and junction of the man and woman being a natural symbol of the union of their lives in love. But there is a further important aspect to this. It is in union with a complementary partner that a person naturally flourishes. But to flourish is to be fruitful. If we say that two people flourish as a couple, that is because in their partnership their lives are made fruitful. And the basic form of human fruitfulness is the production of children. A child is, not inevitably but naturally, the living sign of the loving union of its parents. And it is naturally through the sexual intercourse expressive of that couple's loving union that its fruit comes to be. This need not be so. A child may not be the fruit of love; it may be unfortunate enough to be unwanted, or an accident, or it may not be born to parents who live together in love. But if that is so, it is a sign that something has gone wrong; it means that for its parents sexual union no longer serves, as by nature it does, as an expression of their mutual love.

From this brief sketch it is clear that a whole complex of ideas and metaphors is subsumed under the term complementarity. I now want to take a closer look at some of these, keeping in mind as usual the question of implications for our sexual behaviour: can we find in the idea of complementarity any guide as to how we should or should not conduct ourselves sexually? But the prior question must be what sense we can make of the idea that male and female are complementary.

We may begin by concentrating on the concept of completion implicit in that of complementarity. Nobody is claiming that a man without a woman or a woman without a man is in any sense physically incomplete. Neither, I would suggest, is it profitable to say that they are in any other way, such as mentally or spiritually, incomplete. Normally, when we say that something is incomplete, we mean that part of it is missing, a part that belongs to it as a unified whole. But a man is in no clear sense part of a woman, nor a woman part of a man. Unlike a man who lacks an arm, a man who lacks a woman does not lack part of himself; he lacks somebody else. When people lack other people it is not their wholeness that is in question so much as their needs. If a man has lost his wife, he may say that he feels incomplete without her, but that is an expression of his need for her, which is now unfulfilled. She was a central part of the pattern of his life, and that pattern has now been destroyed. We can equally say that not he, but his life, is now incomplete.

If a man and a woman are complementary, it is not so much that they complete each other as that they go well together. Together they form a pleasing or appropriate whole, and it is that larger whole that is incomplete without one of the partners. It is like strawberries and cream. There are those who think of strawberries and cream as complementary. Because of their respective qualities they go well together, enhancing each other and forming a satisfying whole, the cream offsetting the sharpness of the strawberries and these in turn cutting the bland fattiness of the cream. Cream without strawberries or something similar is hardly to be contemplated, and when strawberries are served without cream, there is something missing. The strawberries, nice as they are alone, lack something. But it is not that the strawberries are incomplete, lack part of themselves. They lack or need something else, cream. Without the cream, it is not the fruit that is incomplete, but the dish.

But complementarity, going well together, is a matter of purpose and function, and these relate to what people want. There is no absolute sense in which coffee and milk are complementary. I may want milk with my coffee if my purpose is to mitigate the bitterness of the coffee, but black coffee with a cigarette may be more to the point if I am trying to stay awake in the small hours. If I am planning a concert and have a Tchaikovsky symphony in the first half, another Tchaikovsky symphony in the second half will be ideal if my aim is to illustrate the composer's development as a symphonist; otherwise, the two will not go well together and I will be better to choose something that will provide a contrast, so that the two halves together will form a satisfactory whole. Similarly, if it is said that men and women are complementary, we have to ask: In what context, and for what purpose?

To say that men and women are complementary is to say that together they form a whole. So our answer to this question is going to depend on our having a particular preconception of what constitutes a whole, a unit. If we take the whole human species as our unit, then there is a trivial sense in which male and female are complementary: that people are by and large divisible into male and female. If we leave out the problematic cases of people of indeterminate sex, those who have both male and female sexual characteristics and those who have neither, then males and females make up the full complement of the species. But note that people of indeterminate sex are 'problematic' just because and only in the sense that they upset such a simple classification, and sometimes also upset the people who insist on it.[1] And we should not forget that we make male and female complementary in this sense only at the cost of ignoring such people. This complementarity is not a true reflection of reality, but at most an approximation that may be convenient for most of us. In just the same way we can say that left-handed people and right-handed people are complementary: if we leave out the problematic cases of the ambidextrous and those with no hands, then left-handers and right-handers together make up the full complement of the species. We can, if we wish, divide people up in any number of ways into separate classes and then say that those classes are complementary. But many of the divisions we could make we do not make, because they are of no interest to us. It does not, on the whole, matter to us whether people are left-handed or right-handed, whether they have freckles or not, whether have curly hair or straight hair. That is to say that we do not do anything with those distinctions. They do not serve any purpose for us, except in very special cases. There is no important human context in which such kinds of complementarity are crucial.

The distinction between male and female is more important to us because it is relevant to a common human objective: to have children. For this purpose men and women are plainly complementary, in that they have complementary roles in the reproductive process. This is a complementarity that goes beyond being a possible way of classifying humanity as a whole; we can say individual couples of man and woman are complementary in this respect. This complementarity is an important one, since the human purpose to which it relates is so important, indeed central to the life of the species. It is also a necessary one, since both man and woman are indispensable for reproduction,[2] and this, not just for the species as a whole, but at the level of each couple. This is such a fundamental part of human life that it may not be misleading to say *tout court* in the light of it that men and women are complementary, without explicit qualification. But it should not be forgotten that if this is done there is always at least an implicit reference to the purpose of having children.

There is a complementary point to be made here. Not only are two human beings indispensable, but they must be of different sexes and their roles are not substitutable. For instance, two men cannot fulfil this important human purpose if they have sexual intercourse together. That is, in relation to the purpose of reproduction, two men are not complementary as a man and a woman are; and neither are two women. It is presumably this point that lies behind a couple of remarks in the *Letter on the Pastoral Care of Homosexual Persons* of the Congregation for the Doctrine of the Faith. At one point we find:

> Human beings are ... nothing less than the work of God himself; and in the complementarity of the sexes they are called to reflect the inner unity of the Creator. They do this in a striking way in their cooperation with him in the transmission of life by a mutual donation of the self to the other.[3]

Leaving aside for the moment the reference to reflecting the unity of God, it seems clear that a particular link is made between the complementarity of the sexes and their roles in reproduction. Later, the *Letter* makes a corresponding point about homosexual activity, which is said to be 'not a complementary union, able to transmit life'.[4] Once again, the link between complementarity and reproduction seems clear. I leave until later a detailed discussion of homosexuality, but one remark needs to be made in this context. The comment that homosexual activity is not a complementary union comes in the context of a very negative evaluation of homosexual behaviour. But if homosexual intercourse is not complementary, this is not of itself a criticism of it, or an argument against it. For complementarity is linked to purpose, in this case the purpose of transmitting life, and as far as this part of the *Letter* is concerned, to say that intercourse is complementary is almost tantamount to saying that it is capable of transmitting life. That sexual activity ought to be complementary is true only if it ought to be capable of fulfilling this purpose. So homosexual intercourse is defective only if it is also a defect that it be incapable of transmitting life, and this is something that has to be shown independently. I have already examined some of the arguments adduced in support of this position. If it were quite acceptable, in the eyes of the church, for intercourse to be incapable of transmitting life, then it would be no criticism of homosexual intercourse, as far as the argument of the *Letter* in these remarks is concerned, that it is not complementary. Thus far, then, the idea of complementarity provides no independent guide to which kinds of sexual behaviour are desirable and which are not.

Psychological complementarity

But the concept of the complementarity of man and woman as normally employed is rather wider than that which appears in these remarks of the *Letter*; it goes far beyond the fact that man and woman have complementary roles in procreation. It is meant to apply to many of the personal qualities of men and women. Men are supposed to have one set of characteristics and women another, complementary set. As an example of this wider concept, here is some of what Henry Peschke writes on the subject:

> Their psychological qualities and spiritual dispositions differ. The male is more active and outgoing; he possesses greater courage to assail. The female is more receptive and protective; she shows greater fortitude to endure. The man is ordered towards things and more concerned with goals of [an?] objective nature. The woman is interested in persons and consecrates herself to those whom she loves with her soul and entire being. The logic of facts and keen penetration are characteristic of the man; the woman is more led by emotion, sensitivity and intuition. He is ruled by principles, she by love.[5]

The significance of these differences from Peschke's point of view is that the sets of qualities he attributes to men and women contain pairs that are not merely different or opposing, but complementary. The outgoing nature of the male is complemented by the receptivity of the female; the man's logical mind is complemented by the woman's feminine intuition. So too people with these different sets of qualities are not merely different but complementary; they go well together. This complementary constitution of man and woman 'results in erotic tensions which have important repercussions on the life of the individual and the community'.[6] Men and women are social beings, and it is not good for them to be alone. Hence, they do not desire to live alone, but seek out a partner with whom they can live well. In seeking to share their lives with each other, they seek relations with somebody complementary, somebody with different qualities such that they go well together. The fullest way of sharing lives is in marriage, and it is here also that a sexual expression of that friendship is appropriate. In this context it becomes significant that male and female have roles in sexual intercourse that can be called complementary: the man penetrates, while the woman opens herself to be penetrated. The way their bodies fit together via the complementary shape and function of their sexual organs is a symbol of the way the partners fit each other, are fit for each other, go well together. Thus the complementary roles of man and woman in sexual intercourse are a natural symbol of the way the couple complement each other in their wider relationship.

Some such scheme, it appears, lies behind much of what is said about the complementarity of the sexes in Christian thought. From a traditional Christian point of view, such a way of thinking has much to recommend it. The notion of complementarity, recognizing the human significance of sex, serves to locate sexual activity firmly within the context of a sharing of life. It also goes a long way towards making the sharing of life between man and woman – marriage – the norm of human life, and marriage the normal context for sexual activity. Hence it also lends weight to a rejection of homosexual relationships. But the important question remains: Is it actually a sound way of characterizing human beings and their relationships, and does it therefore provide the support for traditional Christian sexual morality that it appears to? It seems to me that there are a number of serious objections to it, objections so fundamental as to render it useless as a guide to proper sexual behaviour.

In the first place, once we move into the area of psychological qualities and spiritual dispositions there are grounds for caution in asserting the complementarity of the sexes in the context of a theology of sex. There is no doubt that we do sometimes speak of certain qualities as masculine and others as feminine, and it may also be possible to speak of these differences as complementary. To that extent there is a certain validity in the kind of distinction between the characteristics of men and women that thinkers like Peschke draw. But, to the extent that it is a valid distinction, it is not necessarily one of any theological import. For it is a commonplace of sociology, one to which I drew attention in chapter 3, that many of our perceptions of what belongs to the male and what to the female are socially determined and culturally relative, a product of education and socialization in a particular time and place. This should make us wary of too readily attributing the different qualities of men and women to the work of God, of absolutizing particular gender differences which may well turn out to be the passing work of man. If females tend to be receptive and domestic, it is certain that this is attributable in large measure to their education into a particular role in society; and if men by and large have complementary qualities, if they are outgoing and assertive, it is largely because they have been taught to be. There is no serious doubt about this. The only real doubt is as to whether social forces account completely for these complementary differences. Here the burden of proof seems to be on the theologian who wants to make use of the notion of complementarity; he or she has to show that there is some remnant of character differences that belongs to men and women by their nature, regardless of how they are socialized. Even if it can be shown that there are such natural differences, it remains true that a large proportion of the differences between men and women are the result of social conditioning, the work of man and not God. Many of the qualities conventionally ascribed to men and women as such do not belong to people by nature but are the result of a particular and variable upbringing. Hence, if men and women are complementary, it is only to a very limited extent, if at all, that they are naturally complementary, that their complementarity can be ascribed to God as the author of human nature.

This point is especially important in that the sociological explanation of the formation of male and female characteristics also accounts for the differences between them being precisely complementary differences. According to this explanation, the complementarity of men and women is not accidental. Gender definitions are generally the product of the dominant gender, the ones who have the power to define classes of people and to determine the places they are to occupy. In our society, as in most, the males are dominant. So the men are represented in this vision as dominant – outgoing, active, assailing, penetrating, in general shaping things to their will. To some extent this does reflect reality; men are by and large dominant, have the power. But this is a social reality, and it is by no means necessarily equivalent to a God-given, constitutional reality, valid for all human societies. (This is not to deny that the social reality of male dominance has its roots in nature, in the fact that most men are by and large physically more powerful than most women.) Part of what that means is that, as Jeffrey Weeks says:

> Male sexuality as culturally defined provides the norm and, not surprisingly, female sexuality continues to be the problem. Males, in becoming men, take up positions in power relations in which they acquire the ability to define women.[7]

So the women are defined as subordinate – receptive, passive to the will of men. They are defined, that is, as everything that men, by their self-definition, are not; they are part of the material to be shaped by the men. Hence men and women turn out to be complementary; they fit each other socially because the women occupy the space defined and left for them by the men. Not, of course, that these definitions are always accepted by women or by men, but, as Weeks again points out, the constant battles over sexual meanings

> are against, and within the limits set by, the dominant terms. These in turn are encoded via a social privileging of particular relationships – in marriage and

family arrangements and a host of other social institutions and activities, through
which gender, and sexual, identities are constructed and constantly reaffirmed.[8]

If, then, men and women are complementary in many of their important
attributes, this is not a very lucky coincidence, nor built into nature, a
marvellous piece of planning by the Creator. It is a matter of definition.
This is not to suggest that there are not average physical and even
psychological differences between the sexes, which can perfectly properly
be attributed by Christians to the design of God. But we go well beyond the
design of God when we turn averages into definitional distinctions.[9] These
are definitions, moreover, reflecting a social structure of dominance which
Christians are committed to opposing, as we are committed to opposing all
domination of one person or group by another. Any Christian society has to
be founded not on domination but on mutual service, in imitation of Christ
who 'came not to be served but to serve, and to give his life as a ransom for
many' (Matt. 20.28).

If this is right, then we have to be very careful about how we use the
notion of complementarity in thinking about sex. Any insistence on the
complementarity of the sexes as providing as basis for Christian sexual
ethics is in danger, against the background of these words of Jesus, of
having a peculiarly unChristian ring about it.

Male and female qualities

So far, I have assumed for the sake of argument that there really is a
substantial set of differences between the psychological and spiritual
qualities of men and women, and that these differences are complementary.
But is this so? Let us return again to Peschke. His account of the differences
is admirably plain and straightforward, but it does not fit the case. To begin
with, some of the things he says here could not be right. For example, he
speaks of men being ruled by principles and women by contrast being ruled
by love. But there is not the difference between ruled by principles and
being ruled by love that he supposes, for love demands that people live by
certain principles, those which order behaviour towards the good of others.
Again, men are said to have the courage to assail, while women are rather
receptive and protective. But being protective can actually require the
courage to assail; to protect her children a mother may have to attack one
who is attacking them. Apart from this, ordinary human experience shows
that much of what Peschke says is only true, if at all, to a limited extent.
People are just not divided along sexual lines like this. We may know of men
and women who fit this picture, but we all certainly know of men and
women who do not. We surely all know men who are hardly active and
outgoing at all, and who possess no courage whatever to assail. We also

know women who are not very receptive or who do not consecrate themselves to those whom they love with their soul and entire being. If it is the woman who is more led by emotion, sensitivity and intuition it becomes very difficult to explain the notorious fact that the vast majority of great painters, composers, poets and cooks have been men.

There may well be a statistical tendency for men to be more aggressive and logical, and for women to be more receptive and emotional; but this does not license universal claims about the personal characteristics of men and women. And in order to form any kind of basis for sexual morality the claim has to be all but universal, otherwise the characteristics ascribed to the two sexes cannot be plausibly represented as a natural endowment, even assuming that such characteristics cannot be accounted for by social conditioning. If significant numbers of women are found to be as coldly logical or as outgoing as men are supposed to be, it cannot convincingly be claimed that God made women any less logical or outgoing than men. If not all women have the qualities they are supposed to have by nature, this is not in itself damaging to the theory, for it can be held that in their case nature has been interfered with in some way, or gone wrong: the exceptional women are defective women. But this move becomes less and less plausible as the number of exceptions grows. In any case, we do not normally think of logical or outgoing women as defective, so some justification would have to be given for such a move.

This raises a further important point. Though we do sometimes talk of certain qualities as being feminine and of others as being masculine, we do not thereby normally imply that only women possess the so-called feminine qualities or men the so-called masculine qualities; neither do we regard it as desirable that these qualities be so confined. If we describe, say, emotional sensitivity to others as a feminine quality, this is not to say that it is one only desirable in women; we may, on the contrary, think that it would be well if everybody had such a quality. It is only that we believe, rightly or wrongly, that it is found more often, perhaps much more often, in women than in men. So we may say of an emotionally sensitive man that he has a feminine quality. But this in no way compromises his status as a man, nor does it make us think of him as a defective man. We may indeed think it makes him a much better man than he would otherwise be. Similarly, a woman with the 'masculine' tendency to think logically is none the less a woman, and neither do we think of her as defective. We regard the ability to think logically, like sensitivity to others, as desirable in everybody. Conversely, we regard insensitivity and irrationality as defects wherever we meet them, regardless of sex. Though we sometimes think of certain qualities as typically masculine and others as typically feminine, perhaps because of where we in general expect to find them, we hope to find them universally, and much of our education system is devoted to realizing that hope.

That is to say, many of the distinctions to which Peschke points as fundamental to the natural constitution of men and women are, where they occur in reality, matters of regret for us. It is our hope to mitigate, blur or abolish them. By and large, we think that men are improved by cultivating the qualities we associate with women, and that women are improved by cultivating the qualities we associate with men; this has been popularly expressed by saying that men should develop their feminine side and women their masculine side, so as to become well-rounded people.

But this means that, although there are times when we want to say '*vive la différence*', it is desirable that all people have certain 'masculine' and 'feminine' qualities, not that it is good for, say, the completely active to be complemented by the completely passive. What we hope for when people share their lives with other, complementary individuals is that each partner will acquire some of the complementary characteristics of the other. Suppose a man is very active and outgoing and lacks receptive, passive qualities. It may be good for him to live closely with a more passive person. This may not be the answer, for his too active nature may be accommodated by the passivity of his partner, rather than modified. But let us suppose it works, and that close exposure to the passive qualities of his partner makes him more appreciative of those qualities and develop them himself. This means that he will be made more passive himself. Similarly, his passive partner may come to share some of his active qualities. Thus the end result is that the two partners are no longer complementary in their qualities and dispositions. We can no longer describe the one as active and the other as passive, but both share a mix of active and passive qualities. This kind of complementarity has a dynamic towards its own diminution, or even elimination. The complementary relationship, in so far as it is successful, ceases to be complementary. So we have the somewhat paradoxical conclusion that what is desirable is the reduction or elimination of complementarity, and that relationships of people with complementary qualities and dispositions are desirable not in themselves but only as a means to that end.

If in general we seek a certain blurring of gender differences, this is not universally true. The exceptions that come readily to mind concern clothes, deportment and sexual behaviour. These are distinctions we do not in general hope to mitigate, blur or abolish. Men are not expected to dress or carry themselves like women, nor are they, like women, to find men sexually attractive. Such 'feminine' qualities, unlike others, are often held to compromise a man's masculinity, and hence to be defects in a man. Conversely women are not expected to dress or act like men, or to seek sexual relations with women. I have gone into some of the social reasons why these matters are exceptional and important to us in chapter 3, and I will not repeat them. The point I want to draw attention to here is that it is precisely in the area of sexual behaviour that the idea of the complementarity of the sexes begins to gain plausibility. But it gains plausibility because it reflects antecedently existing views on what counts as desirable sexual behaviour. Since that is so, the appeal to the complementarity of the sexes in order to establish a guide for sexual behaviour contributes nothing: it only becomes credible if we already accept the sexual guidelines it claims to establish.

'The Other'

One of the reasons this idea of complementarity of sexual qualities has been put to work is to flesh out in a sexual context the notion that love means a going beyond oneself in a concern for somebody else. It is a common Christian theme that it is in such love that we are fulfilled, and this is a belief that is shared by many non-Christians. So a sexual expression of this fulfilling love is a physical reaching out to somebody else, somebody different: as it is sometimes put, to 'the Other'. However, its apparent attractiveness in Christian sexual ethics often trades on a simple ambiguity, that between difference of substance – being somebody else, and difference of quality – that somebody else's being unlike you.

It cannot be doubted that much of Christian life is to do with concern for other people; our ethic is in that sense a social ethic, as I have argued since chapter 1. For Christians, relationships with other people are valuable largely because other people are valuable. We are taught to see other people as valuable in themselves, and we are encouraged to learn to be concerned for and open and sensitive to those who are not ourselves. This might be expressed by saying that it is important for us to appreciate the otherness of other people, their simply being somebody else. And if this is true in all our relationships with others, it will *a fortiori* be true in our sexual relationships. But this is quite different from saying that those other people should also have different qualities from ourselves. We can appreciate and be concerned for somebody else who is yet very like ourselves; indeed, that is what Christians are supposed to do. The extent to which another person with whom one is in a close, perhaps sexual relationship should be qualitatively different from oneself remains to be determined; neither is it immediately obvious that this question is one of any Christian ethical significance. What can be said on this question?

Part of the complementarity theory is that, in order that two people who share their lives might go together well, they should have complementary qualities. So far in this discussion it has been assumed that complementary qualities are different qualities, like the qualities of strawberries and cream. But this is a questionable assumption. There are those who think that the best thing to go with strawberries is more strawberries. We normally think that one candlestick is best complemented by another candlestick of the same design rather than a different one, or by a plastic cup. So too it may well be that one particular man finds his complement in somebody else, male or female, with the same qualities rather than different ones. We know that successful relationships can be made by people of similar dispositions. To a large extent similarity is positively desirable.[10] The ability to share is essential to friendship, and that demands a certain likeness between the friends. Part of this sharing is doing things together, and those who have little in common can do little together. If friends need to have a range of interests in common, they also need to have similar tastes. They will find it difficult to eat together if one lives on rare steak and the other is a vegan, or to sit together if one likes to have the radio on all the time while the other likes a lot of silence.

A fundamental element of the desirability of similarity is the obvious fact that it is desirable that the one to whom one relates be a human being, of the same species. It is possible to have a relationship with an animal such as a dog or a cat which we might agree, perhaps with reservations, to describe as a friendship; but such relationships, though they can be very important in the individual case, are of their nature very limited, because a human being and an animal cannot share the range of activities that two people can. A woman can go for a walk with a dog, but she cannot play chess with it or swap complaints with it about the rising cost of living.

In other respects similarity may cause difficulty. For example, two dominant people may not initially find it easy to live well and happily together. But they can manage it, if they are committed enough to each other, through compromise, with give and take. The necessity for compromise does not make it an inferior relationship, for practically all relationships demand compromise, including those between partners with opposite characteristics, for characteristics admit of degrees. Suppose there is a partnership between a dominant woman and a man with the complementary quality of submissiveness. It is still perfectly possible that the man will be a little too submissive for the woman, or not quite enough, and the woman too much or too little dominant from the man's point of view. Here there will need to be give and take if the partnership is to succeed. This implies that the complementarity theory makes altogether too much of natural dispositions. Sometimes difference attracts people to each other, sometimes similarity, but what will make the relationship work is not the natural qualities with which the partners are endowed. True complementarity in a relationship is a matter of will, the willingness to give and take, to take each other's character, likes, dislikes and interests into account, so that the partners can agree on (or naturally fall into) an arrangement that they can both want to continue – an arrangement that enables them both to do things they enjoy (including doing things together, which is why they have a partnership in the first place), and such that each partner does not do, and is happy not to do, what the other does not like. Complementarity in human relationships is not profitably thought of as God-given and related to gender differences. It is something that can be worked at, and its end is that the partners go well together, in that they find their relationship a pleasure. And there is no reason to suppose that such a relationship is possible only between partners of different sexes. The characters and dispositions of the partners may make working out a successful relationship more or less difficult, and from this point of view a person can choose his or her partner wisely or unwisely, but there is little reason to believe that these characters and dispositions are tied at all closely to sexual differences.

Here we can note another reason for the unsatisfactoriness of talking in terms of 'the Other'. If it is important that we relate to human beings, then it is important that our relationships be personal. Seeing somebody simply as a manifestation of 'the Other' depersonalizes them. It is true that we sometimes just want somebody else, anybody 'other'; or a boy may just want a girl, any girl, and this may be a reason for starting a relationship. But we do not expect such an attitude to remain once the relationship develops. We expect it to pass, and its passing is one of our criteria of a real personal relationship being established.

In any case this emphasis on the Other sits ill with Genesis 2, the story of the formation of Eve from the side of Adam. This important passage is sometimes cited (along with the speech of Aristophanes in Plato's *Symposium*) in favour of the idea that in coming together sexually as one flesh people seek a certain wholeness or re-integration. What is indisputable about this passage is that it testifies to a sense that people are social, that they need other people: Then the Lord God said: 'It is not good that the man should be alone; I will make him a helper fit for him.' (Gen. 2.18). God therefore tries to make a companion for the man he has just created. He first makes the animals, but they will not do. Finally he succeeds by making the woman, out of the man's rib. From the way the story moves, the importance of Eve is not that she is sexually different from Adam (this difference is not even mentioned) but that she is more similar to him than are the animals that God has created; it is as if the animals are too different. This similarity is dramatized by giving the woman her origin from the man himself. Adam delights in the woman who is made out of his flesh, who is bone of his bone (v.23), but his words show that it is precisely the sameness of Eve, not the difference, that Adam appreciates and that makes it possible for her to be a fit helper for him.

But supposing nevertheless, for the sake of argument, that there should be differences of some kind between two friends, this would then also be true of those whose friendship is sexual. There seems no obvious reason, however, why those differences should include gender difference. Indeed for most of our relations we do not expect such cross-gender contact, and are not surprised or horrified if we do not come across it. It does not bother us that in non-sexual friendships, work and social activities, people often, perhaps most often, choose partners of their own sex. We expect men to have men as close friends, even to prefer to be with other men most of the time. And similarly with women. A question that has to be answered, then, is: Why should sexual relations be an exception to this; why should gender difference be so vital in this area? Why not gender similarity, since we find similarity so important in other areas of our lives? The conclusion seems inescapable that, if we do want to say that it is indeed important for there to be sexual difference in sexual relationships, it is not because the supposed complementarity of the sexes is in general so vital to us.

Sexual desire when it is directed to other people does not, then, seem well characterized as a desire for completion or fulfilment in somebody who has different, complementary qualities; it is simply a desire for somebody else, whether they are also qualitatively very different or not. So neither are the supposed complementary differences between men and women the source of erotic tension and attraction, as Peschke claims. This is not to say that all we may require for a sexual relationship is that our partner be somebody else, or have interestingly similar or different non-sexual characteristics. A person's sex matters to us as well. We do not for the most part just relate as genderless persons in sex. It happens that people can sometimes develop a friendship to the point where it becomes explicitly sexual quite regardless of the sex of the friend. But this is not the usual case. If we are to entertain the possibility of a friendship's becoming sexual the gender of the friend matters.

This point has to be put with some care, though. It normally matters whether the friend is a man or a woman. But this is not the same as saying that it is gender difference or sameness that matters. It is not sameness or difference that is important but whether somebody is a man or a woman. The notions of sameness and difference contain the idea of comparison. If I find somebody else sexually attractive, that is not because I have compared the other person to myself to see whether or not they are the same sex as me. What matters to me is just what sex they are. It is not the difference of a woman that attracts the heterosexual man, but her femaleness. Or rather, her femaleness is a condition of her being attractive; for of course she may be female and yet remain unattractive. Similarly, it is not the difference of men that is sexually attractive to many women, but their maleness is a condition of their being attractive, just as it is the femaleness of women that is a condition of their being sexually attractive to many men. Precisely analogous points can be made in the case of homosexual attraction.

And for those to whom men are attractive it is not just maleness that is a condition of attraction. People are attracted to different kinds of men. In the same way, quite disparate kinds of women are attractive to different people.

The fat, the thin, the older, the younger, the strong, the vulnerable, the fair, the dark, the reserved, the gregarious, and so on, may each hold a special attraction for various people. Among the many variations that exist among people, some people are drawn to one type, some to others. And the same person can be drawn to people of different types at different times. Facts like these should once again guard us from thinking of difference (complementary or not), or indeed sameness, as the source of erotic attraction.

The notion of complementary difference, then, does not appear to be a help towards understanding or expounding the Christian idea that sexual activity is peculiarly apt for expressing love. I am of course not denying that two people may love each other or be attracted to each other by their complementary qualities, but only saying that love is not to be analysed as attraction to complementary sexual characteristics or other qualities allegedly dependent on them.

If what I have said in the preceding pages is right, then the supposed connexion between sexual activity and the complementarity of the sexes collapses. So it cannot be used, for instance, to support the common Christian contention that sexual relations are legitimate only between people of different sexes, thus ruling out all homosexual practices. Indeed, any attempt to use it in this way may even backfire if, like Peschke and others, we spell out the alleged complementarity in terms of personal qualities. For it makes the criterion for the admissibility of a sexual relationship not the gender but the qualities of a person, whatever the sex of that person. But, for instance, a man may have qualities we regard as feminine, just as a woman can; he may be just as sensitive, emotional, protective and devoted as she. This appears to licence the conclusion that if a woman has the requisite complementary qualities to be my sexual partner, well and good; but if a man has the right complementary qualities (even granting that if he has them he is a defective man), then he too satisfies the criterion of complementarity, and so is a possible sexual partner. Thus the whole attempt to spell out complementarity in terms of personal qualities spells doom for the church teaching that sex can only legitimately take place between people of different sexes.

Complementarity and the image of God

One theological source of the notion of the complementarity of the sexes has been the desire to do full justice to the picture of man and woman as created by God in the opening chapters of Genesis. I have above briefly mentioned the story of the creation of Eve. Now I need to talk at greater length about Genesis 1.26f., which speaks of human beings, male and female, being made in the image of God. We have already come across several examples of a connexion being made between our being created in the image of God and the complementarity of the sexes. It may be remembered from chapter 3 that Bernard Häring, commenting on these verses, writes:

> It is not my intention to give the impression that this text points only to sexuality; it speaks also about the image of God in man's and woman's vocation to be co-creators in ordering the world around them. But sexuality cannot be excluded from the concept of 'image of God'.[11]

And Eric Fuchs writes, more strongly: 'Sexual differentiation has something to do with God's very intention to make man in his own image.'[12] Earlier in this chapter I quoted the Congregation for the Doctrine of the Faith as saying that 'in the complementarity of the sexes they [human beings] are called to reflect the inner unity of the Creator'.[13]

The idea common to all three of these in their reading of Genesis 1.26f. is that our being in the image of God is somehow bound up with there being two sexes, and that it is in the union of the complementary sexes that we mirror the unity of God, particularly in fruitful sexual union. If this is a correct interpretation of these verses, then the idea of the complementarity of the sexes has biblical warrant, and it becomes a serious matter to question it in the way I have been doing in this chapter. So is it a correct interpretation? Has being in the image of God, according to Genesis, anything at all to do with sexual complementarity? To answer this I shall begin by looking a little more closely at the key verses in Genesis 1.

If we first look at the literal meaning of the text, it is very enigmatic indeed. It simply does not elaborate on the idea of the image of God, or give any other obvious clue to what the author has in mind. It certainly does not say that in their complementarity men and women reflect the divine nature. It may be questioned in fact whether the text does mean to impart something significant about human nature by this phrase. Its very failure to go into more detail is an indication of this, as is the fact that the idea is developed nowhere else in the Old Testament.[14] At the level of exegesis, it does not seem possible to extract anything from it without reading into it elements of one or other independently-held anthropology. If the text is read on its own terms, it may well be a mistake to use it as a peg on which to hang a Christian anthropology. Claus Westermann justly comments:

> Without any proper methodological considerations, Gen. 1.26f. has been subordinated to a teaching about humanity in the image of God that is taken for granted. The phrases are taken up into a biblical anthropology and used to construct an Old Testament image of humanity. The presupposition is always that something is being said about human beings which can be taken out of its context and assumed into the very different context of a systematic teaching on human nature.[15]

Despite the vagueness of the text itself, or perhaps because of it, speculation on what it means for people to be created in the image of God has had a long history in the church.[16] The standard interpretation in the Western Christian tradition was the view that we are said to be in the image of God because we resemble him in being rational. For instance, St Augustine, commenting on Genesis, says:

> Here we should not fail to notice that, when he said 'in our image' he immediately added 'and let him have power over the fish of the sea and the birds of the air', and other animals which are devoid of reason. Thus we should understand that man is made in the image of God in virtue of that by which he is superior to irrational animals. But that is reason itself, or mind, or intelligence, or whatever else it might more fittingly be called. So the Apostle too says 'Be renewed in the spirit of your mind, and put on the new man,[17] which is renewed in knowledge according to the image of him who created it',[18] amply showing in what respect man is created in the image of God, that it is by virtue not of bodily shape but of some intelligible form of illuminated mind.[19]

And St Thomas Aquinas agrees that 'only intellectual creatures are, properly speaking, in the image of God'.[20]

According to people like St Augustine and St Thomas Aquinas, we, unlike other animals, are granted a share in the divine wisdom, that rational power by which God created, sustains, shapes and guides the world. That is what sets us apart from the other animals, which are not made in the image of God. It is also what brings us close to God and gives us a special bond with him, and him with us.

This view of what it is to be created in the image of God is closely related to the traditional Christian belief, which formed the basis of chapter 6 of this book, that reason is a distinctive and essential part of human nature. As I noted there, an essential part of the gift of reason is that we have language, and it is language that enables us to communicate. With language we can give information about the world; more importantly, we can share our view of things with each other, and we can communicate ourselves to each other. We can say 'I love you' or 'I hate you' or 'If you want us to remain friends, don't do anything like that again.' Because of language, we can communicate with each other and have communion with each other much more subtly and profoundly than kangaroos or elephants can.

The belief that our being created in the image of God consists in our being rational reflects the belief that our reason, our language, is also what enables us to have a communion with God deeper than he can have with any kangaroo. That we are rational means that God can speak to us and we can speak to him, that the relationship we have with him can have something of the depth of the relationships we have with each other: there can be love, hate, expectation, disappointment. There can be a history of our relationship with God, a history of the kind we write about people and their dealings with each other. A version of that history that is for us authoritative is to be found in scripture, culminating in God's communicating himself totally to us in love when his Word became flesh.

This, then, is what is involved in the traditional Christian view that our being made in the image of God consists in our being rational. It can be summed up by saying that in creating us in his image God made creatures with whom he could enter into a relationship, as he could not with other earthly creatures.

In the next chapter of Genesis, the story of the creation of Adam and Eve, the same point is put in a different way. God makes Adam and speaks to him, blessing him with abundant food; he lives with him in the garden and seeks him when he is not to be found. Even when he later expels him and Eve from the garden, he does not put an end to communication between himself and people. The relationship continues outside the garden. We find God engaged and in conversation with Cain, Noah, and then the patriarchs Abraham, Isaac and Jacob. And this relationship is basically one of love. It seeks the good of the other and communion with him.

Whatever the faults of this approach considered as strict exegesis of the text, this traditional understanding of Genesis 1.26f. clearly has the great merit of making clear the foundation for the possibility of communication between God and people. It would be a pity to jettison it in favour of the view that our being in the image of God consists in sexual complementarity, especially when, as I have tried to show, the concept of complementarity is in any case not entirely unproblematic. This more modern view is in fact equally weak exegetically. It is true that 1.27 says that 'male and female he made them'. But this asserts only that there are two sexes, not that those two sexes are complementary. The most natural reading of Genesis 1.26f. is not that it is in the complementarity of the sexes that the divine image is to be found, but that women as well as men are made in the image of God. The great dignity which God bestows on people is not limited to the male. In this, the greatest gift which we possess, there is no distinction between male and female. What we have here is not an assertion that the sexes are complementary in their relations with each other, but that they are equal in their relationship to God.

There are other difficulties with this line of thought, apart from its treatment of scripture and its break with tradition. If people are in the image of God as members of complementary pairs, that implies that nobody is in the image of God in his or her own right as an individual. That is not only somewhat paradoxical, but also contradicts scripture itself. Genesis 5.1 asserts that God made the individual man Adam in his image,[21] and St Paul, using Adam typology, calls Christ himself 'the image of the invisible God, the firstborn of all creation' (Col. 1.15).

On these grounds the theory that interprets our being in the image of God with our having sexual complementarity is not acceptable. However, at least in the form in which it is present in the CDF's *Letter*, it is an attempt to take seriously the idea that we are 'called to reflect the inner unity of the Creator'.[22] There is surely something right in the idea that we are called to reflect the inner unity of God. For that is just what Christ prays to the Father may come about. According to John, at the Last Supper he prays:

> Holy Father, keep them in thy name, which thou hast given me, that they may be one, even as we are one... The glory which thou hast given me I have given to them, that they may be one even as we are one, I in them and thou in me, that they may become perfectly one, so that the world may know that thou hast sent me and hast loved them even as thou hast loved me (17.11, 22f.).

The unity that Christ is talking about here is the unity of love. That is the unity that subsists between the Father and Jesus, and it is the unity that is to bind the disciples together, and ultimately all people. This is the divine unity that we are called upon to imitate and image in our lives together. If this is what the *Letter* means, it is surely right. But once again, the idea of sexual complementarity has dropped away. Indeed, this union of love is one that is supposed to join together all the disciples, regardless of sex, regardless of sexual difference or sameness. This way in which we are all called to reflect the inner unity of God has nothing to do, either, with sexual activity. The unity of God is not the unity of sexual union, and sexual union has nothing to do with the unity of Christians either, except in the special case of a marriage, which I shall examine in the next chapter.

Fecundity

But before going on to marriage I want to say a few words about fecundity in the context of sex, for it is that fecundity that is one of the major considerations behind the Christian insistence that sexual love be confined to marriage. Love is often seen in the Christian tradition as creative, as bringing to fruition things that were before only latent, or even as bringing into being something out of nothing. It may look not only as if the ability of a sexual relationship between a man and a woman sometimes to result in the creation of new life in a child makes a sexual relationship an especially appropriate expression of creative Christian love, but also as if the essentially fruitful nature of sexual intercourse bound it specifically to marriage. Of course in the context of a loving Christian marriage the birth of a child may well be seen by the parents and by others as God's blessing and gift to them and a sign of the creativity of true love, its fruit; certainly, that is the belief of the church, which will encourage them to see the child in this light.

But once again all depends on context. Just as sexual activity is an expression of love not 'in itself' but only in the context of a relationship of love, so children are the fruit of love only if they are generated in a context of love. This is certainly a view that is found in a number of places in scripture. As an example from the Old Testament, Psalm 128 says:

Blessed is every one who fears the Lord, who walks in his ways! ...
Your wife will be like a fruitful vine within your house; your children will be like
    olive shoots around your table ...
May you see your children's children! Peace be upon Israel! (vv.1,3,6).

Here children are part of the good life that the man who fears the Lord enjoys as his blessing. But note that children are a blessing precisely in the life of one who fears the Lord. The children of one who does not fear the Lord are not a blessing, and are not talked about in terms of fertility and fecundity. The book of Wisdom goes so far as to say that illicit sex will not be blessed with being creative, with children, or that if children do result they will come to no good:

But children of adulterers will not come to maturity, and the offspring of an
unlawful union will perish. Even if they live long they will be held of no account
... For the end of an unrighteous generation is grievous. Better than this is
childlessness with virtue, for in the memory of virtue is immortality, because it is
known both by God and by men (3.16–4.1).

We should also remember that in scripture fecundity, bearing fruit, was something that pervaded the faithful person's whole life. It was not confined to having children, and in the picture of a fruitful life children sometimes did not feature at all. For example, Psalm 92:

The righteous flourish like the palm tree, and grow like a cedar in Lebanon.
They are planted in the house of the Lord, they flourish in the courts of our God.
They still bring forth fruit in old age, they are ever full of sap and green
    (vv.12–14).

This appears not to be about bearing children, for the righteous are old. It is rather that they are still alive, well and vital. This, as opposed to the wicked, who spring up like grass and perish quickly (v.7).

    Fruitfulness in the Old Testament is, then, very much a matter of people's lives, not of their physical fecundity – even if this latter was often seen as symbolic of the former. The book of Wisdom explicitly emphasizes this spiritual fruitfulness by talking of the fruit of the childless:

Blessed is the barren woman who is undefiled, who has not entered into a sinful
union; she will have fruit when God examines souls ... Blessed also is the eunuch
whose hands have done no lawless deed, and who has not devised wicked things

against the Lord; for special favour will be shown him for his faithfulness, and a place of great delight in the temple of the Lord. For the fruit of good labours is renowned, and the root of understanding does not fail (3.13–15).

When we come to the New Testament, fruit is talked of almost entirely in spiritual terms: people's fruits are their deeds, the kind of lives they lead. Think of the parable of the sower, in which those who hear the word and persevere bear much fruit;[23] the Epistle to the Galatians, where the fruit of the Spirit is love, joy, peace, patience, kindness, goodness (5.19); John the Baptist tells his hearers to bear fruits that befit repentance.[24] James writes of 'the wisdom from above... full of mercy and good fruits'; and of 'the harvest of righteousness... sown in peace by those who make peace' (3.17f.); and so on. None of these refer to having children as a kind of fruitfulness.

So in the Christian scriptural vision fecundity is neither confined to sex nor is sex even an essential part of it; sex is fruitful only in the context of a life which is already fruitful in virtue. That is to say, sex is not fruitful in a Christian sense simply by virtue of the biological fact that it sometimes results in children. It is fruitful only in the context of a fruitful life. It does not of its nature, as fertile, demand to be part of a fertile loving relationship; on the contrary, it is such a relationship that makes it fertile. Thus Paul VI writes of married love: 'This love is fecund for it is not exhausted by the communion between husband and wife, but is destined to continue, raising up new lives'.[25] Here the fecundity of marriage is not merely biological, the physical ability of the two partners to produce children. It is their love which is fecund. So a Christian marriage, or any loving marriage, in which there are no children is by no means to be thought of as sterile. Christian fecundity is not the same as biological fertility. Hence also Bernard Häring says:

> Sexuality that is not integrated in mutual love is alienating and alienated. If it is activated only for the biological purpose of fertility it will remain most vulnerable to all kinds of abuses, to the exercise of power over the other, or to base sex appeal.[26]

In the Christian vision reproductive capacity is subordinated to relational significance; it is symbolic of the fecundity of the union in love, rather than constituting it. It is above all life that is fruitful, the life of somebody who is turned towards God, full of love, joy, peace, etc., the life of one who lives in accordance with his or her nature and who therefore, given favourable circumstances, flourishes and is able to nourish the life of others. We might say that the birth of a child is the fruit of a couple's sexual activity; but it is a different thing to say that it is the fruit or fruitfulness of those people. It can only be the latter if they do indeed lead fruitful lives. So what is important is that human beings be fruitful, lead fruitful lives, rather than that their sexual activity be fruitful in the sense that it results in children. Though children will often be part of the fruit of a Christian couple's sexual activity, it is more important that they are part of the fruit of that couple's life together.

In this, Christianity is at one with a common way of speaking about human fruitfulness, which recognizes that it is a very various thing. While, quite apart from Christianity, we may think of producing children as an obviously basic form of human fruitfulness, we recognize things like art and virtue as human fruits, fruits of human living. Thus we talk metaphorically of novels gestating, of symphonies being conceived, of the fertility of somebody's imagination, and so on. Since these usages are metaphorical it might be argued that these other forms of fecundity are not so basic as producing children. But then, it belongs to human living to create things that are not basic. Such things are not inferior, but if anything more essentially human. Pregnancy and giving birth may be archetypal images of fruitfulness in human activity,[27] but that does not testify to their greater value, nor does it show other kinds of creativity to be somehow second-class or substitutes. On the contrary, the use of this archetype testifies to the plurality of truly valuable things, of ways of being creative and fruitful. It can only become an archetype because there are other things whose value we want to express. It is just because these other things are so valuable in their own right that we want to talk about them in this way.

Since human fruitfulness is so various, the possibility arises that human sexual activity can contribute to that fruitfulness in various ways, and not just through procreation. Of specifically Christian interest is the question what part a person's sex life plays in producing virtue. If what a person does sexually makes him more loving, generous and considerate, then his sex life is genuinely fruitful in a Christian sense, even though it may never result in children, and even though it be of a type that could never do so. I am thinking here of things like masturbation, homosexual intercourse and heterosexual intercourse between partners one of whom is sterile. To raise the question is not to answer it. It can and has been argued that such practices can in certain circumstances make people's lives more fruitful in a Christian sense, and that they are therefore in such circumstances good. On the other hand, it can and has been argued, against the first two at least, that they are inadmissible because they do not foster people's development in virtue but of their nature tend to make virtue wither. But the question of their potential fruitfulness must form a large part of the debate on whether indeed such practices are or can be good. There may be *a priori* reasons why we might expect it to be answered in one way or another, but it is basically an empirical question; we need to find out by observation whether homosexuals and people who masturbate are all less virtuous than they otherwise might be, or whether in the lives of some they actually contribute to their ability to love others.

Flourishing

The verses of Psalm 92 that I quoted earlier bring together the ideas of fruitfulness and of flourishing: The righteous flourish like the palm tree, they flourish in the courts of God; they still bring forth fruit in old age, they are ever full of sap and green. The same connexion is made in a number of places in scripture, such as in Psalm 1, where the one who meditates on the law of the Lord is like a tree planted beside streams of water, whose foliage does not wither and which gives its fruit in its season. There is, at the level of this metaphor, a plain relationship between flourishing and fruitfulness: it is the flourishing tree, the vital tree, that brings forth fruit. There is also an obvious aptness to the metaphor, from the biblical point of view. Fruit, which shows the vitality of the tree, is at the same time for others. Others eat of the fruit; it is *for* them to eat.[28] It is what is yielded for another to feed on; it has the quality of a gift that enhances life. Applying the metaphor to people, human beings flourish when they give fruit for others, fruit that others can live from; they flourish when they live in such a way as to enhance the life of others. That is to say, they flourish when they love; for, as Genovesi says: 'When I truly love another, I desire not only to be *with* my loved one, but also to be and live *for* him or her.'[29] Flourishing and loving go together.

8

Sex and Marriage

In this chapter I want to say a little about Christian views on the place of sex within marriage. I am not going to talk about marriage in general, but only about sex in its relation to marriage. This in itself is still a large topic, and my treatment is bound to be partial. What I want to do is to make some remarks that largely follow the lines I have been pursuing in previous chapters. I have argued first that our bodies are loaded with significance by the society in which we live. The structures and distinctions that are important in the social body tend to find expression in the physical bodies of the members of society. Secondly, I argued the complementary point that the meaning of what we do with our bodies, the description of what we do as human act, is dependent on the context within which we act. Though our bodies are naturally highly expressive, we have to look around the body, at the context, to see just what is being expressed. Bodily movements or gestures do not in general have meaning in and of themselves, regardless of context, and that includes sexual gestures. Nevertheless, shared sex does have a kind of natural meaning, since it has a natural context. It is at home within a loving relationship, as the natural physical metaphor for personal intimacy, and if it takes place outside such a setting it loses a meaning that belongs to it. If the Christian view is that sexual activity is properly the expression of love, this is a conclusion as it were read off from the nature of the act, and an insistence that sexual activity take place within the framework of a loving relationship, a close friendship, follows naturally from it. But Christians have generally gone further than this: the normal insistence has been that this friendship be of the kind we call marriage, a friendship between a man and a woman in which they are committed to an intimate and permanent sharing of their lives.

This restriction cannot, I think, be derived by an extension of the kind of argument developed in chapter 6. I argued there that physical intimacy is naturally expressive of personal closeness. It is tempting to go on to say that degrees of physical intimacy express degrees of personal closeness, and that therefore the greatest possible physical intimacy, sexual intercourse, belongs naturally in the context of the greatest personal unity. And that is a life-long, indissoluble sharing of life, a marriage. But this does not seem to work. Principally, it simply does not appear true that degrees of physical intimacy naturally express degrees of personal closeness. Though it may be true that enemies naturally tend to stay apart and friends to gravitate towards each other and perhaps make certain kinds of physical contact, there seems to be no natural scale of physical contact between friends according to the strength of their friendship. On the one hand, the amount and kind of physical contact encouraged or allowed between friends seems to be largely culturally determined and highly variable. On the other hand, many non-married people, including some couples who are not committed to each other for life, and including homosexual couples, do think that sexual expression of their friendship has a natural place in their relationship; it comes naturally to them to unite sexually, even though they are not themselves permanently united, and that not out of sheer *libido* but to express their love for each other.

The Christian restriction of sex to marriage does not, then, appear derivable from human nature and the nature of sex itself. To say that sexual intercourse has one particular meaning and therefore can only legitimately or honestly take place within the friendship that is marriage is, I would suggest, to put things the wrong way round. Christians have not discovered that sex is, necessarily, possessed of a meaning and significance that confine it to marriage, and responded to this discovery by insisting that sex be so confined. Rather has sexual activity been given the very particular significance it has for Christians by being confined among them to marriage. It is easy to see how the mechanism of restriction gives an activity an enhanced significance. For actions to signify, there must be contrast. What I do has meaning because I don't do it all the time, in all circumstances. If my having sex with somebody means something, that is because I don't have sex with just anybody.[1] And the more restricted my sexual activity the more important it is to me when I do actually have sex with somebody. Conversely, the less discriminating my sexual activity, the less it means to me that I have sex with just this person, and the less having sex with any one person expresses. Some years ago there was a slogan: 'Make love, not war.' More sexual coupling was meant to bring people closer together, because of the significance of coupling. But it did not have this effect. As with any activity, the more indiscriminate coupling becomes the less significant it becomes; it did not, in those circles where the slogan was put into practice, signify closeness any more. Closeness is not just sexual coupling, but what was supposed to be signified by it. It involves a certain sharing of life, not just of bed: doing things together, making decisions together, being available to help each other, etc. It presupposes a context in the rest of life; or it signifies the initiation of such a context. And you just cannot share your life closely with that many people.

The Christian insistence that sex be limited to marriage has made sex into a highly expressive range of activities. Christianity has partly created bodily significance, not merely registered it. To a certain extent, in confining sex to marriage Christians have simply taken over existing and prevalent attitudes of the ancient world: the Stoic suspicion of pleasure and emphasis on reproductive purpose, the Jewish horror of homosexuality, the institution of marriage and general disapproval of extramarital sex, and so on. Nevertheless, in making this insistence, and in discouraging other sexual phenomena like premarital intercourse, masturbation, homosexual relations and so on, Christians have given sexual activity a significance much heightened beyond the natural expressiveness discussed in chapter 6. Sex, placed firmly within the context of marriage, has a created, symbolic significance within the Christian system. The following remarks on sex within marriage will therefore have a more theological character than much of what I have said hitherto.

Marriage has not always been held in the highest esteem by Christians. The earliest New Testament writer, St Paul, had some very interesting things to say about it, to which I shall return later. But it is plain he also considered it very much a second-best option. Most of his remarks on marriage are in I Corinthians 7. He himself seems to have been unmarried, and he writes to the church in Corinth:

It is well for a man not to touch a woman (7.1).

And a few verses later:

I wish that all were as I am. But each has his own special gift from God, one of one kind and one of another. To the unmarried and the widows I say that it is well for them to remain as I am.[2] But if they cannot exercise self-control, they should marry. For it is better to marry than to burn.[3]

There seems to be no really positive vision of marriage here. It is simply a remedy for the heat of sexual desire. Paul's idea of marriage as expressed in this chapter is not total mutual self-giving, or anything similar. It is an institution that allows two people to cool their passions together. Paul's opinion here is perhaps influenced by his belief, expressed later in the chapter, that 'the form of this world is passing away'.[4] It is not worth getting married in order to have children, for as likely as not the world will end before they are born. The imminence of the end also makes a single-minded devotion to the things of God very desirable, but being married means you have to be distracted by looking after the interests and needs of your spouse:

The unmarried man is anxious about the affairs of the Lord, how to please the Lord; but the married man is anxious about worldly affairs, how to please his wife, and his interests are divided. And the unmarried woman or girl is anxious about the affairs of the Lord, how to be holy in body and spirit; but the married woman is anxious about worldly affairs, how to please her husband (7.32–34).

The opposition between being anxious about the affairs of a spouse and being anxious about the affairs of God may seem odd to us; surely, to show loving concern for somebody is to be concerned for the things of God. Be that as it may, it is plain that Paul's view of the relative undesirability of marriage is not based entirely on these considerations. It is primarily a matter of its being better not to need sex in the first place, not to suffer from this burning. Here we see perhaps the influence of the Stoic ideal of *apatheia*, lack of passion or suffering. But he does at least not enjoin celibacy. He recognizes that some people do suffer from sexual desire that needs must be fulfilled, and so gives a place to marriage in Christian living. But note that the sole reason he gives for getting married is related to sex. There is no notion of two people marrying in order to share their lives in a union of love, or to have children.

Augustine on marriage

I will come back to Paul later, but I want now to say a few words about Augustine, whose influence on later thought about marriage was immense. In his treatise *On the Good of Marriage* he distinguishes three reasons why people might legitimately be married, three 'goods' of marriage: *fides*, *proles*, and *sacramentum*; fidelity, children and the bond or sacrament.[5] All of these are related in some way or other to sex. *Proles*, offspring, are a good, and, obviously, sexual intercourse is necessary to produce them, however regrettable that may be. And for Augustine it is regrettable. Remember that for him sexual intercourse involves the triumph of the flesh over the mind, and it is the good of children alone that can justify sex. The good of offspring is, however, dispensable. There are already plenty of people around, many of them having children, so that the continuation of human society, which is the point of having children, is ensured.[6] Even married couples do better, therefore, if by mutual consent they abstain totally from sexual intercourse as soon as possible:

> The better they are, the more quickly they have begun by mutual consent to restrain themselves from carnal intercourse; not that it should later be a matter of necessity not be able to do what they want, but that it should be a matter of praise for them at the beginning not to want to do what they could.[7]

All sexual activity must be undertaken for the purpose of reproduction if it is to avoid being sinful. However, Augustine does know that this is not how people actually work. He recognizes that people will have sex just because they enjoy it, or to relieve sexual desire, without procreative intent.

To seek sex for such reasons is sinful, mortally so in the unmarried, but only slightly in the married. If it does happen that one partner in a marriage seeks intercourse just out of desire, then it is the duty of the other partner to give them satisfaction, and in doing so the other partner does not sin. On the contrary, to perform this duty is the good of *fides*, being faithful in rendering service to one's spouse and so preserving his or her fidelity to the requirement of sexual exclusiveness. The spouses' doing this for each other saves them from falling into mortally sinful adultery. So though in Augustine's eyes virginity is a higher state than marriage, and though continence is preferable to intercourse, yet this *fides* is a higher value than continence.[8]

The *sacramentum* or bond is what makes the relationship permanent. The first two goods of marriage are common to all people, but this third good is proper to Christians. In the people of God, the good of marriage also involves

> the sanctity of the sacrament, through which it is unlawful for a divorced woman to marry another man while her husband still lives, even for the sake of having children. Although it is the sole reason for marrying, not even when children do not follow upon the marriage ... is the bond of marriage loosed except by the death of the husband.[9]

There is of course in Augustine's view much more to the relationship of husband and wife than sex. There is a sharing in the responsibility of bringing up the children[10] and the mutual society and love of the spouses.[11] Yet what the sacramental bond does is not to preserve that mutual society and shared responsibility; as Augustine recognizes, there may be cases where unfortunately that is not permanent. But what the bond does is to forbid the partners to have sexual intercourse with anybody else while both are still living, even though everything else has dissolved, even though the partners may be divorced and have no shared life at all.

All three of Augustine's goods of marriage, then, are related to the sexual relations of the marriage partners. But they are, for all that, goods of marriage, not of sexual intercourse within marriage. For Augustine sexual intercourse has only one good, offspring. It was not until the nineteenth century, in Catholic circles, that what he says came to be widely applied to sexual intercourse itself. Only then did sex between marriage partners come to be seen as having values apart from offspring, namely the values of expressing fidelity and the sacramental bond. To say this is to indicate how important and long-term the influence of Augustine's analysis of marriage as having these three goods has been in the church. It was not used by the Second Vatican Council, but as late as 1930 Pius XI in his encyclical *Casti Connubii* bases his whole treatment of marriage on it.[12] So it is largely as a sexual relationship that marriage has been understood in the Christian tradition. Sex has been made central to and symbolic of marriage. This has entered into the way sex is talked of by Christians. Sexual intercourse is referred to sometimes as 'the marriage act',[13] or 'the use of matrimony'.[14] We speak too of sexual intercourse as 'consummating' marriage.

This view of sex as central to marriage is not confined to Christians. If one man asks another: 'Have you been faithful to your wife?' we all know what he means. The question is equivalent to 'Have you preserved sexual exclusivity with your wife?' Fidelity between two people means many things: being with each other, looking after each other's interests, keeping confidences, protecting and supporting each other, and so on. But people are not generally asking about these things when they ask whether somebody else has been faithful to his wife. And we regard it as unfaithful for a married man to have sex with a woman he is not married to, whereas we do not normally regard it as infidelity if he plays tennis or has tea with her, unless we think these innocent activities are leading somewhere. It is not that the other things are regarded as unimportant, but that we make sexual exclusiveness symbolic of marital fidelity. It need not be so and has not always been so. Today there are 'open' marriages in which, so it is said, the partners feel free to have sexual relations with other people. Are people who do not accord sexual activity this symbolic status missing something? If the church makes sex so central to the idea of marriage, is there any particular reason for it?

Marital rights

To attempt a very tentative answer I want to go back to look at I Corinthians 7. Paul says:

> Each man should have his own wife and each woman her own husband. The husband should give his wife what is due,[15] and likewise the wife to her husband. For the wife does not rule over her own body, but the husband does; likewise the husband does not rule over his own body, but the wife does. Do not refuse one another except perhaps by agreement for a season, that you may devote yourselves to prayer; but then come together again lest Satan tempt you through lack of self-control (1.2–5).

This passage reminds us that as far as Paul is concerned marriage is only for those who lack self-control, but it also introduces the notion of the husband and wife having rights over each other, exercising control over each other, evidently sexual rights and control. This is the basis of what Augustine says when, talking of the good of *fides* in marriage, he speaks of the duty of the spouses to give each other sexual service, even when there is no procreative intent in intercourse. It is the idea of what came to be called the marriage debt. It looks at first sight a peculiarly legalistic idea, rather cold, far removed from the concern for love which is so central to the modern

Christian conception of sex and marriage. If we are looking for a starting point from which to talk about the rationale of Christian views on sex in marriage, this one does not at first sight look very promising. But it actually says something important.

First of all we should note that this arrangement is mutual. It places the spouses on the same level. As we saw in chapter 3, much sexual activity and talk of sex expresses male superiority in society, the domination of women by men. The general talk of the male as active and the female as passive in sexual intercourse is a modern example of this. There is a similar way of thinking reflected in Old Testament law. I tried to show that the law forbidding a man to lie with a man as with a woman is a piece of legislation expressing and protecting male social superiority. This superiority was tacitly accepted, or at least remains unchallenged, in Jesus' teaching about adultery in the heart in Matthew 5. What is wrong with looking at a married woman in order to covet her is not that it is an internal sin, damaging the unseen heart of the sinner, but that it infringes the rights of the woman's husband. It is not for the sake of brevity that there is no similar mention of the evils of a woman's looking lustfully at a man. Rather does it reflect the current situation of inequality in Jewish society, in which the husband had rights over his wife which the wife did not have over her husband.[16] When Paul gives the man and the woman equal sexual rights in marriage he is making use of the close connexion between bodily behaviour and society. The sexual equality of men and women in this regard is an expression of the social equality that he sees as central to the gospel. For him, 'there is neither Jew nor Greek, there is neither slave nor free, there is neither male nor female; for you are all one in Christ Jesus' (Gal. 3.28).

This emphasis on the equality of rights of the partners in marriage is not peculiar to Paul. In Matthew 5.27f. Jesus seems to look at things from the point of view only of the rights of the husband, and the succeeding verses too reflect a situation of male superiority. But they also begin to introduce an importantly different note. He says:

> It was also said: 'Whoever divorces his wife, let him give her a certificate of divorce.' But I say to you that every one who divorces his wife, except on the ground of unchastity, makes her an adulteress; and whoever marries a divorced woman commits adultery.[17]

The words of Jesus as given by Matthew presuppose a situation in which a man may divorce his wife but a woman may not divorce her husband.[18] But now Jesus says that this right, which is accorded men in Jewish society and by the law of Moses, is not to be exercised; men have in fact no such right to get rid of their wives, just as wives have no right to get rid of their husbands. A woman is not to be thought of as analogous to a chattel, as disposable. A man is not to have this kind of superior position with respect to his wife.

This thought is amplified in Matthew 19, where Jesus answers the Pharisees' question: 'Is it lawful to divorce one's wife for any cause?' Jesus' answer begins:

> Have you not read that he who made them from the beginning made them male and female, and said: 'For this reason a man shall leave his father and mother and be joined to his wife, and the two shall become one flesh'? (19.4–6a).

The next part of his reply is normally translated 'What therefore God has joined together, let not man put asunder,' and interpreted as a teaching on the permanence and indissolubility of marriage. There is in fact not much doubt that Jesus did indeed believe in and teach the indissolubility of marriage. Whenever he is recorded as speaking of divorce he speaks against it. And in I Corinthians, one of the earliest documents of the church, Paul says:

> To the married I give charge, not I but the Lord, that the wife should not separate from her husband (but if she does, let her remain single or else be reconciled to her husband) – and that the husband should not divorce his wife (7.10f.).

However, it is not clear that this is all that is going on in this part of Matthew 19. The word translated 'man' in 'let not man put asunder' is *anthrōpos*. This is the ordinary word for 'human being', and that is how it is normally taken here, so that Jesus' words are interpreted as saying that God's authority is greater than that of any human being. But *anthrōpos* occurs twice in this passage, apart from this verse, in verses 3[19] and 5 – the latter being the quotation from Genesis. It also occurs in verse 10 in the supplementary dialogue between Jesus and his disciples about the desirability or otherwise of getting married. In each case it is apparent that *anthrōpos* refers to the male, either as such or as husband. So that is the likely meaning in verse 6 too. Probably, *anthrōpos* does not there mean man in general, the species, or a human being, but a man, a male. The prohibition appears to be, not on the dissolution of a marriage, but on a man's divorcing his wife. This seems implied too from the context, which is a discussion of the conditions under which a man may divorce his wife.[20] Hence Jesus' teaching is again about what a man may do with his wife, and is aimed at protecting the wife. She is not to be regarded as for any reason disposable. She is not the property of the man, but his partner. Jesus' emphasis on the permanence and indissolubility of marriage here has the effect of giving security to married women, who might otherwise find themselves divorced at any time, and for any reason.[21] This was at the time a matter of great practical importance. At the time women were economically totally dependent on their husbands. To be divorced could mean suffering not only rejection but also indigence. Jesus goes on to say that 'whoever divorces his wife, except for unchastity, and marries another, commits adultery' (v.9). The adultery the man commits when he divorces his wife and marries another woman is a matter of injustice to his first wife, treating her as if she were a disposable possession. It is not only the man who has rights in a marriage, but his wife also.

This is a significant thing to say in itself. In the Old Testament, to commit adultery was to commit a sin against one of the partners in a marriage, an infringement of rights. Both men and women could commit adultery, but only men could have adultery committed against them. The Hebrew verb 'to commit adultery' is *n'p*. From the use of this verb in the Old Testament[22] it can be seen that the adultery of men is always breaking somebody else's marriage bond, while the adultery of women is always breaking their own marriage bond.[23] The offence is always against a husband, never against a wife. A man's having sexual relations outside the bounds of his own marriage does not count as adultery, and neither is the woman he has relations with guilty of adultery, unless she herself happens to be married. Being married puts a legal restraint on a woman as regards her sexual behaviour, but there is no corresponding legal restraint placed on a married man; he has only to respect the marriage rights of other men. When Jesus says that a man who divorces his wife and marries another commits adultery he is overturning this Old Testament point of view. He is saying not only that a marriage is not dissoluble by decree of the husband, but that a man can commit adultery by breaking his own marriage bond. He can sin not only by infringing the marital rights of another man but also by infringing those of his wife. So in all this Jesus is not giving a teaching about the abstract indissolubility of marriage, regardless of the good of the partners to the marriage. He is not, for instance, saying that if a marriage goes wrong both partners must suffer. What he is concerned to do here is prevent suffering for women and to assert the equality of the partners in a marriage. Like Paul, he sees the sexual activities, rights and duties of the partners as a place where this equality is to be expressed.

Paul again

To return to Paul, and his idea of partners in a marriage exercising authority over each other's body. The word that Paul uses here is a strong one, *exousiazō*. It means to dominate, have power over. It is the same word that Luke uses when he reports Jesus' words:

> The kings of the Gentiles exercise lordship over (*kurieuousi*) them; and those in authority over (*exousiazontes*) them are called benefactors. But not so with you.[24]

It is a matter of being at liberty to do things, holding a position of superiority over inferiors. This is exactly what is not to happen among Christians, according to the gospels. They are not to dominate each other, or have power over each other, but serve each other. Christians have a liberty which no other Christian can take away from them. This Christian liberty is a strong theme in Paul himself. He says to the Galatians: 'For freedom Christ has set us free; stand fast therefore, and do not submit again to a yoke of slavery' (Gal. 5.1). In I Corinthians the theme is no less prominent. He quotes the Corinthians' own claim to freedom and tries to get them to recognize some of the depth of their own words: ' "All things are lawful for me," but not all things are helpful. "All things are lawful for me," but I will not be enslaved by anything' (I Cor. 6.12).

The word translated 'are lawful' here is *exesti*, which is closely related to *exousiazō*; what is lawful for you is what you have the power, authority or right to do. The word translated 'enslaved' is the passive of *exousiazō*, 'be dominated'. Though the Corinthians rightly say that they are free, that they have authority to do what they want, not all things that they might do are helpful to them in their Christian lives; though they have power to do what they want, let them be careful that the things over which they have power do not end up having power over them.

What we have in chapter 7, then, is a rather startling turnaround. From insisting, in line with the Gospels and with most of his own thought, that Christians have authority over everything and are to be dominated by nobody and nothing, Paul now says that a married man is not to have authority even over his own body, which is to be dominated by his wife. Similarly, a married woman has not even the freedom of her own body, but her husband is to have authority over it. How are we to explain this?

What is involved in somebody else having rights over your body? Other people certainly have authority over us: our employers, the police, various officials in various places, all have the right to tell us, up to a point, what to do, to demand certain things of us. But they do not have the right to make use of our bodies. Their authority and rights over us stop short at the boundaries of our body, and normally some way short. To make free with somebody's body, in whatever way, is to assert and express complete domination. If a policeman tells you to move on or asks you what you are doing here, he may just be doing his job. But if he moves too close or if he starts prodding you he is showing you that he has you in his power, and he is therefore humiliating you. The technique of making prisoners strip naked or herding them together to rob them of space around their bodies has the same effect. So also one of the ways we can most effectively lord it over somebody, humiliate him or her, is sexually. It is a standard feature of human relations that men rape women, captors rape their captives of either sex and prisoners rape other prisoners, again of either sex, and that all of these also exercise sexual authority in other ways as a way of expressing dominion. To do this sort of thing to others is significant. It is not just to exercise power – any giving of orders will do that. It is to express your contempt for them and your delight in dominating them; it is, metaphorically, to tell them that you have power over them, that you are master and they are servants, that in relation to you they do not rule even over their own bodies. And that is to rob them of their dignity; if a human being is to be respected, that involves at least his having the disposal of his own body under his own control and the space around his body not infringed. Indeed it seems to belong to the idea of human agency that people have control of their own bodies. While a human act, as I said in chapter 6, is not identical with a bodily movement but also has a large contextual element, most human acts at least involve some kind of bodily movement.[25] To take away somebody's freedom to move, either by physically binding or by binding with authority, is to deprive them of the power of acting, to deprive them of the status of independent human agent. The slave is simply an extension of his master, dominated by and acting according to his will. But now Paul is saying precisely that to married men and women: that in relation to each other they do not even have power over their own bodies.

We are all used to the idea of letting somebody else have the use of our bodies in sex, or indeed inviting them; it can be a liberating and enjoyable thing to do, and allowing somebody else the freedom of your body can be a sign of close friendship. But what Paul is saying is that a married woman does not let her husband have the freedom of her body; he has it as of right. Now if this were a matter of just one partner having power over the other, it would be intolerable, a complete negation of Christianity. But it works both ways; the wife also has the free use of her husband's body, as of right. This means that there can be no domination; while both serve the other, neither lords it over the other. Neither of them is deprived of his or her freedom in this mutual submission. This service is freely given; it does not come from being enslaved but from love. Hence this rather legalistic sounding dictum of Paul's makes the sexual partnership of marriage into an expression of the loving mutual service and the rejection of domination that are central to the gospel. Though marriage may seem for Paul to be only a way of coping with the burning of sexual desire, the way it is to be coped with is significant.

Sexual desire is not, for instance, to be appeased by going to a prostitute. Paul is very clear about this in a passage in I Corinthians 6, and his reasons for ruling out resort to prostitutes are illuminating. He writes:

> Do you not know that your bodies are members of Christ? Shall I therefore take the members of Christ and make them members of a prostitute? Never! Do you not know that he who joins himself to a prostitute becomes one body with her? For, as it is written, 'The two shall become one flesh.' But he who is united to the Lord becomes one spirit with him (I Cor. 6.15–17).

To bring out the force of what Paul is saying here I must first say something about the biblical use of the word 'flesh'. Flesh in the Old Testament does not for the most part mean the squashy stuff out of which people are mostly made.[26] It can mostly be translated 'body'. It is first of all the human being considered as body. In the Psalms, phrases like 'my flesh rejoices' are equivalent to 'I rejoice', except perhaps that they draw attention to the bodily nature of this rejoicing – the shouting, dancing, clapping and so on, that constitute it. When deutero-Isaiah says: 'The glory of the Lord shall be revealed, and all flesh shall see it together,' (Isa. 40.5) he means that everybody, all people, will see it. By extension, 'flesh' can mean a social body. The words of Genesis, 'They become one flesh,' do not mean that two people's squashy bits coalesce, or that the two stick together, or that they become one person, but that they form a social body, a new one where none existed before. The man leaves father and mother, an already existing social body, oneness of flesh, to create a new one with his wife. Here we can compare trito-Isaiah:

> Is not this the fast that I choose: to loose the bonds of wickedness, to undo the thongs of the yoke, to let the oppressed go free, and to break every yoke? Is it not to share your bread with the hungry, and bring the homeless poor into your house; when you see the naked, to cover him, and not to hide yourself from your own flesh?[27]

Here 'your own flesh' means another member of the social body to which you belong. The fast of God is not to hide yourself from one to whom you belong, a member of the same body, but to cover the naked, to hide the flesh of the physical body of that member.

In Paul, the word 'flesh' can sometimes have quite different overtones. It is often a bad thing. He contrasts being in the flesh with being in the spirit (Rom. 8.9). He says in Galatians:

> You were called to freedom, brethren; only do not use your freedom as an opportunity for the flesh, but through love be servants of one another. For the whole law is fulfilled in one word: 'You shall love your neighbour as yourself.' But if you bite and devour one another take heed that you are not consumed by one another (5.15f.).

Using freedom as an opportunity for the flesh is opposed to serving one another in love. 'The flesh' for Paul is again not the squashy stuff of which we are made, nor is it, as it became for Augustine, particularly associated with sex; it is that which works against love. Thus the list of works of the flesh that follows contains, to be sure, fornication, but also enmity, envy, selfishness and the like, while the contrasting list of the fruit of the Spirit speaks of love, joy, peace, patience, and so on.

Let us turn now to I Cor 6.16: 'Do you not know that he who joins himself to a prostitute becomes one body with her? For, as it is written: "The two shall become one flesh." ' Paul is almost certainly talking here about having sexual intercourse with a prostitute for money (not about marrying one, which is what Genesis 2.24 has in view). In linking this with Genesis 2.24 he is extending the scope of that verse. In Genesis it is only man and wife who become one flesh, not man and prostitute; the becoming one flesh is taking on the unity of a shared life, a good thing which a man precisely does not have with a prostitute. In asking his readers whether they know that in having sexual intercourse with a prostitute they become one body with her he is certainly not asking them whether they know that in having sexual intercourse with a prostitute their bodies are physically linked together. Rather is he saying that such sexual intercourse is symbolic of or effects a parody or reversal of the unity of a shared life which a man and his wife enjoy. The unity that the man buys into here is not a sharing of life but the sharing of a way of life which keeps people apart, living according to the flesh, which means living in ways opposed to love; he is perhaps here drawing attention particularly to how the flesh depersonalizes, makes people into commodities.[28] This becoming one flesh is a bad thing, and Paul opposes it to becoming one spirit with Christ (I Cor. 6.17). Sex with a prostitute is a bad thing for Paul because he places such activity, and asks his readers to see it, in the context of the life of the flesh, as expressive of a way of living which they have been called to abandon. It is a bad thing because it expresses not the love to which the disciples are called in Christ but rather solidarity with everything that is opposed to that love. And remember that that love is above all a social love, the love that builds a society that can be perfected in the coming of the kingdom.[29]

In contrast to sex between a man and a prostitute, which expresses solidarity with the world of the flesh, that way of life which is opposed to the spirit, the way Christian partners are to relate to each other sexually is a bodily expression of the way all Christians are to relate to each other in the body of Christ. The sexual union of the marriage partners is to be a physical expression of the union of love which binds together all believers. Of course that union of love includes the partners themselves. They owe each other a debt of love (Rom. 13.8) before they owe each other their bodies. This love will be expressed in the rest of their lives together in the way they do things together, care for each other, put themselves at each other's disposal, and so on. That is to say, they will also be friends. We can expect that this friendship will contribute to the quality of the sexual activities they share, as I tried to indicate in chapter 4. As I showed then, it's better anyway with a friend, and the more they like each other, the more they can actually enjoy doing this precisely with each other. Conversely, if the partners cease to be friends, we can expect their sex life together to suffer, if not to cease. The cooling of the relationship may be expressed in a physical drawing apart, a cooling of physical desire for each other, the distancing of the partners in the distancing of their bodies. It is when the friendship goes or is under strain that we may also expect other sexual trouble, like adultery. On the whole adultery seems to be not something that brings trouble into a marriage so much as a sign that it is already deeply disturbed. If that is so, it is not difficult to see why. Adultery, in a context where sexual activity has been invested with great significance, must itself be a significant act. If you have promised somebody, a friend, sexual exclusivity, to break that promise is, like breaking any promise, an unfriendly or hostile act, a sign therefore that the friendship is not what it was.[30] That is, the fault is not necessarily to be looked for in the uncontrollable lust of the adulterer but in the quality of the non-sexual relations between the marriage partners, and the remedy, if there is one, to be found in the repair of those relations.

In Genesis 2 it is said that when a man goes off and finds his wife the two become one flesh. As I said above this does not mean that they have sexual intercourse. It means that they form a new social unit, come to share their lives, take on special responsibilities to each other. They form now one body. The ambiguity of 'body' here links up with Paul's view of the marriage partners' rights over each other's body. As each no longer has power over his or her own body, he or she is no longer an independent agent, but becomes simply an extension of the other. They form together one body, not just in that their bodies are joined together sexually, but in their being at each other's disposal, and so acting as one, sexually. As friends, they will also act as one in their joint dealings with the rest of the world.

Augustine at times seems to show little appreciation of the aspect of marriage as friendship. For example, in *De Genesi ad Litteram* 9.5, asking in what sense the first woman was a helper fit for the first man, he answers that it is only in the sense that she was necessary to the production of children. Another man would have been better had it been a matter of providing help at work, relief from solitude or companionship. However, at the beginning of *De Bono Conjugali* he picks up the imagery of Genesis 2 in a rather beautiful way:

> Since everybody is a part of the human race, and human nature is social, he also has as a great and natural good the power of friendship. For this reason God willed all men to come from one, so that they might be held together in their society not only by similarity of species but also by bond of kindred. So the first natural bond of human society is man and wife. Neither did God create them as individuals and join them together as if they were unrelated, but he created the one from the other, signifying the power of the bond by the side from which she was taken and formed. For they are joined side by side who walk together and who look together where they are going.[31]

Even for Augustine at times, then, the fundamental thing about marriage is the friendship between the partners, a friendship so close that they form one body. And the friendship that Paul and Augustine are talking about is a Christian friendship, one which is based on the Christian life that we are all to lead whether we are married or not.[32] There may also be a great romantic involvement, which we tend to stress in our culture; but this has not always been so and need not be so. The unity of one flesh that man and wife have is no different essentially from the unity we all have with each other in the body of Christ. The sexual relationship of a couple is an embodiment of their life in Christ. If a sexual relationship gets its meaning from the wider relationship of marriage which is its context, that marriage is itself a mirror of the way in which Christians as a whole are to relate to each other. In its origin the Christian sexual ethic of marriage is not derived from an *a priori* view of the nature of sex 'in itself' but from the general nature of people's relationships as members of the church, the body of Christ. Indeed it is a rather striking illustration of that unity; that is why the church regards marriage as a sacrament, so that a marriage is not just the affair of the partners but of the whole church. A married couple is a sign to the rest of us in the church of the love we all owe each other. This love is derived from and dependent on the love that God has for us, so that the epistle to the Ephesians, which belongs to the Pauline school of thought, can talk of the union of the partners in a marriage as akin to the profoundly mysterious union of Christ and the church (5.31f.).

A married couple and their sexual union are, then, both a picture of the love of Christ and the church and a particular embodiment of the way we are all called to behave towards each other. Up to a point, that is. The huge symbolic significance of this sexual relationship has been achieved at a cost, the cost of making all sexual activity outside marriage illegitimate. It is easy to understand how this came about. At the beginning of Christianity sex outside marriage was not permitted for women anyway. Adulterous married women could be punished, while the unmarried who went with men were simply loose women, and not respectable. Men, married or not, had much greater sexual licence.[33] Forbidding the power of divorce and extramarital relations to men was a progressive move; it ended male superiority and put women on a par with men – theoretically at least: since no society has ever been properly Christianized men have in fact continued to dominate and to enjoy a sexual freedom denied to women. The restriction of the sexual activity of married people to sex with their partners is perhaps also a precondition of its carrying the symbolic weight it does.

However, to say how all this came about is not to show that it is necessary. It might be questioned whether sex should be made to bear quite all the load of significance it does in Christian thought. Even if we want to say that sex within marriage has this deep meaning, that is not to say that all sex has to have such a meaning and therefore that there can be no legitimate sexual activity outside marriage. Even if we want to say that the body is naturally a bearer of meaning and that since we are Christians our bodily behaviour has always to bear a Christian meaning, we could still think of sex rather more widely than has traditionally been done. For though sex naturally expresses love it has no necessary meaning that restricts it to marriage. The significance it has been given in the tradition may be a good one which enables people to express themselves in important ways, but there is nothing to prevent us from considering other meanings, that is to say other contexts for sexual relationships. We might ask, for instance: given that all our relationships are to be, in the appropriate way, governed by Christian love, Christian friendship, why should not a sexual expression of that friendship be appropriate in some non-marital contexts? Paul contrasts being married with going to a prostitute, but there are surely other possibilities in between.

One answer to such a question is to point out the obvious fact that children are sometimes the fruit of sexual relationships, and children need the support of a stable and permanent loving relationship between their parents if they are to grow up properly. And that is what a marriage is. But that invites the obvious counter-argument that it is possible to have a sexual relationship without children, either because one of the partners is sterile or through the use of contraception. It is also possible to have a sexual relationship from which children cannot possibly be born, such a homosexual relationship. It is these I want to go on to look at in the next chapters.

9

Contraception

Scripture and tradition

Wherefore, since there are some who, openly departing from the Christian teaching which has been handed down uninterruptedly from the beginning, have in recent times thought fit solemnly to preach another doctrine concerning this practice, the Catholic Church, to whom God has committed the task of teaching and preserving morals and right conduct in their integrity, standing erect amidst this moral devastation, raises her voice in sign of her divine mission to keep the chastity of the marriage contract unsullied by this ugly stain, and through Our mouth proclaims anew: that any use of matrimony whatsoever in the exercise of which the act is deprived, by human interference, of its natural power to procreate life, is an offence against the law of God and of nature, and that those who commit it are guilty of a grave sin.[1]

Thus Pius XI in 1930, in his encyclical *Casti Connubii*. Many people will think of Paul VI's encyclical *Humanae Vitae* in connexion with contraception, but as this quotation from Pius XI indicates, the preoccupation goes back well before him. Pius, indeed, claims that contraception has been condemned uninterruptedly from the beginning. Certainly Christian antipathy to contraception is very old. But there appears to be no solid evidence that it goes back to the very beginning, to the age of scripture. Various forms of contraception were widely used throughout the Roman world in the time of the early church; there was a practice there to condemn, if it was thought a bad practice. However, the New Testament does not appear to mention contraception at all. It would be a mistake, though, to interpret this as showing that the early church was indifferent to contraception. It seems rather that the New Testament shows little concern with questions surrounding procreation. The apparent lack of reference to contraception may have been due to the belief that since the end of the world was soon to come, procreation was of no importance anyway. Practices surrounding procreation were not morally indifferent; procreation was simply believed to be outmoded.

But though it appears that there are no references to contraception in the New Testament, this is not entirely certain. There are three occurrences of the word *pharmakeia*[2] and two of *pharmakos*,[3] and it is clear that both are considered bad. *pharmakeia* is translated in the Revised Standard Version as 'sorcery' and *pharmakos* as 'sorcerer', and that may well be correct. However, *pharmakeia* is literally the use of poisons, and a *pharmakos* one who makes or administers poisons. It is just possible that these references are to drugs used as contraceptives, but there is no firm evidence to support this. Sometimes one of these words appears in conjunction with *porneia*,[4] 'fornication', so it looks as if it may have a sexual connexion; but even here it appears in lists of sins and is also in conjunction with 'murder' and 'idolatry'[5] Sometimes there appears to be no connexion with any sexual sin.[6] So it is at best speculation to suppose that the references here are to contraceptive practices and practitioners. With regard to *pharmakos* there is also the possibility that it is a general term referring to somebody worthless, the dregs; in earlier times it referred to one who was sacrificed as an atonement for others, a scapegoat, and since it was normally worthless people who were given this office, *pharmakos* became a general term of reproach.[7]

There is in any case a further difficulty in interpreting texts of the New Testament, as well as of the patristic period. In those times knowledge of the reproductive process was more limited than it is now. Today we can distinguish between two different sorts of procedure. First, there are those which prevent the fertilization of the ovum. This can be done by putting a barrier, such as a condom, between sperm and ovum, or by preventing ovulation or by rendering the sperm ineffective. On the other hand, there are practices which prevent the development of a fertilized ovum, for instance by preventing it from becoming properly implanted in the womb. It is clear that there is a major difference between the two cases, since in the latter case there is something which, following on the fusion of sperm and ovum, has a natural tendency, given the right conditions, towards development into one or more human beings. This is prevented by ensuring that the conditions are not right, so that the fertilized ovum is destroyed. Procedures and devices which bring this about are properly described as abortifacient: a pregnancy has begun which is afterwards aborted.[8] Conception has not been prevented but has taken place. Therefore such procedures and devices are not accurately described as contraceptive. Only in the first type of case is there genuine prevention of conception, genuine contraception. In the light of increased knowledge the church now makes a clear distinction between the two kinds of practice, but that distinction was not available in earlier times. There was no possibility of any distinction between drugs or other methods used as contraceptives and those which were abortifacient. Following the modern distinction, it is only with genuinely contraceptive practices that I am concerned here.

If there is no established condemnation of contraception in the New Testament, neither is there in the Old Testament. Pius XI quotes the words of Augustine: 'Sexual intercourse even with a lawful wife is unlawful and shameful if the conception of offspring is prevented. This is what Onan, the son of Judah, did, and on that account God put him to death'.[9] The reference is to this story in Genesis:

> And Judah took a wife for Er his firstborn, and her name was Tamar. But Er, Judah's first-born, was wicked in the sight of the Lord; and the Lord slew him. Then Judah said to Onan: 'Go in to your brother's wife, and perform the duty of a brother-in-law to her, and raise up offspring for your brother.' But Onan knew that the offspring would not be his; so when he went in to his brother's wife he spilled the semen on the ground,[10] lest he should give offspring to his brother. And what he did was displeasing in the sight of the Lord, and he slew him also (Gen. 38.6–10).

It became traditional to use this passage as if it were a condemnation of contraception by *coitus interruptus*, as Pius XI's use of it shows.[11] However, there is reason to think that this is not what the passage is actually about. The text itself, in the context it gives for Onan's act, supplies two reasons for his punishment. First, he has refused to raise up children for his dead brother, and so has sinned by not carrying out his obligations towards him. Second, he has been told to do this by his father Judah, so his act also constitutes filial disobedience. It is indeed through a contraceptive act that Onan both refuses to raise up children for his brother and disobeys his father, but it appears to be for the refusal and the disobedience that he is punished, not the contraception. At the very least, we do not have a reference to contraception pure and simple here.[12]

Once the early New Testament confidence that the end of things was at hand passed, Christian thought began to be pre-occupied again with procreation, and so also with contraception. This is one thing that is clear from Augustine's use of the story of Onan. He was the first major theologian to talk about the subject, and as we see he was completely against any attempt to prevent conception arising from marital intercourse. But we should not forget that Augustine has special reasons for holding such a position. For him, it is the intention to have children alone that justifies the otherwise completely shameful activity of sexual intercourse. To lack that intention, indeed to have an anti-procreative intention, as the use of a contraceptive implies, is deliberately to make the act shameful.

Secondly, Augustine formulated his position as part of his polemic against the Manichees. The followers of Mani, among whom Augustine at one time numbered himself, had a dualist belief of a kind that saw matter as an enemy. Human souls were particles of light trapped in matter by the Lord of darkness. They were trapped particularly in semen. If the semen went to producing a new fleshly human being, what that meant was that the spirit was once more trapped in matter. Hence it was a bad to have sexual intercourse leading to the birth of children. If you were going to have sex at all, and that was a bad thing because it was so irrational and bound up with matter, you had at least to ensure that the spirit did not become trapped again; you had to practice contraception. Here is how Augustine writes to the Manichee Secundinus:

> I know where your indignation comes from. For it is not the prostitute in her fornication who upsets you, so much as that fornication is changed to marriage and converted to conjugal modesty. You believe your God to be bound by tighter bonds of flesh in the procreation of children. You think prostitutes spare God, because they take steps not to conceive in order that, freed from the duty of bearing, they might serve lust.[13]

Thus the Manichean practice of contraception stemmed from a view of matter profoundly opposed to the Christian one, which, following the Jewish tradition, saw the material creation as good, the place of our life and freedom, not of our imprisonment. Hence opposition to contraception became for Augustine a symbol of opposition to the Manichean theology as a whole and of defence of Catholic theology.

In the Middle Ages the influence of Augustine was great, and his teaching on contraception was universally accepted. Among the arguments adduced to support it the most important was the general teaching, based on an appeal to natural law, that the purpose of all sexual activity was procreation. Any sexual activity which was not conformable to this purpose was therefore sinful. So it followed that any measures taken to prevent intercourse from being procreative were sinful.

In modern times contraception has come to seem acceptable to many Christians, but in accordance with Christian tradition it is still strongly opposed in the official teaching of the Catholic church. And the arguments brought in support of it are still commonly of a type that appeals to nature and to purpose. For example, Paul VI, in *Humanae Vitae*, says:

> The Church . . . in urging men to observe the precepts of the natural law, which it interprets by its constant doctrine, teaches as absolutely required that any use whatever of marriage must retain its natural potential to procreate human life.

And a few sentences later:

> The marriage act, because of its fundamental structure, while uniting husband and wife in the closest intimacy actualizes their capacity to generate new life, – and this as a result of laws written into the actual nature of man and of woman.[14]

I have already given reasons for finding this kind of appeal to natural law difficult and unsatisfactory. In brief: Nature is not inviolable to us; we can rightly change the course of nature, and often do. There are problems in understanding the idea that God might have purposes for our free acts. And if we can make sense of God having purposes for our acts, still there is no reason why we should not perform those acts for purposes other than God's: even though the divinely ordained purpose of this object may be to drink whisky from, there is still no reason why I should not use it as a paper-weight, so long as I release it for the purpose God has for it when the time comes. It may be possible to overcome these problems and others, and if so the appeal to natural law will be a sound basis for the traditional Christian ban on contraception. But I do not see at present how they can be overcome. For the moment, therefore, natural law does not appear an attractive place to turn in support of church teaching.

Modern arguments

However, different arguments have been developed in modern times in support of the ban on contraception, and I want to look at a couple of these during the rest of the course of this chapter. First, there is a line of argument developed by Elizabeth Anscombe in her Catholic Truth Society pamphlet *Contraception and Chastity*. This is basically addressed to Catholic married couples, and she sees contraception as inimical to chastity. The argument she uses is based on the idea of types of act. She says:

> If you can turn intercourse into something other than the reproductive type of act (I don't mean of course that every act is reproductive any more than every acorn leads to an oak-tree but it's the reproductive *type* of act) then why, if you change it, should it be restricted to the married?[15]

There are familiar elements in this argument. There is the acceptance of the tradition that sexual intercourse is to be confined to marriage, as well as a variety of appeal to nature: it is because of how things are, in particular how human beings are, that intercourse is by nature a reproductive act. But if the elements are familiar, the shape of the argument is somewhat novel and peculiar. Traditionally (e.g. in Aquinas) intercourse has been confined to marriage because it is 'the reproductive type of act'. That is, the confine-ment of sex to marriage has been seen as a consequence of the nature of sex as reproductive activity. Anscombe now seeks to turn the confinement to marriage into an independent requirement, which demands as a conse-quence that sex be seen as essentially reproductive. Traditionally, sex is reproductive activity, therefore we have to confine it to marriage. Now, according to Anscombe, since we are all agreed that sex has to be confined to marriage, we must make sure that we see sex as reproductive.

We find the same, rather curious reversal of the traditional pattern of argument in another place. She says:

> If contraceptive intercourse is permissible then what objection could there be after all to mutual masturbation, or copulation *in vase indebito*, sodomy, buggery, when normal copulation is impossible or inadvisable (or in any case, according to

taste)? It can't be the mere pattern of bodily behaviour in which the stimulation is procured that makes all the difference! But if such things are all right, it becomes perfectly impossible to see anything wrong with homosexual intercourse, for example.[16]

Traditionally, homosexual intercourse and various other kinds of sex have been condemned because they are thought to be in some sense essentially non-reproductive. Now the argument is not that homosexual intercourse and other forms of sex are ruled out because they are not procreative, but that intercourse has to be seen as essentially procreative so that homosexual intercourse and the rest can be ruled out. It is assumed that we all already, regardless of the procreative purpose of sex, have objections to all these other kinds of sex.

Now let us ask what is meant by saying that intercourse is the 'reproductive type of act'. Note, first, that this can only be true of one particular type of intercourse between man and woman. It is not true of any kind of homosexual intercourse, nor of other kinds of heterosexual intercourse. If Anscombe's argument is going to work at all it is only because it excludes all other forms of sex from its scope from the beginning, or if she regards heterosexual vaginal intercourse as the paradigm, from which all others deviate and in terms of which they are to be judged. In the first case, her argument cannot be used to show the illegitimacy of other, non-reproductive forms of sex, since it presupposes it. In the second case, she has to present a further argument to show that this one kind of intercourse must indeed be regarded as the paradigm, and she does not do so.

But now, limiting ourselves to vaginal intercourse between a man and a woman, what is meant by saying that it is the reproductive type of act? It is most naturally understood as meaning that if you want to have a baby, you will have to perform this act, or would have had to do until the development of *in vitro* fertilization; and, if you don't want a baby, still a baby may result from this activity unless you take precautions. In short, there is a causal relation between acts of this kind and the production of babies. But it is a pretty loose relation, which only holds given that a number of conditions obtain. Think of the following types of act:

(a) Vaginal intercourse between a fertile man and a sterile woman.

(b) Vaginal intercourse between a sterile man and a fertile woman.

(c) Vaginal intercourse between fertile partners not resulting in an orgasm for the man.

(d) Vaginal intercourse between fertile partners, with male orgasm, but in the infertile part of the woman's cycle.

Anscombe, along with the tradition,[17] regards these as conditions which render an essentially reproductive type of act *per accidens* non-reproductive. That is, they are all basically the same type of act as intercourse that leads to pregnancy; though there are differences, the differences are not such as to render the acts different types of act; just as there are differences between left-handed people and right-handed people, but we would not regard those differences as rendering them different types of people. But why should they not be regarded as different types of act? We classify things according to our interests; our classification is not dictated by nature (a nature which we in any case define). Think of chessmen. Is a white knight the same type of thing as a black pawn? – We could answer yes, for they are both chessmen; on the other hand we could answer no, for they are of different colours and move differently. Is a white knight the same sort of thing as a black knight? They are both knights, but again of different colours. Is a white knight the same as a white bishop? – Same colour, but different function. Is a white black-squared bishop the same type of thing as a black black-squared bishop, or the same type of thing as a white white-squared bishop? The answer to these questions depends on what we are interested in, the point of our classification. If what we are interested in is colour we will say one thing; if we are interested in function, we will say another.[18] Things are not just of the same type or of different types. Whether two acts are of the same type or not depends on our interest.

Here what we are interested in is reproduction. Why might we call vaginal intercourse 'the reproductive type of act'? Well, we would call it that because we know that, under the right conditions, pregnancy can result. If pregnancy resulted from anal intercourse, that too would be the 'reproductive type of act'.[19] The reason we classify vaginal and anal intercourse differently, if we are interested in reproduction, is because we know the one kind of intercourse sometimes results in children and that the other never does. So our scientific knowledge is important here. Other societies, which have not made the link between sex and reproduction, though they might still distinguish between vaginal intercourse and anal intercourse and find the one acceptable and the other not, could not make this distinction on the basis of one being the reproductive type of act and the other not.

But we also know that vaginal sex where one of the partners is either permanently or temporarily sterile never results in conception. If our knowledge of the facts of reproduction is the basis of our distinction between vaginal and anal intercourse as different types of act, then our knowledge is relevant in other cases also. Vaginal intercourse which we know to be sterile is a different type of act from vaginal intercourse which, as far as we know, might result in conception.[20]

But is there not an obvious sense in which two infertile partners who have vaginal intercourse are performing the same act as two partners whose intercourse can result in conception? The same organs are involved in the same combination, and the same bodily movements are made. Certainly. The acts can be considered the same if what we are interested in is organs and bodily movements, if that is what is to serve as the basis for our classification. But it is not what we are interested in when examining Anscombe's argument. As she herself says, it can't be the mere pattern of bodily behaviour in which the stimulation is procured that makes all the difference! If the mere pattern of bodily behaviour cannot make all the difference, then neither can it make a relevant sameness. What we are interested in at the moment is whether – as far as we know – a given activity can or cannot result in conception. If that is the basis of our classification, vaginal intercourse between partners known to be infertile is a different type of act from vaginal intercourse between partners known to be fertile. Anscombe's argument would render illegitimate intercourse between partners known to be sterile, as well as homosexual intercourse. And traditional Christian ethics would reject that position.

Natural family planning

Anscombe also has something to say on the distinction between 'artificial' contraception and the rhythm method, otherwise known as 'natural family planning', a method of avoiding conception which has recently gained widespread acceptance in the church.[21] Many people find the moral distinction between these two somewhat obscure; but to Anscombe there is a clear difference, which resides in the difference of intention, making the two different kinds of act. She says:

> In contraceptive intercourse you intend to perform a sexual act which, if it has a chance of being fertile, you render infertile. *Qua* your intentional action, then, what you do *is* something intrinsically unapt for generation... There's all the world of difference between this and the use of the 'rhythm' method. For you use the rhythm method not just by having intercourse now, but by not having it next week, say; and not having it next week isn't something that does something to today's intercourse to turn it into an infertile act; today's intercourse is an ordinary act of intercourse, an ordinary marriage act.[22]

This does not seem satisfactory. Of course today's act of intercourse is not turned into an infertile act by refraining from intercourse next week; but today's intercourse *is* rendered an infertile act by being *timed* so as to be infertile. It is intentionally timed so as to be something unapt for generation. And timing is not something 'accidental' here. The time at which you do something, and the way that time enters into your intention, sometimes makes a very great difference to what it is you are doing. If I shoot a gun thoughtlessly and indiscriminately into the street without looking to see if there is anybody out there, that is very dangerous and reprehensible, and if I hit and kill somebody I have committed manslaughter. But if I deliberately wait until I have somebody in my sights I have committed murder. On the other hand, imagine it is my job in wartime to shoot and kill enemy soldiers as they run past a certain point. If I am inattentive so that when one runs past I fire too late and miss him, then I am incompetent. But if, perhaps horrified at the idea of actually shooting at somebody, I miss by deliberately waiting until the enemy soldier has run past before I shoot, then I have been disobedient, treacherous, a disgrace to my country, and so on. And plainly the timing of intercourse in the rhythm method has as its point to render the intercourse infertile. *Qua* your intentional action, then, what you do is something intrinsically unapt for generation, just as much as if you use an artificial contraceptive device. Paul VI says that '*any use whatever of marriage* must retain its natural potential to procreate human life'.[23] If a woman takes anovulant pills or a man uses a sheath or some other method is used the act no longer, by intention, has any potential to procreate human life. But to time sexual intercourse so as to ensure that it is infertile is also to ensure that it does not have any potential to procreate human life. Of course, you can fail in your intention. You can get the timing wrong so that the act does after all retain its potentiality for procreation, and then you may have a child. But again there is no difference here between the rhythm method and other forms of birth control. If a woman takes anovulant pills, one may not work, or she may forget to take one at the right time. If a man uses a sheath he may put it on inexpertly, or it may have a hole in it. In these latter cases too the act retains its natural potentiality for procreation, but by accident, despite the intention of the participants. There appears, then to be no significant difference between the 'artificial' methods of birth control and the so-called 'natural' rhythm method. As far as Anscombe's argument goes, if the one is illegitimate, then so is the other; and if the rhythm method is all right, then so is using contraceptives.

But surely, we might say, there is an obvious difference. The couple who use artificial contraception perform an act which, but for the contraception, might turn out to be procreative. They obstruct the natural potential of the act. The couple who practise the rhythm method do not obstruct anything. They simply do not perform the act when it might be fertile. Unlike the former couple, they do not do anything; so *a fortiori* they cannot be doing anything wrong.

This sounds all right, and maybe it is; but there seems to me something fishy about it. It is not true that the second couple do not do anything. They do not of course perform any sexual bodily movements, but the matter does not end there. Remember that a human action is not just a bodily movement or set of bodily movements; it is what it is by virtue of its context. Most human actions do involve bodily movements, but because of the contextual element it is possible to perform a human act, an act that might be thought praiseworthy or blameworthy, without moving a muscle.

Here is our little girl in her exercise class. The teacher tells her to lift her arm and she does nothing, that is, she does not move; she just stands there.

But by not moving she is, providing she has heard, defying her teacher. She is perhaps also showing off to her friends, showing how brave she is or how much she can get away with with this teacher. Or to take a different example, we might think of sitting still in a chair as an instance of doing nothing. If somebody asks me what I have been doing for the last ten minutes I could perfectly intelligibly answer: 'Nothing at all, just sitting here.' In this context, just sitting here counts as doing nothing. But now: I am in a room with lots of other people and we are all just sitting there. Now in walks the Prime Minister and everybody stands up – of course: it's a sign of respect. But I remain seated; I do not move a muscle. Though I have not moved, it is not true that I have done nothing. Rather, just because I have not moved I have shown disrespect. Here, in this context, staying seated is a human act, as it would not be in a different context. So too the couple who use the rhythm method do something by not having sexual intercourse during fertile periods. They do not just not have intercourse; they actively avoid intercourse, as part of their plan to avoid children. Anscombe says: 'not having it next week isn't something that does something to today's intercourse to turn it into an infertile act'. That is right, but avoiding having it next week or yesterday is part of what turns today's intercourse into a deliberately infertile act. Together with all the occasions on which intercourse has been avoided because it might lead to pregnancy, they intentionally deprive their intercourse of its natural potential for procreation. It is true that they achieve this result by a different method from those used by a couple using a sheath, but they do the same thing by that different method. And their intercourse is not accidentally infertile, but as deliberately infertile as the intercourse of a couple using a sheath. It is made so not by physical interference with the process of intercourse (pills don't do that, either), but by the pattern of acts of intercourse and avoidances of intercourse that surround it.

The arguments of Grisez, Boyle, Finnis and May

Recently a major contribution to Christian thought on contraception has been made by Germain Grisez, Joseph Boyle, John Finnis and William E. May in their article ' "Every Marital Act Ought To Be Open To New Life": Toward a Clearer Understanding'[24] (already referred to briefly in chapter 2). In this article the authors claim to have established a cogent logical argument for the church's teaching on contraception. In summary, the central argument may be paraphrased as follows: The availability of techniques of contraception means that in an act of heterosexual intercourse between fertile partners those partners are faced with a decision about whether to use contraception or not. Any choice to use contraception is a deliberate choice against the coming to be of a new life; it is 'contralife'. A human life is indisputably a basic human good, though of course there may be circumstances, such as extreme poverty, that may make it inadvisable or even wrong to realize that good. A choice to use contraception is therefore a choice against a basic human good. But the partners can only rationally reject a good if they are making a choice for some greater good. But that means the two goods must be comparable, that is commensurable; it must be possible to choose between them according to some scale. For instance, an airline pilot run out of fuel is faced with a bad situation and must make a choice about the best place to crash. If he has the choice whether to crash on a large town or a small hamlet he has a clear scale in accordance with which he can make a rational choice, namely the numbers of people likely to be killed in either case. Since, as far as he can judge, more people are likely to be killed if he crashes on the town than if he lands on the hamlet, the rational course of action is for him to aim for the hamlet. However, there are no goods commensurable with the good of human life. Therefore no good can be rationally preferred to human life. Hence it is impossible to take a rational decision against human life; that is, it is impossible to make a rational choice to use contraception in sexual intercourse.

This is the argument in outline. I believe it is false. But the article contains much close argumentation, so has to be looked at in some detail if justice is to be done to it. I shall concentrate on those points that seem to me of major importance.

Possible human beings

One of the major sources of difficulty with this argument is the way the authors characterize the decision to use contraception. At one point they say the following about a thoughtful couple deciding on contraception:

> They look ahead and think about the baby whose life they might initiate. Perhaps for some further good reason, perhaps not, they find the prospect repugnant: 'We do not want that possible baby to begin to live.' As the very definition of contraception makes clear, that will is contralife; it is practical (though not necessarily an emotional) hatred of the possible baby they project and reject, just as the will to accept the coming to be of a baby is a practical love of that possible person.[25]

This is of course meant to be a schematic description; GBFM are not suggesting that every such couple actually goes through this process. But still it is misleading in more than one way.

First, the couple are represented as rejecting 'that possible baby'. The use of 'possible' in this way is dangerous. It makes it look as if there are two types of baby, possible ones and actual ones, just as there might be male babies and female ones, or black ones and white ones. But a possible baby is not a kind of baby; it is not a kind of anything. An indication of the way something is wrong here is that the demonstrative adjective 'that' has no function here. Demonstratives are used to pick out particulars, such as individual objects or people. But babies which are not yet conceived are not particulars. The couple who decide on contraception do not reject a particular baby. Later on GBFM write of this same couple that 'they realize that to contracept is to choose contrary to the beginning of a possible person's life'.[26] This again makes it seem as if there is such a thing as a possible person, but a possible person is not a person. It is less misleading to say that to choose contraception is to choose contrary to the possible beginning of a person's life. In choosing contraception the couple do not choose against the life of any person. The baby about whom they are thinking is not a person and does not have any life that may be chosen against.

This is not a minor, grammatical point. Part of the thrust of GBFM's argument is that the couple who use contraception make a choice against life; hence their characterization of such a choice as 'contralife'. That is why contraception is supposed to be so bad. But at the stage where contraception is contemplated there is no life to choose against, because there is no person to choose against, no person to reject. The choice that is made is not against the life of anybody, and certainly not against life in general. It is not against life at all, but against the possibility of a new life. Or, to use GBFM's terminology, it is against a possible life; but a possible life is not a life. In choosing to use contraception the couple are making a decision which might be described as 'contra-possible-life', but their decision is not 'contralife'. Thus this apparently small logical point undermines the entire argument.

This can be seen in another, related way. GBFM attribute to our couple a practical hatred[27] for the possible person whom they reject. How might we make sense of the idea of hating a possible person? I can think of one realistic possibility. We can imagine Andrew saying: 'If a child is born of this activity, I will hate it.' Here Andrew is committing himself to hating another, real person if certain possibilities are fulfilled, namely if that person is born of this act of intercourse. It is not to say that he now hates anybody at all. But this cannot be the sense that GBFM require; for when people use contraception they do not commit themselves to hating any offspring born of their intercourse. They of course do not want any offspring, but may nevertheless love and accept any child of their union; and if they do so, we need not imagine that they have changed or abandoned any earlier commitment to hate the child.

What Andrew does, then, will not do as a satisfactory meaning of hating a possible person; satisfactory, that is, in the sense of coming near to any meaning of that phrase that GBFM require. But now it is difficult to see how there can be any such satisfactory sense, since if Andrew uses contraception they require not that he may possibly hate somebody in the future, but that he actually hate somebody now, for this hatred is the motive of his present contraceptive activity. We would normally say that to hate somebody involves believing that they exist;[28] and there is now no person for Andrew to hate, and neither does he hate somebody whom he falsely believes to exist. So the assertion that the contraception is motivated by practical hatred of a possible baby is false. Just as people who use contraception do not do anything 'contralife', so they do nothing out of hate.

The goodness of human life

Part of GBFM's argument is that those practising contraception always reject a good, because they reject a life. Thus, they write, contraception is of its nature contralife:

> Since contraception must be defined by its intention that a prospective new life not begin, every contraceptive act is necessarily contralife. Those who choose such an act often also intend some further good – for example, not to procreate irresponsibly with bad consequences for already existing persons. But in choosing contraception as a means to this further good, they necessarily reject a new life. They imagine that a new person will come to be if that is not prevented, they want that possible person not to be, and they effectively will that he or she never be. That will is a contralife will. Therefore, each and every contraceptive act is necessarily contralife.[29]

But to be contralife is to be against an important good:

> In itself the coming to be of a new human person is a great human good. To say this is not to say that this good may not be accompanied by many evils that in the concrete can render realizing it repugnant, but only, that, nothing else considered, the prospect of a new person is a reason to act for his or her coming to be and in itself offers no reason to try to prevent that.[30]

Thus every choice to use contraception is necessarily a choice against a great human good.

It seems to me that the term 'contralife' is unhelpful. It is one which GBFM are very insistent on, but it obscures the fact that what we are concerned with is not life in the abstract but the life of people. (So that prolifers are not just in favour of life: they want to protect the lives of people.) What is at stake is whether, in using contraception, one is acting against somebody, a human being, or not. In the case of homicide, to which GBFM compare contraception,[31] being contralife is being against *somebody's* life, and that is being against *that person*. We would normally say that (human) life is always *somebody's* life. The case of contraception is significantly different, for here there is not yet any person to be against, there is no life to be against. To use the word 'contralife' in connexion with contraception, as it might be used in connexion with homicide, is to run the risk of obscuring this important distinction.

More substantially, we have already seen reason to be unhappy with the claim that to use contraception is to reject a life: it may mean deciding against a possible life, but a possible life is not a life. There are also reasons for thinking that, even if they can be shown to be rejecting a life, such a couple are not necessarily rejecting a good. GBFM write: 'In itself the coming to be of a new human person is a great human good.' They acknowledge that this claim is fundamental to their argument, but they make it as if it is all but impossible to disagree with. It seems an unexceptionable claim, but is it? Certainly, any Christian is bound to see human life as a good, and there can be relatively few non-Christians who would disagree. But there is a difference between a saying that a human life is always a good and claiming that a life's coming to be is always a good. I will point to two difficulties in particular which seem to me to be serious.

First, a human good is always a good for or to somebody. Let us accept that the life of a living human being is always a good, a good to the person himself and to those around him. (That the person's life is a good may not be apparent to himself or to others, perhaps because he is very ill or very vicious; but it is in fact so, and the remedy, if there is one, lies in curing the illness or freeing him from the vice.) But to whom or for whom is the coming to be of a new human person a good? It cannot be a good for the prospective new person, for he does not exist yet. Once he does exist, his life will be a good for him, but that is not the same as saying that his coming to be is now a good to him. Now, nothing is a good for him, because he does not exist.

Second, in claiming that the coming to be of a new person is always a good GBFM distinguish between the coming to be in itself and the particular circumstances in which this occurs. Though the former is always good, the latter may be bad, so that it may under circumstances be wrong to bring a new child into existence, a bad thing to realize this good. This distinction has to be made in order to make it possible to say that the coming to be of a new person is always a good. But is it plausible to distinguish thus sharply between the coming to be of a new life considered in itself and the circumstances in which this occurs? In fact a new life never comes into being in isolation. The birth of a baby is an event, and an event always occurs in particular circumstances. In this case the circumstances are not something that 'accompanies' the birth; they may be in large part caused by the birth. A decision about whether to have a baby is always also a decision about whether to accept the causal consequences of having it, whether the present circumstances are good ones in which to have a baby, or about whether to alter them by introducing a baby into them. In claiming that a new life is always a good GBFM mean only 'that, *nothing else considered*, the prospect of a new person is a reason to act for his or her coming to be and in itself offers no reason to try to prevent that'. But to consider things properly is also to consider their consequences, and people rightly think of these when deciding whether to have a child; and it may be that when these things are considered the prospect of a new person is not a reason to act for his or her coming to be. It may be perfectly reasonable to judge that introducing a baby would make things worse rather than better. This is quite compatible with saying that after the child is born its life is a good, that it is always better that it live than that it not.

Matters are somewhat obscured by GBFM's terminology in speaking of 'the coming to be of a new life' always being good. Here they are speaking not about the goodness of human life, which is not in dispute, but about the goodness of an *event*. This is obscured by the use of a substantival form, and this makes it easy to confuse the question of the goodness of human life itself with that of whether it is always good that a new human life begin. 'The coming to be of a new life is always good' is equivalent to 'It is always good that a new life come to be', or perhaps to 'It is always good that a new life has come to be.' In judging the goodness of the coming to be of a new human life we are judging the goodness of an event, not of a human life. But now it is perfectly possible for the realization of a good not itself to be a good event. This is something which GBFM themselves point out. This means that, though a new human life may be a good thing, the event which is the realization of new human life may not be. But this event is precisely what GBFM call 'the coming to be of a new life'. Hence the coming to be of a new life is not always a good. If a couple decide on using contraception and so, in GBFM's terminology, set themselves against the coming to be of a new life, they do not necessarily set themselves to prevent a good. Contraception may, as Christian tradition asserts, be an evil, but not because it implies a choice against this particular good.

GBFM claim that it is not possible to decide rationally to prevent the coming to be of new life. They admit that many people honestly think they make this decision rationally, but claim they are mistaken; they are in fact being irrational. GBFM argue as follows:

> People think of and compare two possible futures: One in which the baby lives and one in which it does not. And they think that the future in which the baby does not live is better. It certainly seems so to them. They feel that the future without the baby will be better than the future with it. But can they know that the future without the baby will be rationally better? Clearly, they cannot. To know that, they would have to know what God knows – not only the immediate, or short-term, or other this-worldly possible futures with and without the baby, but also the place of that possible baby and of everyone else concerned in God's plan for his Kingdom. Human providence does not begin to reach so far.[32]

Do they succeed in showing that the decision to use contraception is not rational? I suggest not. Note first of all an unwarranted suggestion of irrationality towards the beginning. GBFM claim that the couple 'feel that the future without the baby will be better'. But why this talk of feeling here? Simply, the couple think or believe the future without another baby will be better. This is how GBFM themselves describe the matter in the previous sentence. The introduction of 'feel' here is unnecessary and merely obscures the issue; and is designed to imply that people are irrational when they decide in favour of contraception, before any argument to show that has been presented.

They ask of the couple 'But can they know that the future without the baby will be rationally better?' Note first that if they cannot know this, that means that they may believe it, not merely that they may feel it; and they may believe it on the basis of considerable hard thought, even calculation. GBFM follow their question with remarks about the impossibility of being certain of what the long-run future will be like with or without the baby. These are not foolish considerations, but they apply not only to babies but to our knowledge of anything at all in the future, and not only in the long term. If we accept what GBFM say, that prevents us from ever claiming to know the future. Yet in ordinary usage we are quite happy about claiming to know the future. Perhaps GBFM are saying that we ought not to be happy about this. This raises wider philosophical questions, but let us admit for the sake of argument that, if we must have very high standards for claiming to know, we cannot know that the future without the baby will be better than the future with it. But then, as before, that applies to all our actions. We do not know that the future will be better (or worse) for anything that we do or refrain from doing. All we can say is that very likely one course of action will make things better or another make them worse – in the short or medium term. I may think it better that I go to work today, so as to provide for my family, but it may turn out that a child runs into the path of my car and is killed, or that I am caught in a bomb blast and severely injured, so that I and everybody else say that it would have been better had I stayed at home.

Further, because we don't have knowledge of God's plan (except in so far as it has been declared to us), we cannot think about God's plan when we make our decisions about how to act. But our decisions can be rational none the less. The pilot who is about to crash does not know the place in God's plan of each individual on the ground. It may be that a child in the smaller community is otherwise destined for great things, and the pilot cannot know that. Yet he can make a perfectly rational choice. For us human beings, to make rational decisions is to act on our judgments about probabilities in the medium term, according to what it is reasonable to think will happen. If we can make judgments about probabilities in the medium term in the case of contraception, and GBFM do not argue that we cannot, then we can take a rational decision to use contraception.

Here also we meet 'that possible baby' once more, as having a place in God's plan. But possibilities do not have places in God's plan, except in so far as God projects their realization ('predestines them' might be a happier phrase); and if God projects things, they are going to come about. We may want to talk about the place of people in God's plan (even if it is a place we cannot know about), but only the place of people who are or were or will be real people. Otherwise, apart from the general difficulty of identifying possible people, we have to talk about all the ways God has been forced to change his plans by people using contraception and preventing the conception of possible people who had actual places in his plan. God cannot make actual places in his plan except for actual people, or people who will be actual.

People can, then, make quite rational decisions to use contraception. And it is not difficult to see how. They can do so by making reasonable projections about what the future would be like with and without a(nother) baby and making a judgment on the basis of these projections. The chief considerations here might be, say, economic: what an extra baby might reasonably be expected to cost, compared with what the couple can afford. Or for another couple it might be a matter of projected inconvenience, disruption of present plans. A couple may be prepared to tolerate only a certain level of disruption, and judge that a new baby will bring them rather more than that level of inconvenience. This is perfectly rational. Christians may dislike the kind of rationality deployed by the second couple, their decision and the kind of considerations that is based on, and we may think the people who think like that are not very good, that they ought not to think like that; but they *are* thinking, and their decision is rational.

GBFM also have a quite general, theoretical argument against the possibility of choosing to use contraception. It runs as follows:

> If there were a rational method of establishing the rational preferability of the reason for making a choice to the reason against making it (or vice versa), then the reason that the use of that method showed to be less rationally preferable would, by that very fact, cease to be a reason in respect to that situation of choice. But in that case the situation would cease to be a situation of choice between rationally appealing alternatives, and so there would remain no choice between these alternatives. If the reason for making that choice and the reason against making it were the only motives at work in that situation, one simply would act in accord with the now-unopposed reason.[33]

Notice that this argument is quite general; it has nothing to do with contraception or 'contralife will' in particular, but is about any process of decision-making. GBFM see this argument as quite decisive. I may be missing the point, but I cannot see that it has any force at all. First, there is no reason to suppose, as they claim, that the less rationally preferable reason would cease to be a reason; the course of action it is a reason for is simply shown to be the less preferable by the process of judgment. Secondly, though they claim to be describing a situation where rational choice is impossible, in fact they seem to be talking about one in which a rational choice has been made. After the choice between the rationally appealing alternatives has been made, once one alternative has been found preferable to another, of course the choice no longer remains to be made. So the situation ceases to be one of rational choice. But this observation is far from showing the impossibility of making a rational choice.

The failure of contraception

GBFM have a further argument against contraception, this time not based on an abstract conception of reason, but on considerations of charity. Like all arguments based on charity, this argument has a special pertinence to the line I have been pursuing, that it is to the general principle of love of neighbour that we do best to look in our search for a grounded sexual ethic. They argue as follows:

> Every method of contraception, even sterilization, has a failure rate. When the attempt at contraception does not succeed, an unwanted baby comes to be. Today, aborting the baby is likely to be considered. But perhaps the baby will be accepted and loved. Even so, the baby began life as an accident, as someone unwanted. Choosing contraception with the knowledge that it might fail and a baby come to be as unwanted is being willing to put another in a position in which no reasonable person would wish to be. Therefore, choosing contraception is an injustice, even if it succeeds and the harm remains in one's heart.[34]

Some of the things GBFM point out here are right and important. It is true that when a child is conceived through the failure of contraception it is liable to come into being unwanted. The fact that at the time of conception the couple were unwilling to have a baby is reason for thinking that when a baby is conceived this will be a disappointment to them. They may even go to the lengths of abortion in order to remedy the disappointment. But they will by no means necessarily be disappointed, since they may have changed their minds between intercourse and the discovery of the pregnancy and now look forward to having a baby; or the discovery of the pregnancy itself may bring them face to face with the great good of a new life, a good which they feel impelled to recognize. As GBFM say, then, the baby may be accepted and loved. But, as they also say, whatever change in the parents' attitude may occur, the baby actually starts life as someone unwanted.

The main point of their argument comes next. 'Choosing contraception', they write, 'with the knowledge that it might fail and a baby come to be as unwanted is being willing to put another in a position in which no reasonable person would wish to be.' If this is correct, then the use of contraception is simply uncharitable and therefore to be avoided. (I take it that in saying that no reasonable person would wish to be in this position, they mean that every reasonable person would wish to avoid it, rather than the weaker claim that they would simply have no desire to be in it.) But it seems to me that it is not correct, for three reasons.

First, if any baby that comes into being as a result of the failure of contraception might be unwanted and hence unloved, that is not just a brute fact of existence with which those contemplating using contraception have to reckon. It is not a brute fact, because it is up to them whether any such child is loved or not. In using contraception they do not expose any possible child to a risk of being unloved, for whether it is loved or not is entirely within their power. It is simply up to them to accept and love any child that is born from their intercourse, whether it involved the use of contraception or not. It is in their power to love the child, and they should. You can risk having an unwanted child, but you cannot risk not wanting a child you have. Every existing child, whether it was wanted or not before it existed, must be loved by its parents. If a child, when it exists, is unloved, that is a failure of charity on the part of those who should love it. It is surely here that the lack of charity is properly located. It is not the contraception that is properly speaking uncharitable, but the refusal to love a child born of one's sexual intercourse. If I use contraception in my intercourse, I am not being unjust to any possible person (there is nobody to be unjust to), but I may – and should not – be unjust at some future time to my child, if I have one. It is possible to have a baby you didn't want, but you must want the baby you have.

Second, there is a possible ambiguity in what GBFM are saying here. Do they mean that no reasonable person would wish to be in the position of being unwanted, or that no reasonable person would wish to be in the position of having started life as unwanted? If the former, plainly they are right. Any practice that led to putting somebody in that position would indeed be uncharitable. But that does not seem to be what GBFM mean, for they acknowledge that a baby whose conception was unwanted might itself be loved and accepted. So they do not appear to be claiming that contraception makes people unloved and unwanted. That leaves us with the second alternative. But it is not clear that no reasonable person would wish to be in the position of having started life as unwanted. This is certainly true if the start of life is located at birth, for then to start unwanted means living among those who are hostile; and nobody wants to do that or to have done it. But GBFM rightly do not locate the beginning of life at birth. They locate it at the moment of conception. But now it is not clear what starting life unwanted means. Certainly if contraception is used the start of a new life is unwanted, but that does not mean if the contraception fails the newly-conceived child is unwanted; it may well be wanted, as has already been said and as GBFM themselves say. Though the possibility may be shunned, the reality may be accepted when it presents itself. What is necessarily unwanted is not any actual person at any stage of his or her life, but the possible beginning of a person or, to use GBFM's terminology, the beginning of a possible person. But, as already shown, a possible person is not a person.

Third, choosing contraception is not being willing to put another in a position in which no reasonable person would wish to be. The whole point of contraception is precisely trying to avoid anybody coming into being, so that if it is successful there is nobody in that position. It may even be the point of a particular act of contraception to avoid anybody's being put in that position. One or both partners in intercourse may know that any offspring will be unloved, and therefore take steps to avoid there being unloved offspring.

What GBFM appeal to, though, is not the point of contraception but the possibility of its failure. Contraception, like every other human project, carries with it a risk of failure. But failure is precisely not something that is willed; it is something risked. What is willed is the success of the project. So if you use contraception you risk beginning the life of somebody new, somebody who may or may not be unwanted. But of course you are not willing to begin the life of somebody new. So you are not willing to put anybody in the position of being unwanted, not willing to put another in a position in which no reasonable person would wish to be.

What you are willing to do in using contraception is to take the risk that somebody might come into being. But there is nothing necessarily uncharitable about this. A doctor, a general, a sea captain, the leader of a mountaineering party, and many others may all be willing to take risks to obtain their objectives, risks even with their own lives and the lives of those in their charge. There is lack of charity only when the risks are unnecessarily great. Any responsible person will minimize the risks attaching to the project, but need not necessarily abandon the project because of the risk. This can be illustrated by the simple example of driving a car. If Jane goes for a drive she risks causing pain, injury and mutilation to a pedestrian or another motorist. We know that she runs such a risk from statistics of road accidents. No reasonable person would want to be injured or mutilated. But though Jane risks putting others in this position, she is certainly not willing to do so. On the contrary, she devotes all her driving skills to avoiding that eventuality. The risk she runs is a risk of the failure of her skill, and it does not make her act of driving immoral, unless she knows herself to be in an unfit state to drive. The risk of failure does not mean the project should be abandoned, only that she do her best to ensure that she carries it out properly, with due care and skill. So too with the project of contraception. If it carries a risk of failure charity requires only that the risk be minimized, not that contraception be abandoned altogether. It demands, for instance, that if Andrew uses a condom when making love to Jane, then he does so with care: he should make sure he puts it on properly, be vigilant not to tear it, and so on. One may of course argue that unlike the projects of doctors, generals, car drivers, and so on, contraception is an unworthy project, not worth any risk. This is the traditional Christian position. But the point here is that it is not rendered unworthy by being uncharitable because of the possibility of failure.

Natural family planning again

Like Anscombe, GBFM have things to say about the rhythm method of avoiding conception. They refer to it, in common with many others, as 'natural family planning' (abbreviated to 'NFP'). This practice, according to them as to Anscombe, differs in important respects from artificial contraception. But they present rather different arguments which deserve to be examined separately. Writing of a situation in which a couple have reason to avoid having a baby, they say:

> When contraception is chosen, the choice is to impede the baby's coming to be in order that the goods represented by that reason be realized and/or the evils represented by it be avoided. When NFP is noncontraceptively chosen, the choice is to abstain from intercourse that would be likely to result in both the baby's coming to be and the loss of goods and/or occurrence of evils represented by that same reason in order that the goods represented by that reason be realized or the evils represented by it be avoided.
>
> Even when based on good reasons, the contraceptive choice by its very definition is contralife. It is a choice to prevent the beginning of the life of a possible person. It is a choice to do something, with the intent that the baby not be, as a means to a further end: That the good consequences of the baby's not-coming-to-be will be realized and the bad consequences of the baby's coming to be will be prevented. The noncontraceptive choice of NFP differs. It is a choice not to do something – namely, not to engage in possibly fertile sexual intercourse – with the intent that the bad consequences of the baby's coming to be will be avoided, and with the acceptance as side effects of both the baby's not-coming-to-be and the bad consequences of his or her not-coming-to-be. In this choice and in the acceptance of its side effects, there need be no contralife will. The baby who might come into being need not be projected and rejected.[35]

There appear to be two main strands to this argument. First, that practising NFP is not a form of contraception since, unlike contraception, it is not an act. Those who practise contraception both have intercourse and also perform a further contraceptive act, such as taking a pill or donning a condom. In NFP, on the contrary, the couple do precisely nothing. Second, contraception is aimed directly against the good which is the coming to be of a possible person; it sees that good as an evil. NFP on the other hand aims at avoiding the bad consequences of the birth of a baby and accepts the loss of the good of that baby as a side effect.[36]

I have already dealt with the first of these strands in discussing Anscombe's views. It is over-simple to say that the couple practising NFP do nothing. The choice not to have intercourse is itself an act, which constitutes avoiding having a baby. They do not merely not have intercourse; they avoid intercourse. Here is a case where, because of the agents' intention, doing nothing amounts to doing something. It is like not standing up when the Prime Minister enters the room. It constitutes acting against the generation of a new life just as directly as using artificial contraception.

A simple analogy may help to make this clearer. Having intercourse is like going for a walk, and abstaining from intercourse like abstaining from walking. Suppose I go for a walk round the block every day after lunch, except on Thursdays. For on Thursdays there is always somebody on the street collecting for charity. The charity is a good one, so I ought to give money to it if I can; but I don't want to. I also don't want to have to refuse the collector when she asks me, because it embarrasses me and makes me feel guilty. So I just stay in. Let us suppose that my motive for not wanting to give is a bad one; I have plenty of money that I could give if I were at all generous, but I am simply mean and greedy. I ought to give, and my failure to do so is a sinful failure of charity. It would be so if, when asked, I refused a donation, and it is no less true because I never actually refuse. My meanness takes the form of avoiding being asked, and I avoid it by doing nothing, by abstaining from my accustomed walk. My abstaining in this way is an expression of my sinful meanness. Actually saying no looks a much more direct expression of it, a point-blank refusal to do what charity requires; but there is no real moral difference between the two. In the same way, abstaining from intercourse when one might otherwise realize the good of a new life is an act, just as much as having intercourse and refusing to allow the new life to be generated, by means of artificial contraception.

There is a converse point to be made by means of this analogy. Let us now assume instead that my motives for not wanting to give are good ones: I would be happy to give if I could, but I am unemployed and have barely enough to support my wife and children. Now, of course, my failure to give is not sinful. I can stay at home on Thursdays with a clear conscience. But I could equally go for my walk and refuse the charity worker when she asks me. She might think me mean, but in fact I would not be, and I could explain as much. The encounter might be embarrassing for me, but it would not be a sinful one. Similarly, if there is a good reason for not wanting a child, the use of artificial contraception is, on the basis of GBFM's argument, no more sinful a way of avoiding it than abstaining from intercourse. Thus far, then, there is no clear moral difference between NFP and contraception.

But there is a second strand to the argument. This is an attempt to justify NFP by appeal to the principle of double effect. What people are trying to avoid in properly used NFP, according to GBFM, is the bad consequences, such as extreme poverty, that the conception and birth of a baby would cause; as a side effect they are prepared to accept that the baby will not be conceived. But the non-conception of a baby can hardly be thought of as a side-effect of a course of action designed to prevent the consequences of the conception of a baby. If preventing a consequence of a cause involves preventing the cause itself, this cannot be as a side effect. The effect is prevented precisely by preventing the cause, not by doing something else which unfortunately also has the effect of preventing the cause. And what is after all the direct effect of avoiding intercourse? It is not prevention of poverty, but the avoidance of conception.

A precisely similar fallacious argument could be constructed concerning use of the contraceptive pill. We could say that people on the pill do not project and reject a baby, but try to avoid the bad consequences of having a baby, accepting not having the good of the baby itself as a side effect. An argument for NFP which can also be used to justify artificial contraception is surely hardly acceptable as a justification of Christian moral views.

GBFM claim that the vital difference between NFP and artificial contraception is that the latter aims directly against the good of the coming to be of a possible person, while the former aims only at avoiding the bad consequences of the good which is the coming to be of that person. But it seems to me that this distinction cannot be maintained. First, it relies on the dubious notions of a possible person and the good of his or her coming to be, which I criticized earlier. Artificial contraception is not in fact aimed directly against any good. Further, it is in any case an inherently implausible distinction. There is no reason to believe that those who practise artificial contraception see the possible conception of a child as an evil while those practising NFP only see the consequences of such a possible conception as evil. The only reason why the possible conception of a child is ever seen as an evil to be avoided is because of the real or imagined evil of its consequences, because of the poverty it would cause, or because it would disrupt a career or disturb a pleasant life-style or ruin a good figure.

So I think the attempts of Anscombe on the one hand and of Grisez, Boyle, Finnis and May on the other to find a solid detailed basis in reason for the traditional Christian and modern Catholic ban on contraception fail. I have not seen another one that is at all convincing, and I do not know how to generate one myself. However, it does seem to me that a loose general connexion can be made between the church's teaching on contraception and the spirit of the Christian approach to life. The goods that we have in life are, in Christian belief, ones that we see as gifts of God, ones that we have to be open to receive. And that means not always trying to protect ourselves from the world around us, the world of natural causation in which and as part of which we receive the gifts of God. It is one of the merits of the approach of GBFM in particular, though I have found it logically defective, that it stresses the role of human goods in our moral thinking and hence the importance of retaining a spirit of openness, so that we may receive those goods as gifts of God. If we try to control, plan and manage all our contacts with the natural world, including other people, then we can no longer see the goods that come to us as gifts; they appear simply as the result of our management. We have lost the spirit of openness. Loss of that spirit distorts our vision, since it leads us to see the human goods that do come to us outside our control not as life-enhancing gifts but as disruptive interference, not as blessings for which we might give thanks but as threats against which we have to protect ourselves. The standard by which we judge all events and possible events is how they fit into our plans, how they suit our con-venience. Planning and convenience are of course very important aspects of life, but if they come to dominate our attitude this amounts to a grave imbalance in and a severe impoverishment of our lives, for human life does not consist in the greatness of its convenience.

Perhaps one way to understand the church's traditional teaching on contraception is to see it as part of its fight against the impoverishment of human life, against the fearful and thankless spirit that excessive concern with control engenders. It insists on seeing life as the most fundamental of the gifts of God, the one therefore to which we should be most careful to retain a spirit of openness and thankfulness. Neither in its beginning nor in its end is it to be too subject to human control, lest we, to our great loss, come to see it as a mere controlled human product, something which it is in our gift to give and take away when it suits our purposes. (Hence also the church's resistance to *in vitro* fertilization and euthanasia.) New life, when it comes, is therefore a good to which we do well to be open, and when it comes it is a gift to which the proper response is gratitude; it is not properly seen as the result of our good management upon which we are to congratu-late ourselves, nor as a disruptive failure of our management which we must fear and try to guard ourselves against. In so far as the use of contraception – or of natural family planning – diminishes the sense of life as gift and encourages us to see the world in terms of convenience and manageability, it is incompatible with Christianity.

However, we should beware of painting with too broad a brush. If a young wife refuses to have children, and so uses contraception, on the grounds that pregnancy will spoil her figure, we may well want to try to persuade her that she has her priorities wrong, and that her view of life will be transformed for the better if she opens herself up to the gift of new life from God. But this would be entirely the wrong approach to take with a devout, poverty-stricken mother of ten who cares lovingly for her family and who is subjected to periodic rape by her husband. Such a woman may have good reason to believe that another child would mean ruin for her and starvation for her existing children, and so use contraception in order to avoid such a disaster. It would be grotesque to accuse such a one of having her life centred round convenience, or of turning her back on the gifts of God.

With this important limitation, and though I have been critical of the argument in its details, it does seem to me in the light of the above considerations that GBFM are broadly right in the spirit of what they say, if I have understood that spirit aright. Where I think they are wrong is in trying to furnish too cogent a proof of the rightness of the church's teaching, too close a logical connexion between the human goods that any reasonable person will recognize and the church's ban on artificial contraception. But they are surely right in insisting that there must be some connexion between the two. The church's teaching on contraception is only properly understood when it is seen not as an attempted, perhaps unwarranted restriction on people's liberty, but as an aspect of the charity of the church, as part of its loving attempt to preserve and foster human goods. But this, of course, is not to 'prove' that a ban on contraception is right; there is, as far as I can see, no such proof. It is rather to see it in a sympathetic light, as an insistence on openness. Nevertheless, some might still want to say, however much it is true that we do well to be open to the human goods that God grants us, the use of contraception does not mean that we are closed to the gifts of God, merely that we want to receive the gift of children at the appropriate time; and we may also be open in quite other ways.

It is worth remarking that the concerns that appear to lie behind the arguments of GBFM and the approach to the understanding of the church's views on contraception that I have just been sketching fit in with what I was saying in chapter 4 about pleasure. Life, as pleasurable, is largely a participation in pleasurable activity, the unimpeded exercise of our faculties; and activity is always in the world; it requires contact with the world rather than insulation from it. This implies not regarding contact as interference. Some things in the world are actually bad for us, like scorpions and earthquakes, and we do have to protect ourselves from contact with them; there is genuinely harmful interference. But this fact should not be turned into a basic principle of our understanding of the world. Though it may be bad to be continually drenched, yet it is good occasionally to let the rain fall on our face. Nor should the fact that things can interfere with us be allowed to distort our understanding of human freedom. Our freedom is essentially not freedom from the world, but freedom in the world. The circumstances in which we live (generally, and unless we are very unfortunate) do not restrict our freedom but give it form, provide us with an environment, with opportunity, in which to act freely. We can see the Christian dislike of contraception as symbolic of a general determination to see life as in God's world, a disposition to see the things that enter our lives, perhaps unexpectedly, perhaps even against our will, as gifts that give us new opportunities for living, a determination not to insulate ourselves entirely from natural processes. They are gifts which give a new form to our freedom, reshape our field of activity, and so invite us into new pleasures, pleasures whose existence we might not otherwise have recognized and which may be deeper than any of which we may have thought ourselves capable.

10

Homosexuality

In chapter 8 I spoke about sexual activity mostly in the context of the wider relationship of marriage, for this is where, according to the mainstream Christian tradition, the proper place of sex is. As I have shown, there are two main lines of argument leading to this conclusion. First, sex is essentially, by its nature, procreative, so it is only in the context of a relationship that can cope properly with procreation, one which is permanent and close, so as to provide an environment fitting for children, that sex is legitimate. Second, sex is essentially expressive of love between complementary partners, man and woman; in effect, to engage in any explicitly sexual activity with somebody is to tell that person that you are deeply committed to him or her for life, so that if it takes place outside marriage it is a lie. I have tried to show that both of these lines of argument are seriously defective, that there is in no significant sense any natural purpose of sexual activity to which we are bound to conform, and such that all sexual relations outside the bounds of marriage are illegitimate. These two lines of argument are connected with the two possibilities I mentioned at the end of chapter 8. There, while accepting as a demand of love that if children were to result from a sexual relationship they should be born into a stable and loving environment such as a marriage, I mentioned two possibilities of sexual relationship from which no children arise: those heterosexual unions from which children are deliberately excluded by contraception, and homosexual unions, in which the physical possibility of procreation does not exist. In the last chapter we found, considering the first of these possibilities, no valid argument against the use of artificial contraception. At the level of argument, sex is not essentially procreative, since it is possible, without contradicting the nature of the act, to impede the natural procreative potential of heterosexual intercourse by the use of contraception. Hence it cannot be shown that sex must be limited to a permanent relationship; it is not *a priori* confinable to marriage. This is not to say that there is nothing special about marriage or about sex within marriage, but what there is special about it cannot be read off from the nature of the act; it is a specialness Christians have partly created.

We now have to turn to the second possibility adumbrated at the end of chapter 8, that sex may take place outside marriage but within a relationship from which no offspring will result because both partners are of the same sex. Given that it is the standard Christian position that sex may only take place within marriage, a special significance is also given to homosexuality. If sex within marriage has, at least potentially, everything right about it, sex between two people of the same sex has more or less everything necessarily wrong with it.[1] To begin with, there is the simple fact that marriage between two people of the same sex has no place in the Christian scheme. Since it cannot take place within marriage, sex between two men or two women cuts across the traditional Christian determination to confine sex to marriage. Given this determination, there is certainly no room for homosexual practices, even within the context of a relationship of mutual self-giving. But the illegitimacy of homosexual practices has not only been insisted upon on the basis of this determination; it has been argued for on other grounds. This has been necessary because there are those, within the church and without, who see nothing particularly wrong with them, or who attach great potential value to them if they express the love of committed partners. Homosexual men and women, and those who sympathize with them, concede that this goes against the traditional restriction of sex to married men and women, but contend that the traditional attitude should be relaxed to accommodate loving homosexual relationships.

The arguments brought in support of the traditional hostility to homosexual practices have been many and various. I will look at some of them in this chapter. Some of the issues involved have already been covered in earlier chapters, and what was said there is also relevant here. It has been argued that homosexual acts are unnatural, that the very nature and purpose of sex and of our sexual and other organs forbids them. If, to take the example I discussed in chapter 5, anal sex between man and wife is a misuse of their organs, then so is anal intercourse between two men. And no offspring can follow from it; it is thought to be in some way essentially sterile. And that is because it does not involve, either, any complementarity. We found, however, that there was strong reason to doubt the value of any argument based on the nature and purpose of sex. It was also found that there were serious weaknesses in the concept of complementarity, and that our understanding of the fecundity of human beings and relationships, and of sexual activity within those relationships, was not to be limited to procreation.

The use of scripture

But if the arguments surrounding the nature, purpose and meaning of sex, and from complementarity and fecundity do not work, as I have tried to show, if they then fail to produce the results the theologians have wanted to get in their desire to support traditional church teaching, if sexual relationships between people of the same sex cannot be ruled illegitimate on these theoretical grounds, that is not the end of the matter. For the fact remains that theologians and other Christians have wanted to ban homosexual relationships. It is not that they have thought such things perfectly unobjectionable and then changed their minds because they have come across a proof that they are wrong. How such an antecedent desire is characterized will depend on one's point of view. For those sympathetic to the tradition, the desire represents an insight into the nature and purpose of sex and the will of God. For those hostile to it, and who perhaps see themselves as objects of the church's hostility, it is rather a most unChristian prejudice. However it is described, the conviction that such things are wrong has largely been prior to any sort of argument, and then abstract arguments have been developed to support that conviction. Where does that antecedent belief come from?

An obvious answer would be: from scripture. Are there not clear indications in both the Old Testament and the New that such behaviour is to be condemned, and are we not then compelled to condemn it? Surely, to take the best-known texts, the story of Sodom and Gomorrah and Paul's words in the first chapter of the epistle to the Romans leave no room for doubt. Before we look at these texts in any detail, it is well to heed John Boswell's warning on the use of scripture in this area. Writing about the treatment of homosexual people in the Middle Ages, he writes thus:

> Careful analysis can almost always differentiate between conscientious application of religious ethics and the use of religious precepts as justification for personal animosity or prejudice. If religious strictures are used to justify oppression by people who regularly disregard precepts of equal gravity from the same moral code, or if prohibitions which restrain a disliked minority are upheld in their most literal sense as absolutely inviolable while comparable precepts affecting the majority are relaxed or reinterpreted, one must suspect something other than religious belief as the motivating cause of the oppression.[2]

This is in fact something which has happened, Boswell claims, in the Christian tradition with respect to use of scripture. He goes on:

> The very same books which are thought to condemn homosexual acts condemn hypocrisy in the most strident terms, and on greater authority: and yet Western society did not create any social taboos against hypocrisy, did not claim that hypocrites were 'unnatural', did not segregate them into an oppressed minority, did not enact laws punishing their sin with castration or death... In the very same list which has been claimed to exclude from the kingdom of heaven those guilty of homosexual practices, the greedy are also excluded. And yet no medieval states burned the greedy at the stake. Obviously some factors beyond biblical precedent were at work in late medieval states which licensed prostitutes but burned gay people.[3]

The fact is, today as well as in the Middle Ages the attitude of many Christians to homosexual activities and those who take part in them is markedly different from their attitude to prostitutes or to the greedy even though we would all admit that it is sinful to be a prostitute or to be greedy. The point is not to deny that passages condemning homosexual activity can be found in scripture, but to ask why they are looked for and put to the use that is made of them. We do not have to confine ourselves to Boswell's examples. It is traditional to say that in Leviticus there are two places where homosexuality is unambiguously condemned. The first says: 'You shall not lie with a man as with a woman; it is an abomination' (18.22). The second says: 'If a man lies with a male as with a woman, both of them have committed an abomination; they shall be put to death, their blood is upon them' (20.13). Actually, only the first of these forbids sexual relations between men. The second prescribes to the community at large how men who do this are to be treated. Most Christians nowadays have no qualms about disregarding this second law, and would be horrified if it were suggested that gay[4] men should be put to death. Yet failure to kill them is just as much a breach of the law, just as contrary to the text of scripture, as the gay men's sexual activities are. Plainly, that something is laid down in scripture is not what settles the matter.

Again, there are to be found in this same book of scripture passages forbidding all kinds of things. For example, Leviticus 19.9 forbids farmers when harvesting to reap their fields right up to the edge; we do not seek to uphold this law. 19.13 forbids keeping the wages of a hired servant overnight; yet we do not feel obliged to protest against the modern practice of paying people weekly or monthly. 19.19 forbids the wearing of garments made of two kinds of stuff, but we are not worried by people wearing such garments. 19.27 says: 'You shall not round off the hair on your temples or mar the edges of your beard.' Trimming the edge of the beard is in fact considered so serious that it is condemned twice in Leviticus.[5] Yet the church does not feel compelled to speak out against the evils of beard-trimming. Sex between two men or between two women is not condemned by Christians simply because it is condemned in scripture, but because they antecedently want or feel impelled to condemn it regardless. Scripture, in the same way as various abstract arguments, is invoked to support a pre-existing inclination to forbid homosexual relations.

We are all perfectly capable of ignoring the laws and attitudes of scripture when we want to, and we think such a procedure quite legitimate if done for the right reasons. Of course we do not mind if people have their beards trimmed, we would say, because we are not bound by law just because it is law. The controlling principle for us as Christians is that he who loves his neighbour has fulfilled the whole law.[6] All our behaviour is to be judged by that standard, as I said back in the first chapter. We do not in general condemn the trimming of beards or the wearing of polyester/cotton socks because it is hard to think of circumstances in which such activities would offend against the law of love. And of course exactly the same should apply in our attitude to any sexual activity, including same-sex relationships. We should no doubt be ready to criticize sexual activity of any kind that is incompatible with love; and no doubt there is plenty of homosexual activity that works against love, just as there is a lot of heterosexual activity that does. But if it is not against love, Christians have nothing to say about it, except in so far as it is harmful to those who practise it, for then love for those people demands that an attempt be made to dissuade them from it. Yet persistently Christians have refused to think about this subject in terms of the love commandment, in contravention of the explicit and central demands of the gospel. The attitude of many to homosexual relationships and to those who are party to them is not only pre-philosophical, it is also anti-Christian.

Sodom and Gomorrah

However, if scripture as well as reason can be used in an unChristian way in this area, that does not show that they cannot also be used in a Christian way. It may yet be that, if we lay ourselves open to look at scripture honestly, it really does have something to say to us on this subject that differentiates homosexual activity from the trimming of beards. It may also be that there are valid or persuasive rational arguments against homosexuality, regardless of the spirit that inspires them. Let us look first at scripture. The text most famously held to condemn homosexual acts is the story of Sodom and Gomorrah in Genesis 19. To understand this story properly we have to go back to an earlier point in the narrative. In chapter 18 God, sometimes confusingly disguised as three men, appears to Abraham. Seeing the men passing by his tent Abraham asks them to favour him by stopping with him, resting and eating:

> My lord, if I have found favour in your sight, do not pass by your servant. Let a little water be brought, and wash your feet, and rest yourselves under the tree, while I fetch a morsel of bread, that you may refresh yourselves, and after that you may pass on – since you have come to your servant (18.3–5).

They agree to stop, and Abraham gives them not bread and water but cakes, some freshly slaughtered veal and milk, himself standing by ready to serve them (18.6–8). In other words, he shows these strangers exemplary hospitality and courtesy, as one is supposed to do in those parts and as is polite anywhere. This is very important for understanding the Sodom story, which is its contrasting sequel. Most of God – two men of the three, who now become two angels – go on to Sodom and Gomorrah to see if the reports

about the wickedness of the men of Sodom are really true. The beginning of
chapter 19 shows the two angels arriving at Sodom in the evening. Lot,
Abraham's nephew, who has taken up residence there, notices them:

> When Lot saw them, he rose to meet them, and bowed himself with his face to the
> earth, and said: 'My lords, turn aside, I pray you, to your servant's house and
> spend the night, and wash your feet; then you may rise early and go on your way.'
> They said: 'No; we will spend the night in the street.' But he urged them
> strongly; so they turned aside to him and entered his house; and he made them a
> feast, and baked unleavened bread, and they ate (19.1–3).

Lot, like his uncle Abraham, does them proud with his hospitality. But now
the men of the city surround the house:

> They called to Lot: 'Where are the men who came to you tonight? Bring them out
> to us that we may know them.' Lot went out of the door to the men, shut the door
> after him, and said: 'I beg you, my brothers, do not act so wickedly. Behold, I
> have two daughters who have not known man; let me bring them out to you, and
> do to them as you please; only do nothing to these men, for they have come under
> the shelter of my roof' (19.5–8).

It seems clear from Lot's response to the men of the city that what they want
to do when they want to know them is not to find out who they are but to
force themselves on them sexually, to rape them.[7] Their behaviour stands in
contrast to the hospitality first of Abraham, then of Lot. Their great sin is
gross inhospitality.[8] Instead of welcoming the visitors, feeding and shelter-
ing them as Lot does they want to rape them. This is now recognized by
most scholars,[9] but even among those who do recognize it there is sometimes
an ambivalence. For example, the Anglican Board for Social Responsibility's document *Homosexual Relations* says:

> The crime of the inhabitants of Sodom is viewed primarily as a failure to respect
> the duty of hospitality, which was regarded so much more seriously in the ancient
> Semitic world than it would be today. The purpose of the homosexual attack is to
> demonstrate the ultimate breach of the obligation of hospitality.[10]

On the other hand, it accepts that 'the narrative does express abhorrence of
homosexuality'.[11] But it clearly does not. It expresses abhorrence of, if
anything, treating the obligations of hospitality with contempt by attempting to assault and rape a visitor. Sexual assault and rape are not the same as
ordinary sexual relations, whether homosexual or heterosexual. If the
visitor in question had been a woman, nobody would have dreamed of
suggesting that the story expresses abhorrence of heterosexuality.

However, there is indeed significance in the fact that the visitor is a man.
To rape anybody is an exercise in domination; it is to make them your victim
and to let them know they are in your power. There is some evidence,

according to Bailey, that both the Egyptians and the Assyrians raped their vanquished enemies for just this reason.[12] The evidence is only indirect, but it would surprise nobody; it is an obvious thing to do if you want to humiliate somebody.[13] But we also saw, in chapter 3, that Hebrew thought and society are shot through, like those of other peoples, with male domination. Hence the rape of a man is all the more humiliating for him; it is to lie with him forcibly as with a woman, and hence to degrade him to the status of a woman. It is no accident that both in the story of Sodom and Gomorrah and in the parallel in Judges 19 an attempt is made to fend off the attack on the male guest by offering women to the crowd instead. No doubt the continued male dominance in Western societies accounts for the fact that, although theoretically all same-sex relationships are frowned upon by the church and people at large, yet it is male homosexuality that comes in for the greatest and most consistent attention. The Congregation for the Doctrine of the Faith's *Letter to the Bishops of the Catholic Church on the Pastoral Care of Homosexual Persons*, for example, evidently hardly has lesbians in mind at all; and queer-bashers bash male queers.[14]

It is certain, then, that the story of Sodom and Gomorrah is the story of the violation of hospitality and in particular the hospitality to be shown to a male; it is not a condemnation of homosexual acts as such or of people who take part in them. John McNeill has a poignant comment on this:

> If this interpretation of the true sin of Sodom is correct, then we are dealing here with one of the supremely ironic paradoxes of history. For thousands of years in the Christian West the homosexual has been the victim of inhospitable treatment. Condemned by the Church, he has been the victim of persecution, torture, and even death. In the name of a mistaken understanding of the crime of Sodom and Gomorrah, the true crime of Sodom and Gomorrah has been and continues to be repeated every day.[15]

Romans 1

Though lesbians do not feature in this story from Genesis, they are included in the other major text most often adduced in discussions of homosexuality, Romans 1. Here Paul harshly condemns all those Gentiles who reject the true God. Though they claim to be wise, they have not perceived the true God as they ought to have done; they have become fools, and have 'exchanged the glory of the immortal God for images resembling mortal man or birds or animals or reptiles' (Rom. 1.23). Because of their culpable foolishness and idolatry God

> gave them up to dishonourable passions. Their women exchanged natural relations for unnatural, and the men likewise gave up natural relations with women and were consumed with passion for one another, men committing shameless acts with men and receiving in their own persons the due penalty for their error (Rom. 1.26f.).

This passage is often taken as a straightforward condemnation of homosexual acts, impressive in its impartiality in condemning women along with men, and more binding than that implied in Genesis, since it is from the New Testament rather than the Old, and is in the form of explicit teaching rather than narrative. There is indeed no doubt that Paul thinks sex between two men or two women is very much to be regretted, but the reason why is important. Note first a certain symmetry in what he says. Because these people have exchanged the glory of God, whose invisible nature they should know from the world around them, for idols, they have also exchanged natural sexual relations for unnatural ones. Not knowing the nature of God they lose their own nature. But this does not just mean that they go homosexual. We have to read on:

> Since they did not see fit to acknowledge God, God gave them up to a base mind and to improper conduct. They were filled with wickedness, evil, covetousness, malice. Full of envy, murder, strife, deceit, malignity, they are gossips, slanderers, haters of God, insolent, haughty, boastful, inventors of evil, disobedient to parents, foolish, faithless, heartless, ruthless.[16]

The loss of their own nature means that they become full of all sorts of vice. It is not homosexuality to which God has given them up, but a whole way of life. Because they have rejected God, they have become godless. For Paul, homosexual activity is part of that godless way of life. It is indeed singled out for special treatment; this is not, however, because it is so much worse than any of the other things he mentions, but because it has for him a symbolic value. The general unnaturalness and corruption of their lives is expressed in a most dramatic fashion in their sexual behaviour. In view of all we have seen of the natural expressiveness of the body and the peculiar load of meaning we tend to put on sexual behaviour, this is no surprise.[17] For Paul, having sex with a member of your own sex belongs to that godless way of living, and it expresses your belonging to it. It has somewhat the same place in Romans as using prostitutes has in I Cor. 6, which I discussed in chapter 8.

It is therefore significant that homosexual activity is never in the New Testament condemned independently of other kinds of behaviour all of which are condemnable in their own right, from a Christian point of view, and which are condemned independently elsewhere. Homosexual acts are never condemned in isolation. The two other relevant passages are I Cor. 6.9f.:

> Do you not know that the unrighteous will not inherit the kingdom of God? Do not be deceived; neither fornicators[18] nor idolaters, nor adulterers, nor the soft (*malakoi*), nor those who lie with men (*arsenokoitai*),[19] nor thieves, nor the greedy, nor drunkards, nor revilers, nor robbers will inherit the kingdom of God.

And I Tim. 1.8–10:

> Now we know that the law is good, if any one uses it lawfully, understanding this, that the law is not laid down for the just but for the lawless and disobedient, for the ungodly and sinners, for the unholy and profane, for murderers of fathers and murderers of mothers, for manslayers, fornicators,[20] sodomites (*arsenokoitai*), kidnappers, liars, perjurers, and whatever else is contrary to sound doctrine.

The significance of this contextualization of homosexual activities, their being seen as part of a whole way of life, is generally passed over. This is unfortunate, for it leads us to misunderstand what Paul is condemning, which is a whole way of life, a way of life which in Rom. 1 he sees as symbolized and encapsulated in homosexual practices.

So what we find in Rom. 1 is far from a simple condemnation of homosexuality.[21] At the root lies people's rejection of God, their worship of idols. As a result they lose their proper nature and fall into all kinds of sinfulness, a godless life. This passage from Romans is in fact an example of a standard Jewish polemic against pagans and their alleged way of life. It is quite close to the book of Wisdom, chapter 14. For example:

> The idea of making idols was the beginning of fornication, and the invention of them was the corruption of life. (14.12)

> Afterward it was not enough for them to err about the knowledge of God, but they live in great strife due to ignorance, and they call such great evils peace. For whether they kill children in their initiations, or celebrate secret mysteries, or hold frenzied revels with strange customs, they no longer keep either their lives or their marriages pure, but they either treacherously kill one another, or grieve one another by adultery, and all is a raging riot of blood and murder, theft and deceit, corruption, faithlessness, tumult, perjury, confusion over what is good, forgetfulness of favours, pollution of souls, sex perversion, disorder in marriage, adultery, and debauchery. For the worship of idols not to be named is the beginning and cause and end of every evil. (14.22–27)

Because of the importance of the body as an expressive medium, and because Paul sees homosexual relations as wrong, they become for him symbolic and expressive of this whole way of life. Paul condemns homosexual activities because of the significance he sees in them. But all human behaviour has significance in context; it is from its context that what we do gets its meaning. Here this behaviour gets its meaning for Paul from the context of the rejection of God and the generally sinful, because inhuman, life in which Paul situates it. For him, it is just what you would expect from such dreadful people, people who reject God.

This is not to pretend that Paul did not find such sexual behaviour repugnant; it sheds light on why he found it repugnant. But now an important question arises concerning contemporary use of this text and the related ones in I Corinthians and I Timothy. Suppose two twentieth-century people, say two men, have a sexual relationship together but one which is not plausibly locatable in such a context. They have not rejected God, they are not murderers, liars, and so on, but are kind and generous and devout Christians. Now their sexual activity cannot have the same significance as that of all the murderers, idolaters and so on, that Paul is talking about. If the homosexual activity of a corrupt first-century Roman pagan might be seen, as Paul sees it, as the expression of a disordered life that comes from failure to recognize God, the sexual activity of a loving, gay, Christian couple cannot be that. Their homosexuality cannot be a punishment for rejecting God, for they have not rejected God. It cannot be just what you would expect from such dreadful people, for they are not dreadful people; they do not lead the terrible life of which, in Paul's thought, such sexual behaviour is the natural bodily manifestation. Thus what Paul says in Romans 1 and elsewhere is simply not applicable to many modern homosexual people or those of past ages. For him, it was part of a package that embraced a whole way of life; for us, it is not. We do not know how he would have reacted if he was confronted by a pair of pious Christian homosexual men or women. We might guess he would still have been horrified;[22] but his horror would have had its roots in his reaction to the pagan rejection of God, and could not fairly have been expressed in the terms in which he speaks in the passages we have discussed.

'Unnatural'

There is a further point that should be mentioned in connexion with this part of Romans 1. Paul speaks of such behaviour being against nature in some sense. It is not clear exactly what he means; his remarks are too brief. However, it is possible that his thought is connected with the Greek notions that were later developed into a theory of natural law.[23] From at least the time of Plato people have appealed to nature as an argument against sexual relations between people of the same sex, as the extract from the *Laws* cited in chapter 5 testifies: such things do not happen in nature, among animals, so they ought not to be performed by people, either. The application of such arguments to homosexuality is unconvincing, partly because there is in fact plenty of homosexual practice in the animal world.[24] Apart from the failure of such an empirical appeal, I have in earlier chapters voiced doubts about the whole of this line of thought, and those doubts apply in the area of homosexuality as much as elsewhere. Nature is not something to which we have to conform. Much of our energy is devoted to manipulating natural forces or averting them; we dam rivers, and we use the energy we get from those dams to give us light and help us to stay awake when naturally it would be dark and we would sleep. Inventiveness, adaptability and the manipulation of the natural world are part of our nature. To say that homosexual relations are unnatural, even if they did not occur in the animal world, would at most be to say that they are a sign of an inventiveness that is typically human. But this particular piece of inventiveness disturbs Paul, and many other people as well, Christian or not, as other inventions do not. Why? As far as Paul is concerned, the obvious answer lies in his Jewish background. It is obvious enough that same-gender sex acts, between males at least, were much disliked by the Jews, and forbidden in their religious law: remember Lev. 18.22. But we spent a whole chapter looking at this verse. It calls one man's lying with another man as with a woman an abomination, but behind this lies the affirmation of a whole social system which lays great emphasis not only on male superiority but also on gender role and other kinds of classification, division and separation, above all the separation of Israel, the people of God, from the nations. What makes male homosexuality in particular repugnant here is that it is queer: it cuts across distinctions, and so threatens the whole of the Israelite way of life and the ways of thought, including the conception of nature, associated with it.

Something similar probably lies behind much of the homophobia that exists in some modern societies and also, regrettably, in the church, the feeling sometimes expressed by saying that what gay people do is 'unnatural'.[25] Gay people, especially gay men, are often considered a threat – to other men, to young children, to the morals of teenagers and adolescents, to the family, to the state, to civilization. None of this has ever been substantiated, and there is little reason to believe much of it. But the fact that it can nevertheless gain such extensive and uncritical credence, even among Christian writers, does testify to a widespread feeling of being threatened in some way or other. This appears to derive, just as it did in Old Testament times, from the shaking of people's patterns of thought, the ways they see and classify themselves and others. Gay people cut across gender expectations in a way that makes some others acutely uncomfortable. They are unclean because they are anomalous, like many of the unclean animals of Leviticus.[26] They are, in a deep sense, misfits representing a challenge and a threat to important distinctions and cherished divisions which are deeply-rooted in the structure of our society. In this, somewhat ironically, they are like the Jews. Heinz Heger sums up this connexion thus:

> The point is ... to understand why the Nazis picked out for elimination and mass murder certain 'racial' groups (Jews and gypsies), certain ideological groups (socialists and communists, also those Christians who took their gospel seriously enough), and certain sexual groups (homosexuals). At first sight, after all, 'race', conscience and sexual orientation seem three very different categories. But Nazism... had to attack the Jews and gypsies, because they each in their way were international and rejected the arbitrary barriers between states. It had to attack the socialists and communists, who sought to abolish class privilege. And it had to attack gay people, and homosexuality in general, which puts in question the division between the sexes and threatens male supremacy.[27]

The 1975 Congregation for the Doctrine of the Faith's *Declaration* on sexual ethics talks about homosexual people's 'inability to fit into society'.[28] But, if this is true, it is not necessarily the homosexuals' fault. They also failed to fit into Nazi society, just as Jews, gypsies, communists and some Christians did. But this was not the fault of gays, Jews, gypsies, communists and Christians; it was the fault of Nazi society. If it is in some sense true that today gay people still do not fit into society,[29] this need be no judgment against gays. It is social structures and the expectations that arise from them that determine whether people fit or not. Whether somebody is able to fit into society depends very largely on whether people in society are willing to make room for them. 'Society' is not a given, unalterable structure, but consists of people who are capable of either accepting or rejecting others.

The words of the Vatican document can be understood as much as a criticism of the societies into which homosexuals cannot fit as of homosexuals themselves. For, in any Christian view, it is part of love to make room for people. That means we are committed to work for a society in which people are allowed to fit, in which they are not relegated to the margins or despised because they do not fit, a society in which we can be one, a society which positively sets out to make room for those who might tend to be marginalized or despised, the anomalous, the failures and the outsiders. The desire to exclude is a radically anti-Christian desire. Here we should remember that Christianity was first a religion designed for the excluded and that it first flourished among those who counted for nothing. Think of Paul's words to the Corinthians:

> Consider your call, brethren; not many of you were wise according to worldly standards, not many were powerful, not many were of noble birth; but God chose what is foolish in the world to shame the wise, God chose what is weak in the world to shame the strong, God chose what is low and despised in the world, even things that are not, to bring to nothing things that are (I Cor. 1.26–28).

If we are to be true to our origins, that means at the very least not acting in any way that brings division and that marginalizes, causes people to be despised. That means in turn that we are committed to not being threatened by people who cut across our expectations, gender expectations as well as others. Love demands of us that we learn not to be horrified by activities which are not against love. And that means we have to sit lightly on things like our socially determined gender expectations, not let them penetrate so deeply into the structure of our thought and our society.

The gay identity

The question of identity is one that is now often important to people. The question 'Who am I?' or 'What am I?' sometimes assumes great significance and becomes problematic. One aspect of this that seems to be quite modern is the way in which sexual desires have become for many people a large constituent of their identity, determining what kind of person they are, how they think of themselves, how they label themselves, and how they see their place in the world. This importance of sexual preference is in large measure specious, since it is irrelevant to most of us for most of our lives. We recognize this in the way our self-identification varies from context to context. The answer to the question 'What are you?' depends on who asks it and where; it might be 'I'm a bus driver', or 'I'm a Methodist', or 'I'm a Zambian' or 'I'm a weightlifter' or 'I'm a woman'. It might sometimes be 'I'm homosexual' or 'I'm heterosexual', but it might also be many other things, because many features of ourselves are important to us in different situations. We do not so much have an identity as a set of overlapping and shifting identities. What, then, makes sexual preference assume such a disproportionately large role in some people's self-identification? An obvious part of the answer is that people with abnormal sexual preferences, if those preferences are known, are singled out for opprobrium on account of those preferences. Their sexuality becomes socially one of the most important things about them because it is socially problematic for them. So it is normally members of sexual minority groups who tend to identify themselves in terms of their sexuality. For homosexual people the fact that they are homosexual tends to be more important to them than their heterosexuality is to heterosexual people.

One thing any marginalized group does eventually is to form a group identity; denied a proper identity by the society that rejects them, outcasts form their own society, create their own place and their own identity. Hence the development of the 'gay identity'. To be gay does not just mean being attracted to people of the same sex; it means identifying yourself as gay, adopting a characteristic range of attitudes, tastes, activities: going to gay bars, buying gay magazines, maybe wearing a moustache, check shirt, blue jeans and white socks, or whatever the group fashion is at the moment. One tendency of people in any marginalized group is to reject the values of the society that rejects them. The much-reported frantic and exhausting sexual over-activity of many gay men, chiefly in America but also elsewhere, is not best understood as due to their depravity. It, like so much else to do with sex, has a social significance: it is a deliberate rejection of the official sexual values of the society which is seen as oppressive; like the activities of the lesbian sadomasochist quoted in chapter 6, it signifies their rejection of and liberation from those who reject and oppress them. If Christians continue to acquiesce in, and even encourage, the marginalization of gay people, their rejection as an integral part of our society, then we at the same time encourage this sterile and unsatisfying kind of behaviour. For we encourage the perpetuation of this kind of identity and give it false importance. As the CDF *Letter* rightly says:

Today, the Church provides a badly needed context for the care of the human person when she refuses to consider the person as a 'heterosexual' or a 'homosexual' and insists that every person has a fundamental identity: the creature of God, and by grace, his child and heir to eternal life (§16).

The 'Homosexual Condition'[30]

One important shift in church thinking on homosexuality in recent years has been the introduction of the notion of the 'homosexual condition'. In the past church attitudes to homosexual acts and the people who perform them have been openly and deliberately hostile. People who perform homosexual acts have simply been execrated. Now things have changed and the church shows a much more positive attitude. Attempts have been made to insist that homosexuals are integral members of society and of the church. One aspect of this is that recently in the church talk of perversion, sins against nature, and so on, in connexion with homosexual practices has been less to the fore, giving way to a quasi-medical vocabulary, and a way of describing homosexual people has developed which is more consonant with modern thinking. Now they are not so much wicked as sick; they suffer from something called 'the homosexual condition'. The 1975 CDF *Declaration* speaks thus:

> A distinction is drawn ... between homosexuals whose tendency ... is transitory or at least not incurable; and homosexuals who are definitively such because of some kind of innate instinct or a pathological constitution judged to be incurable ... No pastoral method can be employed which would give moral justification to these acts on the grounds that they would be consonant with the condition of such people (§8).

There are many kinds of condition: we speak of social conditions, economic conditions, conditions of hygiene, and so on. But here it is the medical condition that is being taken as a model for homosexuality. That is clear from the reference to possibilities of cure and to 'pathological constitution'. This kind of language was taken up in the CDF *Letter* of 1986. It says in connexion with the 1975 document:

> Special concern and pastoral attention should be directed toward those who have this condition, lest they be led to believe that the living out of this orientation in homosexual activity is a morally acceptable option. It is not (§3).

The reference to 'those who have this condition' makes it clear that a medical model is again being followed (it is only medical conditions that you *have*), albeit one with moral overtones. It is not so much that homosexuals commit horrible sins as that, unfortunately and often through no fault of their own, they have a tendency or disposition to perform such acts. It is still a morally bad thing if they actually give way to this tendency, but it is not sinful that they have it; it is like a tumour on their moral insides.

In the context of the church and the history of church thinking on homosexuality, this approach clearly has a great deal to recommend it. First, it enables a clear distinction to be drawn between homosexual acts and homosexual tendencies. This relieves people of any burden of guilt for having homosexual tendencies (provided that they have not brought them upon themselves). If having these tendencies is properly thought of as analogous to a medical condition, like a tendency to come out in spots or develop fevers, then you are not blameworthy for having them any more than you are for having malaria or tuberculosis – unless you have deliberately exposed yourself to infection. People who have homosexuality are not therefore to be persecuted or belittled, either by themselves or by others. Neither are they to be marginalized, but accepted fully and lovingly into the community of the church. Secondly, it seeks to move away from condemnation towards understanding even of people who actually perform homosexual acts. While official church teaching remains clear that such acts are morally unacceptable and objectively wrong, they can now be seen not as a sign of wilful perversion or depravity but as the expression or symptom of a condition. An active homosexual is a sufferer, one to be understood and cared for. Hence the pastoral concern of the 1975 Vatican Declaration. And the English Catholic Social Welfare Commission's *Introduction to the Pastoral Care of Homosexual People* and the CDF *Letter* both describe themselves as being concerned with pastoral care.

There is, then, potentially much good in this approach. But it does not work. The conception of homosexuality as a condition serves only to introduce more obscurity into an already difficult subject. To begin with, thinking of homosexuality as a condition is unlikely to help the integration of homosexuals into the church. To say that somebody acts or desires as he does because of his condition is also to deprive him of a certain moral autonomy and freedom of action which are essential to the Christian outlook. If the condition is the cause of his being as he is, then he cannot help being as he is, just as one with a physical condition cannot help displaying the symptoms of that condition. The person is seen, and learns to see himself, as a case and as a prisoner of his condition. Hence he is set apart, and sets himself apart, from the normal, the free. He is unnatural, anomalous, and the anomalous has no place in the scheme of things; it is rather a disturbance in the scheme of things, which has to be remedied so that order may be restored. To say that a homosexual has a condition is to say that a normal, 'healthy' person could not act like that. And the healthy, the normal, is central; the abnormal, the sick is the marginal.

If this approach is unlikely to have the desired effect pastorally and is difficult to reconcile with a belief in human freedom, neither is it plausible in itself. There are objections to the idea that there might be a condition called homosexuality. First, such a notion presupposes the division of sexual inclinations into two kinds – heterosexual and homosexual. We are to understand that people are naturally so constituted that they have hetero-sexual inclinations, but in those suffering from homosexuality these natural inclinations are suppressed in favour of homosexual desires, or are trans-muted into homosexual desires. But there is no reason to believe that such a division fits the case. To begin with, homosexual desires are not incom-patible with heterosexual desires in the way that this model presupposes. There are many we would describe as heterosexual who yet have homo-sexual desires, and many we would think of as homosexual who also have heterosexual desires. Homosexuality and heterosexuality are not opposites, and the world is not divisible into heterosexuals and homosexuals. There is a whole spectrum of distribution of sexual inclination. One consequence of this is that homosexual desire is not incompatible with heterosexual desire. It is quite possible to have homosexual desires while still retaining 'normal, healthy' heterosexual desires. To have homosexuality is not to have your heterosexual desires infected. Hence homosexual desire is not correctly described as distorted or perverted heterosexual desire, nor does it suppress heterosexual desire. Neither are homosexual desires plausibly thought of as experienced by people in addition to their normal, heterosexual desires. People who are sexually attracted to others of either sex do not have to cope with having two sets of desires; they are not necessarily attracted to more people than the strictly heterosexual or homosexual are.

There are also many people who may properly be described as bisexual, who are sexually attracted by both male and female in more or less equal measure, and who are simply indifferent to the gender of one they find sexually attractive. If gender does not enter in as a component of their desire, then it would be a mistake to say that they have either homosexual or heterosexual desires. It is at the least misleading; just as it would be wrong to say, if somebody wanted apples, regardless of colour, that he wanted both red apples and green apples. Division and classification of our sexual desires, as of other things, depends on our interests. The division of sexual desire into homosexual and heterosexual reflects the general, but not universal, sexual interest in gender in our society: according to our norms, people are to seek sexual partners of the other sex. Other societies have had other norms.[31] What is wrong with homosexuals and bisexuals is that they do not display the kind of interest in gender that is expected of them. They are properly described not as suffering from a condition but rather as failing to meet the expectations (which may be fully justified) that others have of them.

This is related to a further point. When we speak of something as a sickness we normally imply that it is distressing in some measure; it is suffered. Syphilis is an illness because it is very unpleasant to have it. It is not just a matter of the presence in the system of whatever it is that causes syphilis. If the presence of the syphilis bug had no ill effects, we would not say that somebody who had the bug was sick. Part of its being distressing is that the one who has the sickness would normally be without it if he could be, and this because of the bodily or mental unpleasantness it causes.

Unlike syphilis, homosexuality does not of itself cause suffering or distress. Any suffering on the part of a homosexual stems not from the homosexuality itself but from other people's reaction to it. Somebody who suffers from a sexually transmitted disease like syphilis may also suffer rejection by family and friends and general condemnation from those around him. But such rejection is not part of the disease itself; he could suffer the identical disease without suffering the rejection. The suffering caused by the rejection is social in origin, not a symptom of the disease but a social consequence of having it. Other people's reactions may also be internalized; a man may be led to condemn himself if he contracts such a disease. But syphilis is not called a disease because of any rejection or self-rejection that may be consequent on catching it.

A homosexual person's suffering, if he or she suffers, is not like the suffering which is due to any illness. It is possible to be quite happy and a homosexual. It is not unpleasant just to 'have' homosexuality. It doesn't make you sneeze, come out in boils or give you a fever, and it doesn't kill you.[32] Any suffering involved in being homosexual is rather a matter of other people's reactions and general social attitudes. These reactions and attitudes may of course be internalized; the social climate in which we all grow and live, particularly what people say about us and people like us, and whether they say anything about us at all, is likely to have a powerful effect on the way we regard ourselves. Of course, if a gay man does reject himself because of his homosexuality, there is something internal about this; he carries his condemnation around with him, in a way similar to that in which he carries a virus around with him if he has a cold. He is never going to be happy and may well wish he was not gay. This can, if you like, be regarded as a condition, a sickness. But his condition is his tendency to reject himself, his inability to accept himself, not his homosexuality. And that means that it is his self-rejection that he needs to be cured of, if anything, not his homosexuality. The fact is that, if I am a gay man, my homosexuality does not of itself cause me distress; but it may distress other people, and then it is they who call it a disease.

The traditional unacceptability of homosexual activities from the viewpoint of the church is better understood much more straightforwardly: such activities are not symptoms of a condition but a breach of an aspect of the sexual discipline which the church seeks to encourage in its members.

Because of the way people vary in the range of their sexual desires, this discipline will be much harder for some to keep than for others; but there is no reason to think that there is something wrong with a person because he or she finds it difficult to a accept a particular discipline. If the church insists on this rule for whatever reason (and one must assume that this is because it believes homosexual activities to be bad for people in one way or another), then it must regard breaches of the rule as wrong, even if it is breached by those who find it specially difficult to keep it. But we have no need to suppose that people who do wrong therefore have something wrong with them. There is no reason to think that homosexual practices are in this respect any different from many others. The church similarly discourages people from masturbating or committing adultery. This is much easier for some people to accept than for others. But if we say that those who masturbate or commit adultery do wrong, we would not normally want to say that they do these things because there is something wrong with them, because they suffer from a condition. Quite normal people can masturbate or commit adultery, or very much want to, even if they ought not to. If we do not speak of a 'masturbatory condition' or an 'adulterous condition', there is no reason for us to speak of a homosexual condition, either.

The argument from inferiority

I now want to move away from talking about Christian attitudes to homosexuals and turn to some specific criticisms of homosexual activity. I take these from Lawler, Boyle and May. They write:

> Genital activity ... has a life-uniting or person-uniting dimension or meaning. Genital acts serve to join two persons, two lives, by a special kind of love. This is marital love – a love that has an exclusive and enduring quality about it, precisely because it has reference to the life-giving end or meaning of genital sexuality. This is a love which opens those whom it unites to what is other than themselves, to a transcendent goal or good toward which they can commit themselves and their shared lives. But this sort of love is simply incapable of being expressed in homosexual activity. In the homosexual union 'the authentic human sense of the other, as nourished by the enriching and complementary otherness of the other sex, is conspicuously absent'.[33]

This criticism of homosexual union springs from a central vision of the value and importance of sex which pervades their whole book, and which, in line with church teaching, takes marital love as the norm. Some of what Lawler, Boyle and May say here relates to points we have discussed earlier. For example, it appears to rely on views of the essential meaning of sexual activity which we have already seen to be questionable. Genital activity sometimes has a life-uniting or person-uniting dimension or meaning, which the church seeks to encourage, but sometimes it does not; it all depends on context.

This also might be said about the remarks on the enduring quality of married love: Marital love does not have its exclusive and enduring quality precisely because it has reference to the life-giving end or meaning of genital sexuality. This is shown by infertile marriages, which may be just as exclusive and enduring as any other. In any case what has to be shown is that marriage or other relationships cannot get that quality from elsewhere. That they can indeed get it from elsewhere is again shown by infertile marriages. So there is no reason why relationships between people of the same sex which include sexual activity might not be just as exclusive and enduring as fertile marriages. In fact, some of them are. And is there any evidence that fertile marriages are any more stable, exclusive and enduring than other relationships *for precisely that reason*?

But this passage also raises some other questions, which are more general in their import. The argument deployed here is an example of a prominent strategy which is used in arguing the impermissibility of same-sex sexual relations: to claim that they are inferior to heterosexual relations in that they lack certain beneficial features of the latter. For example, homosexual activity may be criticized, as it is here, as lacking the complementarity which, it is claimed, is such an important feature of heterosexual activity. Before looking in detail at this particular argument from complementarity, one general remark on this whole style of argumentation is in order. If the goal is to show the impermissibility of homosexual activity, there must be serious doubts about the strategy of relying on any argument designed to show the inferiority of homosexual practices, since there is a large difference between inferiority and impermissibility. Even if it can be proved that homosexual activities are of themselves inferior to heterosexual ones, it would by no means follow that they are to be discouraged or condemned. Simply, even if it can be shown that what happens in heterosexual intercourse is better than what happens in homosexual intercourse, homosexual intercourse may still be good; it may indeed be very good. All that will have been shown is that it is not as good. If heterosexual sex is the best, still we have no licence to make the best the enemy of the good. If we establish that homosexual sex is inferior sex, that is not, *prima facie*, any reason why it should be discouraged, let alone combatted. We might regret it when people evince erotic attraction to members of their own sex, since what they are inclined to is not as good as it might be, and we might encourage them in another direction. In the same way, we may be convinced that Hummel is an inferior composer to Mozart. If Andrew showed a marked preference for Hummel over Mozart, and spent all his spare time listening to the one rather than the other, we might deploy arguments to show the superiority of Mozart and encourage him to give up Hummel and listen to Mozart instead;

but if we failed, we should hardly have grounds for saying that he should not listen to Hummel at all.

If homosexual activity is to be legitimately discouraged, then it needs to be shown to be not merely inferior but vicious. Unfavourable comparisons will not do if they amount only to showing homosexual activity's lack of good points. It has to be demonstrated to have bad points.

One way of claiming that it is positively vicious might be to argue that it promotes vicious habits or in some other way inclines people who perform homosexual acts towards other actions which we all agree are bad. But this would be an unfruitful way of proceeding. An obvious drawback is that it cannot plausibly be maintained that practising homosexuals are more inclined to vice than anybody else. We would have to ask: does being a practising homosexual make you particularly neglectful of the needs of others, or violently aggressive? Does it turn you into a thief or a murderer? We have no reason to expect a positive answer. And there is no evidence to show that practising homosexuals are less virtuous or more vicious than anybody else. In fact, the Congregation for the Doctrine of the Faith's *Letter*, while seeking to discourage homosexual behaviour, does not seek to show that homosexual activity does have these moral consequences. Indeed the *Letter* itself acknowledges that 'homosexual persons are... often generous and giving of themselves'.[34] The claim that practising homosexuals are more vicious than they otherwise would be appears, then, to be a non-starter, and is acknowledged as such in a recent high-level church document.

But one might attempt to argue in a more subtle way, in terms of human development. The claim would be, not that homosexual behaviour of itself inclines people to sin, but that it prevents those who practise it from attaining a fullness of life they might otherwise enjoy. To put it crudely: practising homosexuals stunt themselves. They may not harm others, and in that sense be uncharitable; but they do prevent themselves from developing into mature people capable of appreciating as others can the various gifts of God and playing their full part in the shared movement towards the kingdom of God. Though charity may not demand of them that they cease their sexual activity, yet charity may demand of others, including the church, that they encourage practising homosexuals to a greater maturity. Those who engage in homosexual practices would then be, again crudely, like children who have to be drawn by their parents out of the cosy world of childhood, not because as children they are uncharitable, but because something greater lies before them. Parents who by their own fault fail so to draw their children into adulthood neglect their duty towards them and so are failing in charity. Similarly, it might be said, others have a duty to try to wean practising homosexuals from their immature ways.

This kind of argument is lent some plausibility by views of human development which see the process of sexual maturing as involving a homosexual phase. The goal of mature heterosexuality, it is held, is one which, for most people, is achieved after passing through a homosexual stage, normally in adolescence or early adulthood. If models like this are accepted, homosexuality is understood as a sign of immaturity, even the homosexuality of people of mature years. Homosexuals are those who have got stuck at a transitional stage of development. There is in this sense something wrong with them. This justifies trying to treat them, to unstick them so as to allow them to reach full development.

However, theories of this kind are not unproblematic. Principally, they involve the large assumption that heterosexuality is an element of maturity for everybody. The assumption is certainly not justifiable empirically. Many people who in all other respects are as mature as anybody else are homosexual. There would seem to be no reason for taking their homosexuality as a sign of immaturity rather than acknowledging that some people mature as homosexuals; for even if it is true that all or most people go through a homosexual stage while they are immature, it by no means follows that all homosexuality constitutes such a stage, that there cannot be mature homosexuals. The assumption that homosexuality is a sign of immaturity begins to look like an *a priori* principle, and one that lacks justification.

An interesting variant on such an approach is that of John Milhaven in his article 'Homosexuality and Love'.[35] In arguing the wrongness of homosexuality, he relies on a psychological theory, but he does so in order to show that homosexual practice is a failure in love. He agrees with the position for which I argued in chapter 1, that the commandment to love is the only absolute commandment of God, the one on which all others depend. For him, all homosexual acts are contrary to love. His argument is as follows:

> According to the Christian who is moved only by love and relies on the experience of the community, homosexual behaviour is wrong in that it frustrates the man himself. It fixates him at a stage far short of the full emotional and sexual development of the 'living man' who is 'God's glory'. In other words, a Christian for whom love is the only absolute understands that love is free, strong, open. (One might think of the analyses of Erich Fromm.) If I act in a particular way basically because I am afraid to look a woman in the eye, to relate with her independently as one grown person to another, if, for example, the affection I am seeking by my homosexual actions – though I may not realize it, but as psychological analysis finds – is Mommy's love for her little boy, then I must say to myself that I am not acting out of love. I am fleeing from love. Which is the greatest sin and the greatest failure for any man and, in a special way, for any Christian.[36]

A Christian who agrees that all our acts are to be judged according to the criterion of love will readily agree that if homosexual acts represent a flight from love, then they are to be shunned. But it is a big if. It is a large claim, too, that psychological analysis finds them to be such. To begin with, there are many different and competing schools of psychology. Milhaven does not say to which one he is referring – it appears to be a kind of 'depth psychology' – but to make such a large generalization in an area where there is so much difference of opinion seems unwarranted. There are also well-known doubts about the status of such psychological theories. They may be seen as heuristic models rather than as attempts to represent reality accurately. And their appeal to hidden mechanisms and unseen forces in the mind is at best problematic; some critics see them as the product of confusion rather than insight. Whatever the right in this matter, the claims of depth psychology are not to be presented as indisputable facts. It is very unclear indeed that a homosexual man is searching for 'Mommy's love for her little boy'.

Milhaven's only appeal to actual behaviour is that he relates (male) homosexual behaviour to the fear of looking a woman in the eye, the inability to relate with her independently as one grown person to another. Such fear and inability may indeed show lack of love, but there is no reason to believe that it is found universally or even typically in homosexual men; many are quite happy to look women in the eye, and enjoy happy and mature relationships with women.

Further, love is not a hidden psychic force. If somebody is not a loving person, this is not to be deduced by reference to putative hidden states of mind as interpreted by a disputed theory; it can be seen at the level of that person's behaviour. If homosexuals or anybody else are in flight from love, we can see this by the fact that their behaviour is unloving. But, while there are unloving gay men, there are also loving ones, including many who are sexually active. As I remarked above, this fact is freely acknowledged by the CDF *Letter*. There are many homosexuals, just as there are many hetero-sexuals, who devote themselves to the good of others – of their partner, if they have one, or of their neighbours or of those in special need. An indication of this is the well-known prominence of homosexuals in the 'caring professions'. If Milhaven's test is love, it cannot be said that homosexuals, as such, are any less likely to pass it than heterosexuals as such; still less is it true that, as Milhaven wants to show, they are bound to fail it because of the very nature of homosexual desire and activity as purportedly shown by a disputable psychological theory.

Homosexuality and complementarity

Christian thought on homosexual behaviour would do well, then, to be cautious about yoking itself to such theories as those just discussed. However, there is a kind of Christian analogue to these theories of psychological development, which I have already spent some time on: the idea that human moral maturity demands that we all be enriched by engagement with the complementary qualities of the other sex. It is sometimes said or implied that homosexual relationships are inferior because they lack the element of complementarity which is such an important feature of heterosexual relationships. The partners, being both of the same sex, are unable to provide for each other the enriching personal difference that a man and a woman can provide for each other. I have already, in discussing complementarity, given reasons for being dissatisfied with this line of argument in general. But there are additional reasons why appeal to the complementarity of the sexes should be viewed with caution when dealing with homosexuality, even if my earlier, more general arguments are rejected and we assume that complementarity is indeed a significant concept. I will try to illustrate this with reference to the argument of Lawler, Boyle and May.

The authors quote with approval somebody who says that in sexual relationships between people of the same sex 'the authentic human sense of the other, as nourished by the enriching and complementary otherness of the other sex, is conspicuously absent'. Here we encounter 'the other' again. Of course partners to a homosexual union do not thereby have their appreciation of the other sex sharpened, but that is not the same as 'the authentic human sense of the other'. As I argued in chapter 7, this can be nourished just as well by their same-sex partner, who is another person, with a different history and different qualities.

But let it be admitted, for the sake of argument, that it is desirable that people be exposed to the company of members of the opposite sex, so as to help them become more fully developed human beings. This is of course very different from saying that in order to reach maturity people in general need to have a sexual relationship with a member of the opposite sex, and it by no means implies it. Personal relationships are much wider than sexual ones. Men and women friends may chat together over cups of coffee, go to concerts or football matches together, work together in the same office, school or factory. If men and women by their nature enrich each other, they do so not only in bed. If that were not so, all chaste single people – including priests and religious – would be defective in this 'authentic human sense of the other'. In fact people of different sexes meet and enrich each other in shared projects of many different kinds and in the common round of everyday social intercourse, an intercourse shared not only with their sexual partners but with friends, colleagues and acquaintances of all degrees of intimacy.

If it is not necessary to have a sexual relationship with a member of the opposite sex in order to be exposed to the beneficial influence of the opposite sex, neither does a person have to be living with somebody of the opposite sex to get that benefit, and for the same reasons. Indeed if that were the case the conclusion would be that, if they are to be properly mature people, all men should be living with women, and all women with men. But nobody would subscribe to such a view. The Catholic church, with its long tradition of male and female monasticism, could not do so. Even apart from religious institutions, there is no moral objection to a number of men, even a couple of men, living together and sharing their lives; nor is there any objection to women doing the same. That is to say, the kind of argument deployed by Lawler, Boyle and May is in danger of trying to prove too much, that relationships acceptable to the church and in ordinary human society are in fact inadmissible.[37] What many, both inside the church and outside it, object to is not people of the same sex living together but their having sexual relations with each other.

This leads on to the second point. What is important in this line of thought is social exposure to people of the other sex, not sexual intimacy with one of them. Homosexual people tend to be averse to sexual intimacy with members of the opposite sex, but that is irrelevant to whether they benefit from social contact with them. Whether they have sexual inter-course with one of their own sex is similarly irrelevant. Those who are engaged in homosexual relationships, who not only live with or significantly share their lives with another or others of the same sex but actually have sex with them, are not thereby debarred from enriching and maturing contact with people of the other sex. There is no reason why they should not appreciate members of the other sex and their qualities from ordinary social contact. Practising lesbians may appreciate the qualities of their men friends and acquaintances just as much as other women do, and be broadened by them. The friendship of women may be very important to practising gay men. In fact, openly homosexual people often get on very well with members of the other sex, partly because there is no hidden sexual agenda in their relationship.

Engaging in homosexual activity does not, then, render impossible a proper appreciation of the other sex. But it might be argued that practising homosexuals are in fact less likely to develop such an appreciation than are heterosexuals and chastely continent homosexuals. I do not know whether such an argument has been or could be empirically substantiated. Suppos-ing it could, the conclusions to be drawn from it would be rather limited. If it is desirable that we all properly appreciate the qualities of people of the other sex, and if this is more difficult for practising homosexuals, what follows is that practising homosexuals have to be rather more careful to acquire this desirable appreciation than do others. It will not come so naturally to them and they may have to work harder for it than do others. The moral imperative for practising homosexuals would then be not to give up their sexual practices but to be vigilant about their attitude to the other sex.

Thus appeal to complementarity as a foundation for rejection of homosexual practices appears to be of little value. The argument from the complementarity of the sexes at most shows, if it shows anything, the desirability of social intercourse between the sexes, not the undesirability of sexual intercourse between members of the same sex.

Lawler, Boyle and May raise another important point here. They talk about openness: marital love 'is a love which opens those whom it unites to what is other than themselves'. The importance of this idea of openness has been emerging in the last couple of chapters. But it cannot, I think, be used to argue against homosexual activity in the way that Lawler, Boyle and May do. In a trivial sense all humans are open to what is other than themselves. We all interact with our environment and are human only as worlded. More importantly, most of us are open to and care about other people, as well as about obvious human goods, the gifts of God. But this has nothing in particular to do with marriage. Anybody can devote themselves towards a 'transcendent goal or good'; e.g. social reformers, nurses, those who look after the poor, politicians, musicians, teachers, priests, writers, etc. We do not have to get married to do that, to have a special kind of love that comes with marriage. Homosexuals are as capable of it as anybody else. Those who share their lives with others can devote their lives jointly to such a goal – e.g. the oft-cited partnership of Britten and Pears. If doing this jointly requires love then of course homosexuals can have this love and that is what they express in their sexual activity. What Lawler, Boyle and May seem to imply here is that it is children who are the only thing that qualifies as 'other', the only possible 'transcendent goal or good'; and that must be wrong.

Because of this supposedly necessary lack of such a transcendental goal or good, Lawler, Boyle and May conclude that there is a manifold unhappiness connected with homosexual relationships:

> There is, in short, a frustrating sterility in homosexual liaisons, an absence of any reference to the procreative good of human genital sexuality and a very impoverished and truncated mimicking of its unitive good ... Homosexual life is a bitter form of life, for it is founded on actions which pursue not the real goods of human persons but only the mere appearances of these goods. The unhappiness of many homosexuals is a sign that their lives are not properly orientated toward what is truly good.[38]

If what they say here were true, it would indeed constitute an argument against homosexual relationships. If they were necessarily unhappy in the ways indicated, it would be an act of charity to wean active homosexuals from their present liaisons to ones which are more fulfilling. But we have no reason to believe that it is true. There is no frustrating sterility in homosexual relationships as such. Despite all the enormous social pressures and much hostility from within the church as from without, there have been and are fertile and fulfilling homosexual unions, including between Christians. (When the authors write of the unhappiness of many homosexuals, this amounts to a tacit admission that there are indeed happy homosexuals.) It is false to assume that, important though it is, procreation is the only kind of creativity and fulfilment people are capable of or want. It is true that homosexual activity cannot be procreative in the way that heterosexual activity can. It is fair enough to point this out, and to resist any attempt, by homosexuals or others, to trivialize or treat with contempt the human ability to procreate. Children are a great good in human life which homosexual men and women normally cannot share in, and that inability is regretted by many of them. This is indicated by the fact that some homosexual couples adopt children with whom they can share their love, in the same way as childless married couples.

And while there may be no reference to the procreative good of human genital sexuality, there can well be reference to its other goods – the mutual giving of pleasure, the expression of mutual commitment, etc. And homosexual people cannot fairly be said to seek to mimic any unitive good. The physical intimacy of sexual intercourse can be expressive of intimacy of life for people of the same sex just as it can be for those of opposite sexes. Here, as in marriage, sex can express love. Modern church teaching since *Humanae Vitae* insists on two important dimensions to sex: as procreative and as a sign of personal union, and it insists that these two be held together. Sex between people of the same sex does not hold the two together, since it cannot be procreative. It must lack one dimension which the church insists is essential, and this is a major reason for the church's condemnation of it. But the two dimensions are separate and in fact separable, even if the church says they ought not to be separated. That homosexual relations lack the one does not imply that they lack the other.[39]

Lawler, Boyle and May speak of the 'bitterness of homosexual life'. This is an important consideration. If living life as an active homosexual necessarily leads to bitterness, then it is bad for people, and the church should certainly in its love for them try to persuade them to give it up. But does homosexual life lead to such bitterness? It must be said that 'homosexual life' is not a form of life; there are many forms of life lived by homosexuals, just as there are many forms of heterosexual life. It is no doubt true that some of these forms, whether homosexual or heterosexual, are bitter. It is equally true that some (not just one) are not. The authors seem to have in mind the hedonistic American gay subculture of bars and gyms in which a main activity is the search for irresponsible sex. One might well imagine that a life like this, centred around sex divorced from any enduring personal bond or other lasting values, becomes, exciting though it may be at first, frustrating and perhaps even bitter. But this is different from supposing that the bitterness of such a life is due to its being homosexual. Irresponsible hedonism and individualism of this sort may be bitter in the end whether practised by homosexuals or heterosexuals. But many homosexuals, like many heterosexuals, completely reject such a way of life and are concerned to live a responsible and productive life based on solid and lasting relationships. They may therefore lead happy and fulfilled lives. It is no doubt true that some homosexuals, like some heterosexuals, lead lives that are not properly orientated towards what is truly good. But that has not the least tendency to show that sexual relationships between people of the same sex are as such antithetical to what is truly good.

And so neither is the unhappiness of many homosexuals necessarily 'a sign that their lives are not properly orientated toward what is truly good', if by that is meant being an active homosexual. As there are many factors that can contribute to human happiness, so there are many and various reasons why somebody can be unhappy. In addition, given social attitudes prevalent at many times and places there are obvious reasons why you would not expect homosexuals to be as happy as others. Rightly or wrongly, many societies deny homosexuals a free and open place within them, and even persecute them. Any homosexual in such a society is liable to feel rejected, alienated and oppressed. These are not conditions which make for happiness. If in such circumstances we find that homosexuals tend to be less happy than others, it is *prima facie* plausible to ascribe that not to the nature of their homosexuality in itself, but to their being marginalized and despised.

Conclusion

I conclude with a brief account of the principal points of this survey, and of what I see to have been achieved and, as importantly, not achieved in it. In chapters 1 to 3 I have tried to make a case for saying that Christian sexual ethics are social in nature: what they fundamentally have in view is love of neighbour, that is, that we should behave in a loving manner towards one another. Such a conclusion is in the first place what we would expect given the general Christian emphasis on love of neighbour, which was stressed in chapter 1. In chapters 2 and 3 I was concerned to show that this approach is consonant with what the Bible has to say about sex. While a comprehensive treatment of biblical sexual ethics would be beyond the scope of a book such as this, I took two examples of biblical teaching which looked at first sight to run counter to my general thesis, namely Matt.5.27f. and Lev.18.22. I argued that these, far from being concerned only with what goes on in the head of an individual or with private sexual conduct, have deep social concerns: they concern respectively the property rights of others and the stability of the social structure, upon which people depend for their place in society. In order properly to understand the bodily activities referred to here, they have to be seen in their social context.

This treatment raised the broader question of whether the social structures which are presupposed by and give meaning to some of the biblical laws are themselves just, whether they allow people the kind of place within society that encourages others to treat them in a Christian way. Some aspects of the social structure of Old Testament Israel, such as the low status accorded to women, do not seem to be ones that Christians can emulate or approve of. If as Christians we wish to develop, because of the love of neighbour to which we are called, a society which is structured differently from ancient Israelite society, then we cannot take our sexual ethics over from that society wholesale.

To look at two biblical texts in the way I have done in these chapters does not prove the case that all biblical sexual ethics are dependent on social considerations, even taken in conjunction with the other texts to which I have alluded throughout. A much more detailed and comprehensive study of biblical sexual ethics along similar lines remains necessary to do that. Nevertheless I hope that I have presented sufficient material here to render the case a plausible one. In any case, the point was not simply to try to establish a general thesis by taking a small sample. Perhaps more importantly, both of these texts show how easy it is to fall into confusion when studying sexual ethics, and how necessary it is to make use of insights from sociology, anthropology and philosophy.

In the central section of the book, chapters 4 to 7, I have been concerned with more abstract, conceptual matters, examining the concepts of pleasure, natural law, purpose and meaning as applied to human sexual activity, and going on to discuss the conceptualization of gender difference in terms of complementarity. Here I have tried to come to grips with some of the arguments, both traditional and modern, which have been employed to underpin and render attractive the demands of traditional Christian sexual ethics. In general, the arguments from purpose and from the intrinsic meaning of sexual acts were found wanting, especially the former. We found that by taking seriously the natural importance of pleasure in human life some weight could be restored to natural law arguments; and similarly, appeal to the notion of the natural expressiveness of human gesture lent persuasiveness to more modern arguments couched in terms of the meaningfulness of sexual acts. However, it is only to a limited extent that acts have meaning in themselves. In order properly to appreciate the meaning of sexual and other acts we have to see the body and its gestures in context, the context of the relationship between the people involved, and once again of the wider society in which they live. Though this approach showed that traditional Christian sexual ethics had a solid basis in reason, it would not by itself take us as far as Christians have wanted, and still want, to go. The arguments, if sound, showed that sex has a proper place within a close friendship, but fell short of showing that that friendship must be of such an intimacy and committed permanence as to be what we would recognize as a marriage. The failure of arguments from complementarity meant that such a relationship could not even be shown to be necessarily one between two people of different sexes.

That did not show that sex is not properly confined to marriage, but only that such restriction cannot be read off from the nature of the act. Christians have every right to say that sex should be confined to marriage, but in doing so they do not merely register the significance of sexual acts, they partly create it. Sex within marriage is given a symbolic, specifically Christian significance by being so confined. At this point Christian sexual ethics must appeal not simply to reason and argument, but to revelation. Hence any further steps in developing a Christian sexual ethic are liable to be accepted only by those who also accept the validity of Christian revelation in general. In chapter 8 I tried to draw out some of the significance accorded to marital sex within the Christian system. It is not only expressive of the love of the partners for each other and of Christ for his church. It also, in contrast to the law of Lev. 18.22 which was studied in chapter 3, asserts the fundamental equality of the sexes which is so important an element of the Christian view of a loving relationship and a loving society.

One argument often put forward to the effect that the restriction of sex to marriage is not a creative gesture of Christians but springs from the nature of sex itself is that sex is essentially procreative, and therefore demands a suitable environment for the rearing of children. And that is marriage. Some arguments against this position were advanced in chapter 5. It remained to consider arguments surrounding two non-procreative kinds of sex: that in which children were deliberately excluded by means of contraception, and that in which they were naturally excluded because the partners were of the same sex. This was done in chapters 9 and 10. The arguments examined, against both contraception and homosexuality, were all found to be defective.

The question of contraception has been a particularly disputed one in the church. If I am right, and the arguments against contraception do not hold water, that may be considered a blow against the traditional church teaching on this matter. However, what I have shown in chapter 9, even if my own argumentation is correct, is very limited. To begin with, I have not examined all possible arguments against the practice of artificial contraception. I have taken those that appeared to me most careful and most interesting, but there may be others, ultimately more compelling, of which I am unaware. I can only repeat that I myself have no idea how to generate such an argument. Secondly, if it is not a truth of reason that contraception is wrong, and if it cannot be shown from scripture, still the ban on contraception is broadly consonant with the Christian view that the human goods we receive on earth, including the good of our own life and the life of our children, are gifts of God. The wrongness of contraception does not follow from this fundamental Christian attitude, yet it does fit it. Third, what I have been concerned with throughout is what is derivable, in the field of sexual ethics, from scripture or, more often, from argument of a more or less abstract kind. But there are plenty of things we can know are right or wrong neither from scripture nor through argument but from experience. The church, committed to love, seeks that human beings may flourish. It may be that a link can be shown between contraception and a lack of human flourishing, shown not logically but empirically, through long-term scientific or common-sense observation. This point applies, as I have stressed throughout, to many of the things people want to say in the realm of sexual ethics. In the end we may have to stop arguing and simply look with open eyes and see. There may, for instance, be no valid *a priori* argument against masturbation, but that is not the end of the matter. What matters is whether, as a matter of observable fact, people who masturbate do or do not flourish as they otherwise might, or whether they impede or promote the development and well-being of others around them and of society as a whole.

However, there appear at the moment to be no firmly empirically established conclusions as to whether masturbation is good or bad for people, or whether it has any appreciable effect at all. And the same is true of the practice of contraception. In the meantime, until such conclusions are established by research or ordinary observation, the church, if it to convince the doubtful, must rely more on argument. If the arguments that have so far been adduced are inadequate, as I believe I have shown some of them to be, then that is undeniably a problem for the church.

Similar and further general points can be made in the context of the arguments of chapter 10. Official church teaching has set itself against homosexual practices with increasing firmness in recent years. This has been much resisted, both by homosexuals themselves and by heterosexuals, Christians and others, more sympathetic to homosexuals and their desire for free acceptance within the church and in society at large. Whatever the sympathies of individuals in this dispute, it seems from the brief survey of chapter 10 that the actual arguments, based on scripture and reason, that have been deployed in support of church teaching are seriously deficient. Somebody who is in doubt about church teaching in this area will not be convinced by them, and will be right to remain sceptical.

I have not in chapter 10, as I have in some other chapters, sketched any argument which I believe gives firmer support to church teaching, for I myself have been unable, as when discussing arguments about contraception, to find any which is more cogent. However, again as in the case of contraception, this does not amount to vindication for those who oppose the church's teaching and are sympathetic to the desire of homosexuals to be allowed the freedom to enter into loving relationships in accordance with their emotional and sexual inclinations. Apart from the considerations raised in connexion with contraception above, there are other points to be made. As I remarked in the introduction to this book, genuine intuitions are often very difficult to articulate and substantiate in formal argument. And the church's authority to teach does not lie in its ability to argue cogently, but in the commission of Christ. Whatever the status of the arguments employed, it remains part of the life of all followers of Christ to listen sympathetically to what the church has to say, and to attempt to grasp any insights the church claims to teach, without abandoning the critical rational faculties that are proper to human beings. On the other hand, the divine commission to teach imposes on the church the obligation to teach as well as possible, adapting content and method so that not only may the faithful be confirmed in their faith but the hostile may have a change of heart and doubters be convinced. The effort to find good arguments to vindicate the church's position to those who need convincing is a sign of its taking that commission and that obligation seriously. If those arguments fail, as I believe they do, that may not invalidate the church's teaching, but it does render it unpersuasive to those who need to be persuaded.

These considerations apply to the church's teaching not only on homosexuality, but on sex in general. I have throughout this book examined major arguments brought to bear in support of the church's sexual teaching. Some I have found wanting, and I have tried to go some way towards strengthening them or providing alternative arguments. I have contended that these arguments take us some way, but that they do not, as a matter of logic, succeed in establishing incontrovertibly what the church wants to say. For those who fully accept the authority of the church in this area, this is no problem. But there are those who have difficulty with it, as well as those who reject it outright. Here the church must argue; and if I am right in my assessment of the available arguments, they are deficient. This is a serious impediment to the church's fulfilment of its commission. To those who question the church's teaching, or flatly disagree with it, it may also be a sign that that doctrine cannot be substantiated or defended and that it needs to be modified. The church needs to do more thinking about sex.

Modern Works Cited

A. Anscombe, *Contraception and Chastity*, Catholic Truth Society, London no date.

D. S. Bailey, *Homosexuality and the Western Christian Tradition*, Longmans 1955.

J. Boswell, *Christianity, Social Tolerance and Homosexuality*, University of Chicago Press, Chicago 1980.

H. Brierley, 'Gender Identity and Sexual Behaviour' in K. Howells (ed.), *The Psychology of Sexual Diversity*, Blackwell 1984, pp.63–88.

M. P. Carroll, 'One More Time: Leviticus Revisited' in B. Lang (ed.), *Anthropological Approaches to the Old Testament*, SPCK/Fortress Press 1985, pp.117–126.

J. H. Charlesworth (ed.), *The Old Testament Pseudepigrapha*: vol. 1, *Apocalyptic Literature and Testaments*, Darton, Longman and Todd 1983.

L. W. Countryman, *Dirt, Greed and Sex*, SCM Press and Fortress Press 1989.

J. Dominian, *Sexual Integrity*, Darton, Longman and Todd 1987.

M. Douglas, *Implicit Meanings*, Routledge and Kegan Paul 1975.

M. Douglas, *Natural Symbols*, Penguin 1973.

M. Douglas, *Purity and Danger*, Routledge and Kegan Paul 1966.

D. Field, *The Homosexual Way – A Christian Option?* Grove Books 1980.

J. Finnis, 'Natural Law and Unnatural Acts' in *The Heythrop Journal* vol. XI no. 4, October 1970, pp.365–387.

M. Foucault, *The Use of Pleasure* (*The History of Sexuality*, volume 2), Penguin 1987.

E. Fuchs, *Sexual Desire and Love*, James Clarke & Co. 1983.

V. Genovesi, SJ, *In Pursuit of Love*, Gill and Macmillan 1987.

G. Grisez, J. Boyle, J. Finnis and W. E. May, ' "Every Marital Act Ought To Be Open To New Life": Toward a Clearer Understanding', in *The Thomist* vol. 52, no. 3, July 1988, pp.365–426.

B. Häring, *The Law of Christ*, The Mercier Press 1963.

B. Häring, *Free and Faithful in Christ*, St Paul Publications 1979.

H. Heger, *The Men with the Pink Triangle*, GMP 1986.

M. Heidegger, *Being and Time*, Blackwell 1962.

R. Lawler, OFM Cap., J. Boyle and May W. E., *Catholic Sexual Ethics: A Summary, Explanation and Defense*, Our Sunday Visitor Inc., Huntington, Indiana 1985.

M. H. Masters and V. E. Johnson, *Human Sexual Response*, Little, Brown and Company, Boston 1966.

J. McNeill, SJ, *The Church and the Homosexual*, Darton, Longman and Todd 1977.

J. G. Milhaven, 'Homosexuality and Love', in E. Batchelor (ed.), *Homosexuality and Ethics*, Pilgrim Press, New York 1980, pp.63–70.

G. Moore, 'Are Homosexuals Sick?' in *New Blackfriars*, January 1989, pp.15–19.

J. T. Noonan, *Contraception*, Harvard University Press, Cambridge, Mass. 1986.

C. H. Peschke, *Christian Ethics*, volume 2, C. Goodliffe Neale 1978.

T. Radcliffe, OP, '"*Glorify God in your bodies*": I Corinthians 6, 12–20 as a sexual ethic' in New Blackfriars July/August 1986, pp.306–314.

C. M. Taylor, *Theories of Meaning* (1980 Dawes Hicks Lecture on Philosophy), The British Academy 1982.

P. A. Tyler, 'Homosexual Behaviour in Animals' in K. Howells (ed.), *The Psychology of Sexual Diversity*, Blackwell 1984, pp.42–62.

P. Veyne, 'Homosexuality in Ancient Rome' in Ariès and Béjin, *Western Sexuality*, Blackwell 1985.

J. Weeks, *Sexuality*, Tavistock Publications 1986.

J. Weeks, *Sexuality and its Discontents*, Routledge and Kegan Paul 1985.

C. Westermann, *Genesis 1–11*, SPCK 1984.

L. Wittgenstein, *Zettel*, Blackwell 1967.

L. Wittgenstein, *Philosophical Investigations*, Blackwell 1953.

L. Wittgenstein, *Culture and Value*, Blackwell 1980.

Notes

Full bibliographical details of most titles will be found in the list of Modern Works Cited. They are not repeated here.

1 Sex and Ethics

1. What we do habitually we mostly do naturally, spontaneously, without thinking about it. That means we do not particularly notice what we are doing. This is one of the reasons why we often do not know ourselves very well, even though we may think we do. Often, our behaviour and our habits are much more obvious to others than to ourselves, and in knowing how we act those others know what sort of person we are.

2. Rom. 13.8–10. See also Gal. 5.14: 'The whole law is fulfilled in one word: "You shall love your neighbour as yourself"'; and James 2.8: 'If you really fulfil the royal law, according to the scripture, "You shall love your neighbour as yourself," you do well.'

3. Cf. Matt. 22.34–40; Mark 12.28–34.

4. *Confessions* 1.1.

5. David Field, *The Homosexual Way – A Christian Option?*, pp.18f.

6. Ibid., p.19.

7. *In Epistolam Ioannis ad Parthos* 7.8.

8. 15.2 objection 4.

9. 3.122.

2 The Lustful Eye

1. Field, *The Homosexual Way – A Christian Option?*, p.19.

2. Lawler, Boyle and May, *Catholic Sexual Ethics: A Summary, Explanation and Defense*, pp.26f.

3. This behaviour may indeed, in a perfectly straightforward sense, not be observable. It may, for instance, be going on behind closed doors. But if it is hidden, it is hidden inside a room, by a door, not inside somebody's head.

4. I Enoch 6.1f.; 7.1. In J.H. Charlesworth (ed.), *The Old Testament Pseudepigrapha*, vol. 1, pp.3ff.

5. Josh. 7.21. See also e.g. Micah 2.2; Prov. 1.22; 6.25ff.

6. Understanding these verses in this way would also bring them into line with Matt. 5.21–26, where a similar method is followed of connecting different actions by placing them in a spectrum. Killing, which is mentioned first, is an extreme of hostility, an extreme form of anger with one's brother. But anger may have many degrees, and may amount to no more than hurling an insult.

7. For a more systematic treatment see L. William Countryman, *Dirt, Greed and Sex*, pp. 147–167.

8. And it confirms that the verb *epithumeo* has in this context more to do with possession than with sexual attraction: we are not to suppose that what is being forbidden here is wanting to have sex with your neighbour's manservant or his ox, let alone his house.

9. E.g. Prov. 5.18–20: 'Let your fountain be blessed, and rejoice in the wife of your youth, a lovely hind, a graceful doe. Let her affection fill you at all times with delight, be infatuated always with her love.'

10. Probably, this also has consequences for the way we should understand the absence of any corresponding saying against a woman setting her desire on another woman's husband. Perhaps it is merely for the sake of brevity; perhaps we are meant to generalize what Jesus says to cover the desires of women. More likely the explanation is to be found in the property relationship. The designs of a woman on another woman's husband would not involve any infringement of that other woman's property rights over her husband, for she has none.

11. Lawler, Boyle and May take this perfectly good English word and split it in two, producing 'one's self'. No point is served by doing this. Indeed, a considerable disservice to clarity of thought is done, since it is intimated that one has something called a self, whose nature remains to be specified.

12. Lawler, Boyle and May, op. cit., p. 27.

13. *dialogismoi*. Here the Greek, following the Hebrew root *ḥšb*, has the meaning of plan, machination, intention. Here your thought is what you are thinking of doing. It is not something going on independently of behaviour, but is on the contrary directed at and normally issuing in or even consisting in, doing something (see e.g. the use of *maḥᵃšebet* in Esth. 8.5). If this were not the case, or something like it, it would be difficult to understand how evil thoughts could come out of the heart.

We should bear in mind, too, that to have an intention is not a matter of having a particular kind of thought, of thinking, of having a thought going through your head. The concept of intention is a much more subtle one. See e.g. the remarks in Wittgenstein, *Philosophical Investigations*, §631ff.

14. Matt. 15.19f. See also the longer list in Mark 7.21f.

15. In *The Thomist*, vol. 52, no. 3, July 1988, pp. 365–426.

16. Ibid., pp. 372f.

17. This possibility serves to remind us that imagination is not necessarily something that goes on in the head. It may take the form of acting something out in the classroom or on the stage. There is nothing necessarily 'internal' about it.

18. Though once again, legalistic only in a somewhat stretched sense. In the last example, from Mark 7, Jesus is himself, just as in Matt. 5, thinking in terms of the Law, criticizing the Pharisees for not keeping a central commandment of the law of Moses. That they do not keep the law they preach is also the thrust of the criticism in Matt. 23 and elsewhere.

3   The Treatment of Men

1. See e.g. Lev. 10.8–11; 22.10ff.; 19.5–8; Num. 3.6–10, 38. The Hebrew words regularly translated 'holy, 'holiness', 'consecrate', 'sacred', etc., come from the root *qdš*, whose original meaning seems to have been 'separate'.

2. E.g. it is death for unconsecrated people to touch the holy instruments of the cult. See Num. 4.15; 18.3.

3. E.g. Lev. 20.23.

4. See e.g. Ex. 20.8–11. We should note that the sabbath also has the function of separating the weeks from each other.

5. Bernard Häring, *Free and Faithful in Christ*, vol. 2, p.497. In this context Häring approvingly quotes Karl Barth: 'Men are simply male and female. Whatever else they may be, it is only in this differentiation and relationship. This is the particular dignity ascribed to sex relationship' (*Church Dogmatics* 3.1, p.186).

6. Eric Fuchs, *Sexual Desire and Love*, p.43.

7. See e.g. Prov. 31.10–31.

8. Not as relaxed as all that. Some of the apparent relaxations have simply been shifts in gender expectations. When people – particularly men – do things not in accord with their gender role, we can still get upset: at least, most of us do sometimes. People were upset in the '60s when young men started wearing their hair long and so started looking 'like women'. After a while most people didn't mind so much. This was not because it became acceptable for men to look like women, but that a shift occurred in the image of men; it became acceptable for *men* to look like that, so that men who did no longer looked like women, as they had done earlier.

9. Jeffrey Weeks comments: 'The imposition of identity can be seen as a crude tactic of power, designed to obscure the real human diversity with the strict categorizations of uniformity.' He refers to Michel Foucault's edition of the 'tragic memoirs' of the nineteenth-century hermaphrodite Herculine Barbin, a 'gentle hymn to the "happy limbo of non-identity" and a warning of the dire consequences of insisting upon a true identity hidden behind the ambiguities of outward appearance' (*Sexuality and its Discontents*, p.187).

10. Mary Douglas gives some (to us) extreme examples of the removal of anomaly:

> When a monstrous birth occurs, the defining lines between humans and animals may be threatened. If a monstrous birth can be labelled an event of a peculiar kind the categories can be restored. So the Nuer treat monstrous births as baby hippopotamuses, accidentally born to humans and, with this labelling, the appropriate action is clear. They gently lay them in the river where they belong .... The existence of anomaly can be physically controlled. Thus in some West African tribes the rule that twins should be killed at birth eliminates a social anomaly, if it is held that two humans could not be born from the same womb at the same time. Or take night-crowing cocks. If their necks are promptly wrung, they do not live to contradict the definition of a cock as a bird that crows at dawn (*Purity and Danger*, p.39).

11. And in parts of Poland, for a while under Nazi occupation, hair colour too could be a matter of life and death. Blonde children might be sent to labour in Germany while the dark-haired were sent to the death camps.

12. Mary Douglas, *Natural Symbols*, p.93.

13. Mary Douglas, *Implicit Meanings*, p.84.

14. Ibid., p.87.

15. This does not occur in scripture, but is to be found in later tradition. For example, in the thirteenth century Albert the Great had this to say about sexual positions:

> None of those things that a married man does with his own wife using the proper organ is in itself a mortal sin. But it can be a sign of mortal concupiscence; when the posture that nature determines by disposition of the organs is not enough for them and they get into the positions of brute animals. That it may be better understood what the natural way is, and deviation from it, according to Aristotle only man has a long, wide body, and the male member is above the tendon of the leg while the female member is at the end of the belly, so that nature teaches that the proper position is that the woman should be on her back and that the man lie on her belly ... And women conceive more easily in this position than in others ... Intercourse sideways is a minor deviation from this, sitting is greater, greater still is standing, and the greatest is backwards, like beasts of burden. So some have said that this last is a mortal sin, which I disagree with (*Sentences* 4.31.24).

Notice here the tendency to invoke 'nature' in defence of what is a social convention.

16. E.g. Epigrams 2.47,62.

17. Poem 100.

18. Poem 56. See also, among others, 15 and 21.

19. Suetonius, *Divus Iulius* 49. For this reference, as for others in this paragraph, I am indebted to John Boswell, *Christianity, Social Tolerance and Homosexuality*, p.75.

20. 'Homosexuality in Ancient Rome' in Ariès and Béjin (ed.), *Western Sexuality*, Blackwell 1985, p.30.

21. Michel Foucault, *The Use of Pleasure* (*The History of Sexuality*, vol. 2), Penguin 1987, p.215.

22. For a parallel view of the Greek unease at sexual relations between men and boys see Foucault's *History of Sexuality*, vol. 2, p.222. Note in particular the following: '[Although there was a sense of the naturalness of the desire of one man for another male, especially a boy] one could take exception to the very act that was carried out between two male individuals on the grounds that it was *para phusin* – because it *feminized* one of the partners.' This expresses well how breach of socially imposed gender roles is at the same time seen as a going against (or beyond) nature. What is conceived as natural is socially determined.

23. It is true, though, that he can be accused of a certain inconsistency on this point. In one place, I Cor. 11.2ff., he appears to press, for certain purposes, a very rigid gender distinction.

24. See Ezra, chapters 9 and 10. Another piece of legislation that could not command Christian support is the Immorality Act formerly in force in South Africa, which forbade sexual relations between white and black.

4   The Pleasures of the Flesh

1. *De Bono Conjugali* 10.

2. *De Nuptiis et Concupiscentia* 1.9.

3. *De Bono Conjugali* 13.

4. For a survey of the relevant biblical texts, see J.T. Noonan, *Contraception*, pp.31–46. It is true that in the book of Tobit Tobias, on his wedding night, says to God:

> And now, O Lord, I am not taking this sister of mine because of lust (*dia porneian*), but with sincerity,

but this is about his motives for marriage, not about his reasons for his wanting sexual intercourse.

5. For a brief review of stoic and other views on sex and marriage, see Noonan, *Contraception*, pp.46f.

6. Noonan summarizes: 'In the case of such an early and influential teacher as Clement of Alexandria, the direct descent is obvious; his work on the purposes of marriage is a paraphrase of works of Musonius. In the second century, Origen's standard for intercourse in pregnancy is clearly Seneca's. In the third century, Lactantius' remarks on the obvious purpose of the generative faculties echo Ocellus Lucanus. In the fourth century, Jerome's most austere remarks are taken from Seneca. It is not a matter of men expressing simple truth which common sense might suggest to anyone with open eyes. It is a matter of a doctrine consciously appropriated. The descent is literary, the dependence substantial' (*Contraception*, p.48).

7. Denzinger, *Enchiridion Symbolorum*, 31st edition, §1159.

8. Bernard Häring, *The Law of Christ*, vol. 3, p.371.

9. E.g. Psalm 119.16,35.

10. Plato, *Republic* 9.577d.

11. *City of God* 14.12.

12. *City of God* 14.24.

13. *De Nuptiis et Concupiscentia* 1.6. Augustine's language has survived into this century. Pius XI, in his encyclical *Casti Connubii* 102–104, says: 'Since man cannot acquire mastery over his passions unless he himself is submissive to God, obedience to his Creator must consequently be his first care, according to the order divinely established. For it is an invariable law which, with the help of God's grace, he is able to exert that he who submits his will to God feels joy in the mastery over his passions and concupiscence; whereas, on the contrary, he who rebels against God has a painful experience of the interior conflict which the violence of his desires lets loose in his soul ... Since, therefore, man cannot achieve the needful restraint of unruly passion unless he himself first yields to his Creator the humble homage of piety and reverence which is due to Him ...' We should note, however, that Pius' point is much more general than Augustine's. Though the focus is on sexual desire, it is the passions in general which are unruly here, and it is the passions which are out of control, not the penis. Further, for Pius this is not an inescapable state of affairs, to which we are condemned because of the Fall. We can bring out passions under control if we submit to God.

14. See, e.g., *City of God* 14.16.

15. See, e.g., *City of God* 14.19: 'Lust has in a sense taken the genital parts of the body as its own property, so that they have no strength to move if lust is absent, and if it has not arisen spontaneously or through some stimulus. It is this that causes shame.'

Compare the related view of Thomas Aquinas: '*Pudicitia* is properly concerned with those things people feel most shame about. People feel most shame about sexual acts... even to the extent that conjugal intercourse, which is adorned with the honour of marriage, does not lack shame. And this is because the movement of the genital organs is not subject to the command of reason as is the movement of other external members' (*Summa Theologiae* 2–2.151.4c).

16. *City of God* 14.16.

17. *Sermons* 62.2.

18. *Soliloquies* 1.10. Aquinas echoes this sentiment centuries later: 'Sexual pleasures are more vehement and press on the mind more than do pleasures of food. And because of this they are more in need of correction and restraint, because if they are consented to the power of concupiscence grows yet stronger and the power of the mind is brought down' (*Summa Theologiae* 2–2.151.3 ad 2).

19. E.g. *Contra Faustum* 22.30: 'The eternal law, that is, the will of God the creator of all things, having regard for the conservation of natural order, not that the satisfaction of lust might be provided for, but to arrange for the preservation of the race, solely for the propagation of children, allows the delight of mortal flesh to be released from the domination of reason in intercourse.'

20. *Summa Theologiae* 1.98.2 ad 3.

21. See, e.g., *City of God* 14.24: 'Then [had there been no sin] the man would have engendered his offspring and the woman would have conceived the child when and in so far as necessary, when their genital organs had been moved by the will, not excited by lust. For we move at our command [*ad nutum*] not only those members which are jointed with bones ... but also those which are loosely constructed of soft tissues ... Is there any reason why we should not believe that before the sin of disobedience and its punishment of corruption the members of a human body could have served the human will without any lust, for the procreation of children?'

Cf. the analysis of internal conflict in *Confessions* 8.9: 'Whence this monstrousness? And why this thing? The mind commands the body and it is obeyed at once. The mind commands itself and is resisted ... And thus there are two wills, because neither one of them is whole.'

22. *Summa Theologiae* 2–2.153.2 ad 2.

23. Not that female orgasm is not recognized, but that sexual pleasure has generally been regarded from a male point of view. So that when sexual pleasure has been seen as problematic, it has been a male problem. As an example of this, and of the point that pleasure was identified with orgasm, Noonan quotes the twelfth-century authority Huguccio, struggling with the question how it is possible for a man to satisfy his wife sexually without sin. For Huguccio intercourse is normally sinful, since it involves the always sinful pleasure that accompanies ejaculation. Here is his solution: 'To render the conjugal debt to one's wife is nothing other than to make for her a plenty of one's body for the wifely matter. Hence one often renders the debt to his wife in such a way that he does not satisfy his pleasure, and

conversely. Therefore, in the aforesaid case, I can so render the debt to the wife and wait in such a way until she satisfies her pleasure. Indeed, often in such cases a woman is accustomed to anticipate her husband, and when the pleasure of the wife in the carnal work is satisfied, I can, if I wish, withdraw, not satisfying my pleasure, and not emitting my seed of propagation (*Summa* 2.13, quoted in Noonan, *Contraception*, pp.296f.).

24. The Song of Songs is full of obvious sexual delight the lovers get from the exploration of each other's body.

25. Masters and Johnson claim to have established empirically that orgasms obtained through masturbation are generally better than those resulting from sexual contact with other people. If orgasm were the sole or the most important pleasure of sex, then we would expect people to prefer masturbation to sex with other people. It is significant that the researchers state that 'subjects report that usually the experience with orgasm induced by masturbation is more intense than, *though not necessarily as satisfying as* (my italics), that resulting from coition' (William H. Masters and Virginia E. Johnson, *Human Sexual Response*, p.118.)

26. *Nicomachean Ethics* 10.4.1–10.5.5.

27. For a full exposition of this theme, see Heidegger, *Being and Time*, §§ 12–24.

28. None of this is to say that we cannot be mistaken about what we feel or hear, etc., or just not know. We might just say: 'I hear a noise,' but what we hear is the noise of some unidentified thing. We could equally say: 'I hear something, but I don't know what it is.' In the same way, we might say: 'I can feel something in my shoe.' Our hearing, smelling, etc., is of the world.

29. Hardly as the climax of it. An activity you do not want to do does not in this sense have a climax. The climax of your activity is the climax of your involvement in it, your goal. An activity you do not want to take part in does not have such a goal; it is merely a relief when it comes to an end.

30. On the notion of common space, see C.M. Taylor, *Theories of Meaning*.

31. It may perhaps be slightly more accurate to put things the other way round: to be together is to be doing something together, and the pleasure of being together is the pleasure of doing something together. It is true that a couple may be together doing nothing in particular, but still their doing nothing together is different from two strangers each doing nothing in the same place. There is a jointness about what the couple does, derived from shared intention to do the same thing or to do nothing, that makes it appropriate to talk of shared activity.

32. This might make it pleasurable for a number of reasons. E.g. it might give the sex the significance of cocking a snook at or liberating himself from those who he feels oppress him and who hold, among other things, that sex is only permissible within the context of a certain kind of friendship, say marriage. He may be saying it to himself, or maybe to others, in which case it becomes important to *publicize* his sexual activity. Here the activity has a social meaning, almost as an assertion about himself and his place in society, and the activity is pleasurable in the same way that saying something may be pleasurable. And so it may cease to be pleasurable in the same way that it can cease to be pleasurable to say something, when you no longer need to say it, when you have grown tired of saying it. Here we begin to see connexions between pleasure and meaning, in particular the beginning of the notion of the pleasures of *significant* action. For more on meaning, see chapter 6.

33. Parallel remarks could be made about the identification of pleasure with fun. Though having fun is one important way of enjoying oneself, it is only one way. Many kinds of enjoyment cannot properly be described as fun, and to look always for fun is to limit the range of pleasures open to one. There may often be elements of fun in sex, but they are only elements in a wider range of pleasures.

34. These two cases do not, of course, exhaust all the possibilities concerning the ways we can care or fail to care about the identity of our partners. They are extremes, at or near opposite ends of a spectrum. As an intermediate case, I might study my intended partner across the bar for a couple of hours, and it might become important for me to get *him* or *her*, just for this evening, or for the next few days.

35. This could be said even of their dead body. The way you treat somebody's corpse shows your attitude towards that person. It is important, from a Christian point of view, that a person's dead body be treated with respect, for that is a way of treating the person with respect.

36. See *Summa Theologiae* 1.76.3,4, especially 4c.

37. I do not know how to determine whether this is simply a matter of culture, or whether there is a closer, conceptual connexion between the soul, the appreciation of a person as a person, and the eyes. Certainly, if it is a cultural matter, it is very widespread. Here I simply register that, for whatever reason, a connexion does exist.

38. Wittgenstein, *Philosophical Investigations*, §286f.

39. Wittgenstein, *Culture and Value*, p.23.

40. Wittgenstein, *Zettel*, §222.

41. Barring shame or any taboos there might be in various societies regarding eye contact during sex. Such things themselves testify to the importance of eye contact. My point is that in sex it is not a matter of indifference whether you look at people's faces or not.

5 Sexual Purposes

1. Henry Peschke, *Christian Ethics*, vol. 2, p.379. We can in fact note in this passage a mixture of two ideas that are commonly found: first, that the purpose of sex is reproduction because of our physical nature – 'the whole sexual structure and inclination' – and second, that sex is for having children because God has ordained it so. These two ideas may be differently related. It may be held that our physical structure and inclinations are themselves expressive of God's intention, that we can in fact read off God's intentions and purposes from nature; or that God's purposes supervene on nature, that the divine purpose cannot be read off from nature itself but is known only because revealed. In the Catholic tradition it is the former that has prevailed, so that the two can for practical purposes be treated as one.

2. Op. cit., p.378.

3. *The Nature of the Universe*, 44. Quoted in Noonan, *Contraception*, p.47.

4. See *De Bono Conjugali* 16: 'What food is to the health of a man, intercourse is to the health of the species, and neither is without carnal delight which, if moderated, with temperance restraining it and bringing it back to its natural use, cannot be lust. But what unlawful food is to supporting life, this fornication or adulterous intercourse is to seeking offspring. And what unlawful food is in the excess of the belly

and gullet, that is illicit intercourse in the lust that seeks no offspring. And what is, in the area of lawful food, the somewhat immoderate appetite that some people have, this is that pardonable intercourse in spouses.'

5. This is not the same as saying that it is good to be a self-indulgent person. Being a self-indulgent person implies paying too much attention to one's own desires, and so being insufficiently alive to the desires and needs of others. So it diminishes the capacity to love, and hence is unChristian. This is one reason why self-control is such an important virtue. But a loving and self-controlled person may nevertheless indulge himself or herself from time to time, be occasionally self-indulgent, and indeed may need to do so. To drink a long gin alone is to indulge oneself; it is to give oneself a pleasure purely for the sake of the pleasure. A gin has no food value, or if it has it is certainly not drunk on account of it. But taking a drink in this way is something any devoted doctor or pastoral worker, for example, might do, and might need to do, when arriving home after long hours of work in the service of others. It is quite understandable that relaxation for such a person might involve giving himself a treat, indulging himself. And such self-indulgence makes him no less devoted, no less loving. It is in danger of doing that only if he becomes undisciplined about when he allows himself this luxury, if instead of having a gin in the evening he begins to have one also at various points during the day, so that his concern to indulge himself begins to interfere with his devotion to those he serves. It is possible to be disciplined in one's self-indulgence, and many people are. It is undisciplined self-indulgence that is a bad thing, not self-indulgence in itself. Being self-indulgent does not make one into a self-indulgent person.

6. Lawler, Boyle and May, *Catholic Sexual Ethics*, p.20.

7. Gen. 15.1,5. Cf. 12.2; 17.2. In other contexts, see e.g. Psalms 127 and 128. Conversely, childlessness was reckoned a great misfortune. See e.g. Gen. 15.2f.

8. Plato, *Laws* 8.836C.

9. Plato, *Laws* 8.836D–E.

10. Foucault finds this concern with gender role a pervasive factor in Greek attitudes towards sex between men. If this kind of activity was problematic for them it was not because they could not understand how a man might want pleasure with another man or with a boy, but because of the threat to the status of one of them as male. While relationships between males were valued, there was also current the opinion that all sex between men was *para phusin*, 'against nature': 'The very possibility of these two opinions was probably owing to the fact that while people deemed it quite natural that one might find pleasure with a boy, it was much harder to accept as natural that which made a boy an object of pleasure. So that one could take exception to the very act that was carried out between two male individuals on the grounds that it was *para phusin* – because it *feminized* one of the partners, whereas the desire that one could have for beauty was nevertheless regarded as natural' (*History of Sexuality*, vol. 2, p.222).

11. See *Summa Theologiae* 1.2.91.2.

12. *Summa Theologiae* 1–2.94.2c. In describing the natural law as 'what nature has taught all animals' Aquinas is following the formula of the Roman jurist Ulpian (d.228).

13. See *Summa Theologiae* 2–2.154.11c.

14. See e.g. *On the Sentences* 4.31 Expositio Textus; *Summa Theologiae* 2–2.154.

11c. Albert the Great criticizes those for whom 'the posture that nature determines by disposition of the organs is not enough, and who get into the positions of brute animals' (*Sentences* 4.31.24).

15. For a review of research on homosexual behaviour in animals see P. A. Tyler, 'Homosexual Behaviour in Animals.'

16. *Contra Gentiles* 3.122.

17. It is worth saying here something about Aquinas' distinction between an inability to result in procreation *secundum se* and a *per accidens* inability. Emission of semen in vaginal intercourse with a sterile woman is not going to result in conception, but only *per accidens*, for this is the sort of activity that would result in conception in the normal case; women are not normally sterile. On the other hand anal intercourse never normally results in conception; it belongs to anal intercourse to be without issue; it is non-procreative *secundum se*. To put it another way, vaginal intercourse between man and woman can serve a procreative purpose whereas anal intercourse cannot; you can hope for a child from vaginal intercourse, but you cannot hope for a child from anal intercourse.

This distinction seems right enough at first sight, but note that it depends on our knowledge of the facts of reproduction. We classify anal intercourse as non-procreative *secundum se* because we all know that you cannot generate offspring through anal intercourse. So you cannot have a procreative intention in performing such an activity; you cannot intend to do something you know you cannot do. It is possible that somebody might be ignorant of this, and have anal sex in the hope of having a child from it. They would not be sinning thereby. But according to Aquinas the knowledge that the act could not result in offspring would make it a sin. But we also all know that sex between a man and a sterile woman cannot generate offspring either. Her sterility may be an unfortunate accident, but still a man cannot hope to have a child from intercourse with a woman he knows to be sterile. He cannot perform this activity with procreative intent; and neither can she. If it is not known that she is sterile there can be hope of offspring, but not if she is known to be sterile. The waste of semen is just as sure, and just as known, so it ought to be judged just as sinful as any anal intercourse.

18. There is an obvious sense in which you can reproduce defectively, namely by engendering or giving birth to a child who suffers from defects. But that case is not relevant here.

19. It should perhaps here be noted that I have been conducting this argument in terms of things and their uses. Theologians and church documents have tended to assimilate activities to things by talking about the 'use' of sexual activity as one might talk about the use of a glass. See e.g. Pius XI, *Casti Connubii* 56:

> Any use of matrimony [i.e. the activity of sexual intercourse] whatsoever in the exercise of which the act is deprived, by human interference, of its natural power to procreate life, is an offence against the law of God and of nature, and... those who commit it are guilty of a grave sin.

This language is echoed by Paul VI in *Humanae Vitae* 11:

> God has wisely ordered the laws of nature and the incidence of fertility in such a way that successive births are already naturally spaced through the inherent operation of these laws. The Church, nevertheless, in urging men to the

observance of the precepts of the natural law, teaches as absolutely required that *any use whatever of marriage* must retain its natural potential to procreate human life.

I do not think that this variation of terminology makes any substantial difference to the argument. After all, bodily activities involve the use of bodily organs. One can, it seems, translate talk of the use of activities without loss into that of the use of the organs involved in those activities.

20. There may even be some Christians who do not regard our sexual faculties as a gift of God. But I take it that these are not typical of the central Christian tradition.

6   Sexual Gestures

1. *Casti Connubii* §8.

2. In the New Testament and elsewhere the English word 'love' is used to render the Greek verbs *agapao* and *phileo*. The use of one English verb to cover two Greek verbs is not misleading, since *agapao* is not unusually used as equivalent to *phileo*, sometimes in contexts which speak of or imply affection. At other times it signifies attachment or longing; this usage is particularly striking when it appears in connexion with material things. For examples see Arndt and Gingrich, *Greek-English Lexicon of the New Testament*, Zondervan, pp.4f. Hence there is no linguistic justification for setting up Christian *agape* as a special emotionless, disinterested kind of love and opposing it to ordinary human love, as has sometimes been done. It is ordinary human love. Ordinary human love is very important to us, and that is why what Christians have to say about it, when they talk about *agape*, is so important. *Gratia non tollit naturam, sed perficit.*

3. *Familiaris Consortio* §11.

4. Vincent Genovesi, *In Pursuit of Love*, p.147.

5. Ibid., p.154, quoting John F. Dedek, *Contemporary Medical Ethics*, Sheed and Ward, New York 1975, pp.82f.

6. Jack Dominian, *Sexual Integrity*, p.67.

7. John Finnis, 'Natural Law and Unnatural Acts', p.381.

8. Ibid.

9. Jeffrey Weeks, *Sexuality and its Discontents*, p.208.

10. Ibid., p.237.

11. Connected with this is the fact that gay men and women sometimes assume non-sexual characteristics of the opposite sex, as socially defined; some gay men adopt 'feminine' ways of behaving, even women's clothes, and lesbians sometimes cultivate an appearance that would be conventionally described as masculine. This is not to be interpreted as a matter of their feeling they belong to the opposite sex or wanting to – the opposite sex does not generally interest them. It is better understood as another way of crossing gender roles, refusing to conform to the behaviour pattern expected of them as men or women, a rejection of the gender role imposed upon them rather than the positive adoption of the role of the other sex: the 'femininity' of some gay men, for instance, is actually not like the femininity of women, but is rather a deliberate non-masculinity. Thus the meaning of such behaviour is at one with the meaning of their sexual activities.

12. We should also note that speaking is itself an activity, and a verbal action can replace (not translate or explain) a non-verbal one. See Wittgenstein, *Philosophical Investigations*, §244f.

13. Paul VI makes a similar point in different language when, in *Humanae Vitae*, he writes of the *significationem unitatis* of the marriage act (§12), of sex as a sign and expression of the unity of a married couple. The act has its proper place in a relationship of two people who have been unified. It then expresses or signifies that union.

7   The Other Half

1. See for example the case cited by Harry Brierley in 'Gender Identity and Sexual Behaviour', pp.83–85.

2. At some stage in the process. Because of modern technology physical union of man and woman is no longer necessary to produce a child: there are sperm banks and *in vitro* fertilization. But nevertheless a man is necessary to provide the sperm and a woman to supply the ovum. Hence the advances of science (whether themselves desirable or not) have not yet affected the complementarity of male and female in this respect.

3. *Letter on the Pastoral Care of Homosexual Persons*, §6.

4. Ibid., §7.

5. Henry Peschke, *Christian Ethics*, vol. 2, p.377.

6. Ibid.,

7. Jeffrey Weeks, *Sexuality*, p.60.

8. Ibid., p.59. Weeks quotes a study of Mica Nava which shows the process of formation of gender identity among boys and girls, the process being dominated by the boys: 'The regulation of girls is enforced largely by *boys* through reference to a notion of femininity which incorporates particular modes of sexual behaviour, deference and compliance ... In this culture outside the home, girls are observers of boys' activity and *guardians* of girls' passivity ... Such power is located in groups of boys (and girls) who, through reference to certain discourses and categories – like 'slag' and 'poof' – are able to ensure 'appropriate' masculine and feminine behaviour.'

9. In this context Weeks complains: 'To say that on average men have more sexual activity than women is tantamount to saying that some women are more sexually active than some men. Average statements are both true and not particularly useful. Yet they carry an enormous weight, in part at least because we prefer clear-cut divisions to ambiguity. Nature herself, however, can be very ambivalent, as the very idea of 'averages' suggests. Why aren't we?' (op. cit., p.51).

10. On this see Aristotle, *Nicomachean Ethics*, book 8, especially 8.5.

11. Bernard Häring, *Free and Faithful in Christ*, vol.2, p.497.

12. Eric Fuchs, *Sexual Desire and Love*, p.43.

13. *Letter on the Pastoral Care of Homosexual Persons* §6.

14. Gen. 5.1 and 9.6 both reiterate that God made people in his image, but say nothing further by way of explanation.

15. Claus Westermann, *Genesis 1–11*, p.156.

16. For a brief survey of some Christian as well as Jewish interpretations of the passage, see Westermann, op. cit., pp.148–155.

17. Eph. 4.23f.

18. Col. 3.10.

19. *De Genesi ad Litteram* 3.20.

20. *Summa Theologiae* 1.93.2c.

21. Although in chapters 1 and 2 the Hebrew *'adam* is used generically to mean 'human being', from chapter 3 onwards, including chapter 5, it functions as the name of the first human being, Adam.

22. Jack Dominian similarly sees a connexion, though a slightly different one, between married love and the unity of God. Writing of Gen. 2.23–25 he says: 'This passage directs our attention to the fact that the essence of sexuality points to relationship between the sexes, whose ultimate consummation is the oneness of coitus. This in turn reflects the mystery of the Trinity where the three persons are constantly in a relationship of love, which makes them one, and yet they retain their separate identity, just as the couple do' (*Sexual Integrity*, p.131).

23. Matt. 13.23; Mark 4.20; Luke 8.15.

24. Matt. 3.8; Luke 3.8.

25. *Humanae Vitae* §9.

26. Bernard Häring, *Free and Faithful in Christ*, vol.2, p.517.

27. Though we should not lose sight of the fact that children, too, are only metaphorically described as fruit, and the womb as bearing fruit.

28. See e.g. Gen. 1.29, where fruit trees, as well as other plants, are given to people by God for food.

29. V. Genovesi, *In Pursuit of Love*, p.152.

8 Sex and Marriage

1. Unless I am thereby taking up a stance against the social convention that you don't have sex with just anybody, that sex is significant. And now my activity signifies nothing about my relationship with the one I am having sex with but something rather about my relationship with 'society', i.e. parents, the dominant social ethos, etc.; or with myself: I may be punishing or degrading myself.

2. The Revised Standard Version has 'remain single as I do,' but there is no word for 'single' in the Greek text.

3. I Cor. 7.7–9. For 'burn' the Revised Standard Version has 'be aflame with passion'.

4. v.31.

5. *De Bono Conjugali* 24.

6. See *De Conjugiis Adulterinis* 2.12: 'In this time of refraining from embrace it is not necessary to beget children.'

7. *De Bono Conjugali* 3.

8. *De Bono Conjugali* 6.

9. *De Bono Conjugali* 24.

10. Augustine sees the good of *proles* as including that of bringing up the children properly, that is giving them proper care and inducting them into the faith. Cf. *De*

Genesi ad Litteram 9.7: 'Concerning offspring: they are to be received lovingly, nourished generously, and educated religiously.'

11. E.g. *De Bono Conjugali* 3.

12. At the beginning of his treatment (§11) he says, quoting *De Bono Conjugali* 24: 'These are the blessings which make matrimony itself a blessing: offspring, fidelity, sacrament.'

He immediately follows this with a quotation from *De Genesi ad Litteram* 9.7: 'Fidelity signifies that outside the matrimonial bond there shall be no sexual intercourse; offspring signifies that children shall be lovingly welcomed, tenderly reared, and religiously educated; sacrament signifies that the bond of wedlock shall never be broken, and that neither party, if separated, shall form a union with another, even for the sake of offspring. Such is the law of marriage, which gives lustre to the fruitfulness of nature and sets a curb upon shameful incontinence.'

13. E.g. *Humanae Vitae* §12.

14. E.g. *Casti Connubii* §56.

15. *tēn opheilēn*. The Revised Standard Version has 'conjugal rights'.

16. It no doubt also reflects the connected assumption, still common today, that it is the place of women to be passive in the realm of desire, to receive the sexual attentions of men and be objects of desire, rather than subjects who might set their desires on men.

17. 5.31f. We may note in passing that divorce is criticized here on the basis of what it does to somebody else, not as the infringement of some independent divine law. One who divorces his wife 'makes her an adulteress'. This relates back to the concerns of chapter 1. Divorce is wrong because it does something bad to the divorced woman.

18. The parallel in Mark 10.10–12 is set rather against the Roman background, in which a wife also had the right of divorce.

19. In some manuscripts it is absent here – hence the Revised Standard Version translation – and some others have *aner*, 'man' (male human) instead.

20. See vv.3,7,8,9,10.

21. The rabbis were divided over what counted as sufficient reason for a man to divorce his wife. The school of Shammai thought that some shamefulness in the wife was necessary, while the school of Hillel held that a man could divorce his wife 'even if she has burnt his food in cooking it' (Mishnah, *Gittin* 9.10).

22. There are 29 occurrences altogether: Ex. 20.14; Lev. 20.10; Deut. 5.17; Isa. 57.3; Jer. 3.8; 3.9; 5.7; 7.9; 9.1 (x2); 13.27; 23.10; 23.14; 29.23; Ezek. 16.32; 16.38; 23.37; 23.43; 23.45; Hosea 2.4; 3.1; 4.2; 4.13; 4.14; 7.4; Ps. 50.18; Prov. 6.32; 30.20; Job 24.15; Mal. 3.5.

23. The situation is complicated a little by the use of the verb in the metaphorical context of the marriage between God and Israel. Here it is the men of Israel who commit adultery by breaking their own marriage bond, but here they are being cast collectively in the role of God's wife.

24. Luke 22.25f. Matt., in his parallel (20.25f.), uses the emphatic variant *katexousiazō*.

25. Not all human acts. As I have also remarked, you can act, do something, by doing nothing, by not moving. But for doing nothing to be at the same time doing something there has to be the possibility of doing something by moving, a possibility which is deliberately not realized.

26. It does sometimes mean the fleshy substance of animals; e.g. Gen. 41.4; Ex. 12.8; 16.3; Lev. 8.31. But even in reference to animals, it sometimes means simply the living animal; e.g. Gen. 7.15.

27. 58.6f. There is some word-play in the Hebrew. *kissah*, here translated 'cover', can have the sense of 'conceal' in the same way as the root *ʿlm*, here translated 'hide'.

28. Cf. my remarks in chapter 4 about prostitution.

29. For a rather different view of this passage, and one related to the views discussed in chapter 6, see Timothy Radcliffe OP, ' "Glorify God in your bodies" ': I Corinthians 6, 12–20 as a sexual ethic'.

30. This is very different from promising sexual exclusivity to a master, who then enjoys quasi-proprietorial rights over you. Then adultery is an infringement of those rights, and you can be disposed of – violently, according to Jewish law. See Lev. 20.10.

31. *De Bono Conjugali* 1. See also section 3 on why marriage is a good: 'This seems to me not only because of the procreation of sons, but also because of the companionship natural between those of different sexes. Otherwise it could no longer be called marriage in the case of old people, especially if either they had lost sons, or had given birth to none. But now in good if aged marriage, even if the youthful heat that exists between male and female has died down, yet still the order of charity flourishes between husband and wife.'

32. But the similarity between Paul and Augustine should not be exaggerated. If for them both a main purpose of marriage is sexual, for Paul the only purpose of sex he mentions is to relieve desire and fend off sexual temptation. For Augustine, as we saw, the only legitimate purpose of sex is procreation, and sex out of desire is sinful. So he has trouble coping with Paul. This is what he says in *Enchiridion* 78, on sex without procreative purpose in marriage: 'It would have been possible ... that this should not be thought a sin, if he [Paul] had not added, "But I speak this as a concession, not as a commandment." And now who will deny this to be a sin, when it is admitted that a concession is given on apostolic authority to those who do this?'

33. As I remarked earlier, men's sexual activities with women are subject to no legal restriction in the Old Testament apart from their being forbidden other men's wives. It is true that men are sometimes advised to be faithful to their wives; but this is definitely advice, not command, and prudential reasons are given for fidelity. For example, in the book of Proverbs a young man is advised to be faithful to his own wife as a way of avoiding other men getting to her: 'Drink water from your own cistern, flowing water from your own well. Should your springs be scattered abroad, streams of water in the streets? Let them be for yourself alone, and not for strangers with you. Let your fountain be blessed, and rejoice in the wife of your youth, a lovely hind, a graceful doe' (5.15ff.).

Even when it comes to the injunction not to commit adultery, the approach is still prudential. The young man is advised to eschew getting mixed up with other men's wives as a way to avoid coming to grief: 'A harlot may be hired for a loaf of bread, but an adulteress [Hebrew: a man's wife] stalks a man's very life. Can a man carry fire in his bosom and his clothes not be burned? Or can one walk upon hot coals and his feet not be scorched? So is he who goes in to his neighbour's wife; none who touches her will go unpunished ... He who commits adultery has no sense; he who does it destroys himself. Wounds and dishonour he will get, and his disgrace will not be wiped away. For jealousy makes a man furious, and he will not spare when he takes revenge. He will accept no compensation, nor be appeased though you multiply gifts' (6.26ff.).

9   Contraception

1. Pius XI, *Casti Connubii* 56.

2. Gal. 5.20; Rev. 9.21; 18.23.

3. Rev. 21.8; 22.15.

4. Rev. 9.21; 21.8; 22.15.

5. The connexion with idolatry should also make us cautious about the possible significance of the occurrence of the word 'fornication' in these contexts. Fornication is a well-known image for idolatry in scripture, so here the word may well have a religious rather than a sexual sense.

6. Gal. 5.20; Rev. 18.23.

7. In this paragraph I am indebted to Noonan, *Contraception*, pp.44f.

8. This is not to prejudge any moral questions surrounding these practices. There is an important debate about whether the fertilized ovum which is destroyed by these methods is or is not a human being. If not, that is reason for saying that abortion at this early stage of pregnancy has a different moral status from abortion at a later stage, when it is clear that the developing child is indeed a human being. In this latter case the stance of the church has been that since abortion is the deliberate taking of the life of a human being it is a kind of murder. If abortion at a very early stage of pregnancy does not involve taking the life of a human being, it cannot be described as murder. However, it may still be seriously wrong for other reasons.

9. Pius XI, *Casti Connubii* 55, quoting Augustine, *De Conjugiis Adulterinis* 2.12.

10. Literally 'corrupted/spoiled on to the ground'; there occurs in the Hebrew text no word for 'semen'. LXX translates 'he poured on to the ground'.

11. For a mediaeval use to the same effect, see Albert the Great, *On the Sentences* 4.31.18.

12. Sometimes reference is made in connexion with this story to the law of levirate marriage laid down in Deut. 25.5–10. There are obvious similarities, but, as Noonan points out (*Contraception*, p.34), there are also important differences. In Genesis the father is living and the punishment for failure to perform the duty severe. In Deuteronomy the law refers to a situation in which the father is dead, and the penalty is shame rather than death: His brother's wife shall go up to him in the presence of the elders, and pull his sandal off his foot, and spit in his face; and she shall answer and say: 'So shall it be done to the man who does not build up his brother's house.'

13. *Contra Secundinum* 21.

14. *Humanae Vitae* §11, 12.

15. Elizabeth Anscombe, *Contraception and Chastity*, p.5.

16. Ibid., p.18.

17. E.g. Aquinas, *Contra Gentiles* 3.122.

18. See Wittgenstein, *Philosophical Investigations* §17.

19. Would we then have two reproductive types of act or only one? Would they be one in that they are after all both reproductive, or two in that the place of penetration is different? Does it matter what we say here? Our interest will determine what we say.

20. It would not be to the point to appeal to the possibility of miracles here, claiming that God might miraculously make an otherwise sterile intercourse fertile. Miracles put limitations on human knowledge perhaps, but it is our knowledge that must guide our actions, and therefore our classifications. If it is not, then we have no basis for distinguishing between reproductive and non-reproductive acts (or indeed acts of any kind). For anal intercourse – even between two men – or oral intercourse or masturbation could, by a miracle, also result in conception.

21. It is interesting, if nothing more, to note in this connexion these words of Augustine, written against the Manichees, words which amount to a strong attack on the rhythm method which is so favoured today. 'Is it not you who used to warn us to watch as much as we could the time when a woman is fitted to conceive after her period, and at that time to refrain from intercourse, lest a soul be bound up in flesh? From this it follows that you consider that having a wife is not for procreating children, but to satisfy lust ... Whoever says that to procreate children is a worse sin than to copulate thereby prohibits marriage; and he makes the woman no more a wife but a harlot' (*De Moribus Manichaeorum* 18).

On these words Noonan comments: 'In the history of the thought of theologians on contraception, it is, no doubt, piquant that the first pronouncement on contraception by the most influential theologian teaching on such matters should be such a vigorous attack on the one method of avoiding procreation accepted by twentieth-century Catholic theologians as morally lawful. History has made doctrine take a topsy-turvy course' (*Contraception*, p.120).

22. Elizabeth Anscombe, *Contraception and Chastity*, p.18.

23. *Humanae Vitae* §11.

24. In *The Thomist* vol. 52, no. 3, July 1988, pp.365–426. Henceforth, for the sake of brevity, I refer to the authors collectively as GBFM.

25. Art. cit., p.373.

26. Ibid., p.377.

27. The use of the word 'hatred' seems to me a misuse of language here, despite the authors' defence of it in their succeeding paragraph. Hatred of something is not equivalent to not wanting it or to rejecting it. It is perfectly possible to decide against something, to reject it, without hating it. It can be rejected even if it is very desirable; it has only to be less desirable than what is actually chosen. In English, 'hatred' just is an emotional term, and its use here muddies the waters unnecessarily.

28. We might make an exception for dead people, and be prepared to say Andrew hates Mary, even if she is dead and he believes her to be dead. But still Mary was a definite person who is still identifiable even though she is dead. It makes sense to say that Andrew hates that person and not another. With the prospective 'possible' baby that is impossible.

29. GBFM, art. cit., p.371.

30. Ibid., p.374.

31. Ibid., pp.372–374.

32. Ibid., p.379.

33. Ibid., p.378.

34. Ibid., p.385.

35. Ibid., p.401f.

36. Or so it does when properly practised, according to GBFM. But NFP can be used illegitimately, as a form of contraception if those who practise it do not see the coming to be of a new person as a good in itself.

10 Homosexuality

1. Not quite: at least these are sexual relations between people. Bestiality would be considered worse, but gay sex is certainly considered one of the most seriously wrong of the common forms of sex, the ones that we know go on all around us all the time.

2. John Boswell, *Christianity, Social Tolerance and Homosexuality*, p.6.

3. Ibid., p.7.

4. I use the terms 'gay' and 'homosexual' indifferently throughout this chapter. Neither word is all that satisfactory, and for various reasons different people object to one or other of them; but I know of no others. In using both, I have no wish to offend anybody.

5. The priests are also forbidden to do it in 21.5.

6. Rom. 13.8–10; Gal. 5.14; cf. Matt. 7.12.

7. Bailey, in *Homosexuality and the Western Christian Tradition*, pp.1–6, thinks it likely that this is not what the Sodomites want, but only to find out who these strangers are. The argument turns on the interpretation of the verb yd^c, 'know'. It normally has the range of meaning it has in English, but is used a number of times in an obviously sexual sense: Gen. 4.1; 4.17; 4.25; 38.26; Judg. 11.39; 19.25; I Sam. 1.19; I Kings 1.4. Thus, apart from the disputed one in Gen. 19.5 and that in v.8 there are eight occurrences of the verb in a sexual sense, all heterosexual apart from Gen. 19.5. Apart from the occurrence in v.8 knowing is always what the man does to the woman, not the woman to the man, nor what the man and the woman do together. It seems likely, especially in the light of the use of 'know' in v.8, that this is what the men want to do to Lot's visitors. (The use of 'know' in the parallel story in Judg. 19 is important here.) It could be that, as so often elsewhere in the Old Testament, there is a play on words here, 'know' being used in a cognitive, non-sexual sense in v.5 and in a sexual sense in v.8. But if that is the sense in v.5, it is hard to see why Lot should consider it such a terrible thing for the men of Sodom to want to know the identity of two strangers who turn up in the evening in their town and stay in the house of one who is not a citizen but an alien, and why he should beg them not to do anything to them.

8. This also seems to be how it is understood by Christ as by the Jewish tradition before him. See Matt. 10.14f. and the parallel in Luke 10.11f., in which Christ sends out the disciples on a healing mission. He likens the fate of those places that do not offer them hospitality to that of Sodom and Gomorrah. This understanding of Gen. 19 does better justice, too, to the similarities of this story to that of Philemon and Baucis in Ovid's *Metamorphoses* VIII, 618–724. Because of their hospitality to visiting gods the aged couple alone escape the doom visited on their inhospitable city, and are later both transformed into trees.

9. The Congregation for the Doctrine of the Faith's *Letter to the Bishops of the Catholic Church on the Pastoral Care of Homosexual Persons* of 1986, however, takes a different line. See §6.

10. Anglican Board for Social Responsibility, *Homosexual Relations*, §91, p.27.

11. Ibid., §95, p.28.

12. Bailey, op. cit., pp.31ff.

13. Lawler, Boyle and May go some way to recognizing this point. They write (*Catholic Sexual Ethics*, p.24): '[Scholars] agree ... that the Old Testament is unequivocal in condemning homosexual activities as an abomination, a form of idolatry, and a base attempt to gain sexual power. Moreover, the motive for the moral condemnation seems to be the character of homosexual acts themselves.'

It is not clear exactly what they mean here by 'the character of homosexual acts themselves'. Is it meant to imply that this condemnation is independent of context? The very motives for condemnation that they cite imply the opposite. If homosexual acts were condemned as a form of idolatry it is clear that they were ascribed a particular significance in the context of Old Testament religion. If they were a base attempt to gain sexual power, this shows they were accorded (naturally, given the expressive powers of the body) a significant place in power relationships; e.g. raping somebody, male or female, was a sign you had them in your power.

14. Until not long ago all male homosexual relations were illegal in Britain, but female ones were not. The story is often told that reference to lesbians was excluded from the Victorian legislation owing to Queen Victoria's ignorance of lesbianism. But why was she ignorant of it, if she was aware of male homosexuality? A natural assumption is that it was because the male, and hence what are considered male aberrations, have a much higher profile in our society.

15. John McNeill SJ, *The Church and the Homosexual*, p.50.

16. Rom. 1.28–32. Though it is lost in translation, there is wordplay here similar to that which Paul uses in the preceding verses: Because they did not see fit (*ouk edokimasan*) to acknowledge God, he gave them up to a base (*adokimon*) mind.

17. This is a point which the CDF *Letter* misses. Speaking of the disharmony between creator and creatures that Paul is talking about here, it says simply: 'Paul is at a loss to find a clearer example of this disharmony than homosexual relations' (§6) The idea that Paul is at a loss here is unwarranted, in view of the long list of pagan vices which he gives a few verses later; there is no reason at all to think he finds homosexual relations any clearer an example of disharmony than murder, deceit, etc. Rather do they for him sum up and express the horribleness of those other things. It is as if he is saying: you would expect such dreadful people – idolaters, murderers, heartless – to do *that*.

18. *pornoi*. The Revised Standard Version translates 'the immoral'.

19. The Revised Standard Version links this together with *malakoi*, some editions translating the two words as 'homosexual', others as 'sexual perverts'. Neither the linking nor the translations have any warrant. *Arsenokoites* appears to be a word coined by Paul, probably referring to those who, contrary to Lev. 18.22 lie with a man as with a woman. The word reflects the LXX translation of this verse. We have no way of knowing for certain how that verse was understood by Paul, nor therefore the exact class of people he refers to by this term, if he is referring to a precise class at all. *Malakos* is the ordinary Greek word for 'soft'. Here it is probably used in a sexual

sense, meaning those who lack self-control and so masturbate. There is no suggestion in the term that the masturbator is also homosexual.

20. Again *pornoi*; Revised Standard Version translates 'immoral persons'.

21. Indeed, it is questionable whether it is best thought of as even including
condemnation of homosexual practices. See the interesting analysis by Countryman
in *Dirt, Greed and Sex*, pp.110–117. He contends that Paul treated homosexual
behaviour as 'an integral if unpleasingly dirty aspect of Gentile culture. It was not in
itself sinful, but had been visited upon the Gentiles as recompense for sins, chiefly
the sin of idolatry but also those of social disruption' (p.117).

22. He might, though, have thought it good, or at least better, that they should be
a stable couple in a way somewhat analogous to partners in a marriage. It is the
punishment of idolaters not merely that they turn to homosexual relations, but that
they are 'burned up' (*exekauthesan*) by their desire for each other (Rom. 1.27).
Clearly it was important for Paul to avoid or mitigate the heat of passion. He
advocates marriage for those who cannot contain their passion, for 'it is better to
marry than to burn (*purousthai*)' (I Cor. 7.9). The regular sexual service to each other
of gay partners, though not sinless, would have the same cooling effect as in
marriage.

23. For the later tradition see Aquinas, *Summa Theologiae* 2–2.154.11c; 2–2.154.
12.

24. See P. A. Tyler, 'Homosexual Behaviour in Animals'.

25. This is felt to be true not only of their sexual behaviour, but also the way they
dress, walk, talk, etc. And many people would be upset at the sight of two men (not
women!) holding hands, or with their arms around each other (except when playing
sports).

26. See Mary Douglas, *Purity and Danger*, especially chapter 3, and, for a slightly
different view, Michael P. Carroll, 'One More Time: Leviticus Revisited'. The
connexion between unclean animals and sexual impurity was made already in the
early Christian period. See *Epistle of Barnabas* 10.6–8.

27. Heinz Heger, *The Men with the Pink Triangle*, p.15.

28. *Declaration on Certain Questions concerning Sexual Ethics*, §8.

29. I am not sure what the CDF means by saying this. In the most obvious sense of
the words, it is not true. Most gay people lead, despite the pressures on them, quite
well-adjusted lives, fitting in and making as good a contribution to society as anyone
else. Hence the 'invisibility' of so many gay people. But the CDF may have had
something else in mind.

30. I have written briefly on this topic elsewhere ('Are Homosexuals Sick?'). Here
I summarize the main thoughts offered there, with some additional observations.

31. Cf. these remarks of Foucault on Greek attitudes to sex in *The Uses of Pleasure*,
vol. 2 of his *History of Sexuality*: 'We can talk about their "bisexuality", thinking of
the free choice they allowed themselves between the two sexes, but for them this
option was not referred to a dual, ambivalent, and "bisexual" structure of desire'
(p.188).

'The enjoyment of boys and of women did not constitute two classificatory
categories between which individuals could be distributed; a man who preferred
paidika did not think of himself as being 'different' from those who pursued women'
(p.190).

32. The CDF *Letter* does see homosexuality as mortally dangerous to those who have got it. It speaks of the self-denial of homosexual people as something 'which will save them from a way of life which constantly threatens to destroy them' (§12). But notice that it is not now a disease, a condition, that is supposed to threaten to destroy them, but a way of life. A way of life is not akin to a condition. Here we are back with moral discourse, and have veered away from the incompatible medical model.

33. Lawler, Boyle and May, *Catholic Sexual Ethics*, p.200.

34. §7. This acknowledgment is particularly interesting in the context in which it is made; the sentence continues: 'but when they engage in homosexual activity they confirm within themselves a disordered sexual inclination which is essentially self-indulgent'. This seems to imply that homosexual activity itself is self-indulgent. If so, then the *Letter* interestingly implies that people who engage in self-indulgent activities may nevertheless be generous and giving of themselves, i.e. not self-indulgent. Engaging in self-indulgences does not make one into a self-indulgent person, as I argued in chapter 5.

35. John Milhaven, 'Homosexuality and Love'.

36. Ibid., p.68.

37. Something similar seems to happen in some comments of Lawler, Boyle and May on same-sex relationships. They admit that these can be enduring and loving, but then go on to write of such: 'Even these homosexual relationships, if they involve homosexual actions, are deeply flawed. They do not and cannot have the inner dynamism toward permanence and fidelity which the marriage relationship can have' (p.201). But this seems to imply that such relationships are deeply flawed whether they involve homosexual actions or not. For the flaw that is mentioned is that they lack the 'inner dynamism toward permanence and fidelity which the marriage relationship can have'. It is implausible to argue that a relationship between two men or two women would have this inner dynamism if it involved no homosexual actions, since it is difficult to see how such actions would deprive the relationship of such a dynamism. In any case, for Lawler, Boyle and May this dynamism appears to come from an orientation towards the production and raising of children, and this is lacking in any relationship between homosexuals, whether they express their relationship sexually or not. Indeed, it is lacking in *any* relationship between any two people sharing their lives who do not perform heterosexual actions together. So it turns out that any two people living together, homosexual or not, have a flawed relationship if they are not committed to having children. Such a conclusion is surely unacceptable.

38. Lawler, Boyle and May, op. cit., p.200f.

39. Peschke, however, has an argument which attempts to link the two together logically. He argues: 'Advocates of homosexual liaisons often claim that the sexual act can also serve as an expression of love between two persons of the same sex. But a closer inspection reveals that this is not so. The sexual act is apt to be an expression of love and appreciation in the last analysis because it is able to generate new human life. Every man and every woman would like to have a child only with a partner whom they sincerely esteem. The readiness of a man and a woman to unite together in the sexual act is therefore a sign of their mutual esteem, at least if they do not superficially plunge into the sexual encounter, but do so in a responsible decision.

Sexual acts between two persons of the same sex however are never apt to procreate offspring. Therefore they can also not be the expression of a love and esteem which is based on the possibility to give life to a child. The precondition is missing which imparts to the sexual act the quality of a sign of love' (*Christian Ethics* vol.2, p.435.). This is unconvincing. The sexual activity of a biologically sterile married couple is not able to generate new human life, but it is still apt to be an expression of love and appreciation. There is a straightforward logical mistake here, too. If nobody would like to have a child except with a partner they sincerely esteem, that does not imply that you do not sincerely esteem somebody if you cannot, or even do not want to, have a child with them. If love is a condition for wanting to have a child, that does not make wanting to have a child a condition for love.

Index